FUN WITH THE FAMILY™

in PENNSYLVANIA

HUNDREDS OF IDEAS
FOR DAY TRIPS WITH THE KIDS
FOURTH EDITION

EMILY PAULSEN

and

FAITH PAULSEN

The Globe Pequot Press

GUILFORD, CONNECTICUT

To buy books in quantity for corporate use
or incentives, call **(800) 962–0973, ext. 4551,**
or e-mail **premiums@GlobePequot.com.**

The prices and rates listed in this guidebook were
confirmed at press time. We recommend, however,
that you call establishments to obtain current
information before traveling.

Text design by Nancy Freeborn
Maps by M. A. Dubé

ISBN 0-7627-2233-9
ISSN 1539-8730

Manufactured in the United States of America
Fourth Edition/Third Printing

To our parents, who taught us the love of travel
and the joy of discovery.

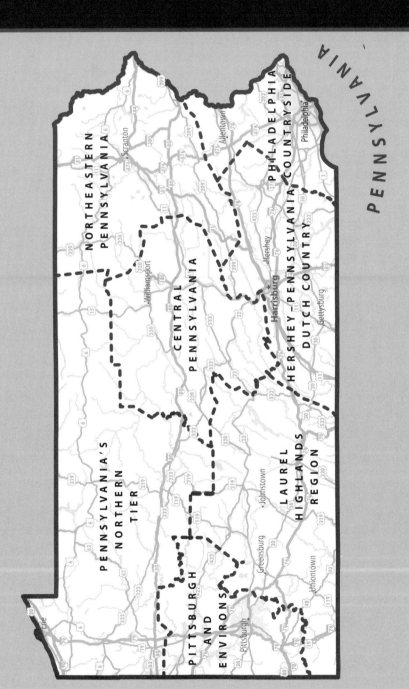

Contents

Acknowledgments

Our names may be on the cover, but there are a lot of people who have helped make this book possible. We'd like to thank all the people at the tourist boards and sites who took extra time to answer our questions and point us in the right direction. We'd also like to thank our husbands, Martin Livezey and Bart Sacks; Faith's children, Judah, Seth, and Gideon Paulsen-Sacks; and Emily's children, Eli and Maya Livezey, for their enthusiasm and support.

Introduction

Pennsylvania's history reflects America's history. Today it is more important than ever for families to learn about the background, and the responsibilities, of the freedoms we cherish.

In Pennsylvania it is easy to take our historical sites for granted, but this is a great time to explore Old City Philadelphia, Independence Hall and the Lights of Liberty sounds and lights show, as well as places like Valley Forge, Washington's Crossing, and Gettysburg National Military Park. Historic landmarks and living-history sites can be found in every corner of the state. There's no better time to discover them than now.

But liberty is not just something from the past; it is a living legacy that requires regular care. The new National Liberty Museum gets kids thinking in new ways about the responsibilities of citizenship. Looking for a place to start? The Web site at www.experiencepa.com is a great jumping-off point for your adventure in Pennsylvania.

When we first visited Pennsylvania on a family vacation in 1969, neither of us realized that someday we would each adopt the state as our home, and we certainly never dreamed we would write a book about it. As children then, we saw the Liberty Bell and the Franklin Institute with our parents and our brother, Bruce. Now we take our own children to these places and many more.

Between us, we have five children, three dogs, and four cats. Our homes are in two different regions of Pennsylvania. Together and separately, we've enjoyed many family adventures here. But until we began to write it all down, we never fully appreciated the richness of this state.

Whether you're looking for a place to hike, bike, camp, ski, horseback ride, or just take a Sunday afternoon drive, Pennsylvania has a park for you. We've tried to cover the highlights of the state park system in this book, but to devote the space each deserves, we'd have to write another book on the subject. If you want more information about Pennsylvania state parks, call their special toll-free number, (800) 63–PARKS, or check the Web site www.dcnr.state.pa.us.

Pennsylvania has nine major caves open to the public, including the only water-filled cave in the country. Many of the caves offer educational programs on such topics as geology, bats, and Native American history—all geared especially for children.

In 1969, when we walked through the beating heart at the Franklin Institute, it was exciting because it was our first experience with hands-on, interactive science education. Today, the Franklin Institute Science Museum joins a host of other "user-friendly" science centers, including the Carnegie Science Center, Williamsport's Children's Discovery Workshop, Erie's expERIEnce Children's Museum, and Harrisburg's up-and-coming Whitaker Center, to name just a few. Some of the best family adventures can be adventures in learning.

Many parents are afraid to take kids to art museums, but we've found that our children respond well to art museums as long as they experience them in small doses. Sometimes we visit the gift shop first, pick up a few postcards, then see who can find the pictured artworks in the galleries. Pennsylvania has some first-rate art museums, large and small, from the Philadelphia Museum of Art to the Carnegie Museum of Art.

Families across the country have discovered First Night, and Pennsylvanians have led the way. First Night is a family-oriented, alcohol-free event that takes place in many cities and town on the evening of New Year's Day. In fact, more towns in Pennsylvania enjoy First Night than any other state. In all, nineteen Pennsylvania municipalities celebrate First Night, including Bethlehem, Bradford, Carlisle, Doylestown, Erie, Pittsburgh, Scranton, and State College.

No matter what the season, whether you like your adventures indoors or outdoors, Pennsylvania is a wonderful destination for families. We're certainly enjoying what the state has to offer, and we hope you will, too.

Please note that some sections of Pennsylvania have "ten-digit dialing." In these areas it is necessary to dial the area code before dialing any telephone number, even if you're only calling next door. This is true in the 610, 215, 412, 724, 878, 267, 445, 484, and 835 area codes. Another note: Exit numbers on major roads throughout the state are being changed. Check recent road maps or call ahead to avoid confusion.

LODGING, RESTAURANT, AND ATTRACTION FEES

Each chapter in this book gives a list of accommodations and restaurants for the area. This list is not meant to be complete, and we also recommend checking with the local tourist bureaus for other options. In general, we recommend advance reservations. Lodging prices can vary depending on the season and other factors, so make sure you understand in advance how much you'll be expected to pay.

Because admission fees change frequently, we offer a general idea of the prices charged by each attraction. Keep in mind that even though many preserves and museums offer **Free** admission, a donation is often expected to help the facility with the costs of keeping the lands and buildings open to the public.

Rates for Attractions

$	under $5
$$	$5 to $10
$$$	$10 to $20
$$$$	over $20

Attractions Key

The following is a key to the icons found throughout the text.

 Swimming

 Animal Viewing

 Boating / Boat Tour

 Food

 Historic Site

 Lodging

 Hiking / Walking

 Camping

 Fishing

 Museums

 Biking

 Performing Arts

 Amusement Park

 Sports/Athletic

 Horseback Riding

 Picnicking

 Skiing/Winter Sports

 Playground

 Park

 Shopping

 Plants/Gardens/
Nature Trails

Help Us Keep This Guide Up to Date

Every effort has been made by the authors and editors to make this guide as accurate and useful as possible. However, many changes can occur after a guide is published—establishments close, phone numbers change, hiking trails are rerouted, facilities come under new management, etc.

We would love to hear from you concerning your experiences with this guide and how you feel it could be made better and be kept up to date. While we may not be able to respond to all comments and suggestions, we'll take them to heart, and we'll make certain to share them with the author. Please send your comments and suggestions to the following address:

The Globe Pequot Press
Reader Response/Editorial Department
P.O. Box 480
Guilford, CT 06437

Or you may e-mail us at: editorial@globe-pequot.com

Thanks for your input, and happy travels!

Philadelphia

The City of Brotherly Love has long been a popular family destination, chock-full of great things to do and see together—and it's about to get even better. The Liberty Bell is moving to a new home, a new visitors center provides a gateway to the entire region, and a new National Constitution Center is opening. A new performing-arts complex has just opened, and there are new sports stadiums in the works.

Condé Nast Traveler magazine has rated Philly "America's Friendliest City" and one of the two "most honest" cities. FBI statistics name Philadelphia as the safest of the nation's twelve largest cities.

More than one and a half million visitors see the Liberty Bell each year. The bell will soon be moved to its new home, a "Bell Chamber" from which the bell will be visible all the time. The chamber will be part of a new Liberty Bell Complex, near Sixth and Chestnut

Faith & Emily's
Favorite Philadelphia Attractions

1. Franklin Institute Science Center
2. Academy of Natural Sciences
3. Please Touch Museum
4. Independence Hall
5. Liberty Bell
6. Betsy Ross House
7. Philadelphia Zoo
8. Insectarium
9. Elfreth's Alley
10. Lights of Liberty
11. National Liberty Museum

across from Congress Hall, to include an exhibit hall and sheltered queuing area. According to a new master plan, the bell will be linked with a brand-new visitors center, the National Constitution Center, and Independence Hall.

Thanks to a donation of more than $1 million from the Pew Charitable Trust, the West Wing of Independence Hall will feature a new exhibit of historical documents older than anything in the National Archives in Washington, D.C. This exhibit will also highlight the original Syng inkstand used for the signing of the Declaration of Independence.

By spring of 2003, the new National Constitution Center will open on Independence Mall between Arch and Race Streets. The new center will be the first-ever museum honoring and explaining our Constitution. Its Web site is already up and running at www.constitutioncenter.org. The site offers a Kids Corner with lots of useful information for school projects, including a place to order a pocket copy of the Constitution.

If you're Web-savvy, you can do some great research on the Internet before your trip. (And if you're not computer literate, ask your kids to show you!) The Web site of the Greater Philadelphia Marketing Corp., www.gophila.com, offers itineraries, walking tours for specific interests, events, and much more.

Faith & Emily's
Favorite Events in Philadelphia

- **Mummer's Day Parade** (January 1, summer version in June), (215) 336–3050.
- **Philadelphia Flower Show** (late February through early March), (215) 988–8839; www.theflowershow.com.
- **Philadelphia International Children's Festival** (last week of May), (215) 898–6791 or (215) 898–6683.
- **Philadelphia Orchestra Concerts at Mann Music Center** (outdoor summer series), Fifty-second and Parkside Avenue, (215) 893–1995 or (215) 893–1999; www.manncenter.org.
- **Summer concerts at Penn's Landing** (June through August), (held at Festival Pier through 2002), (215) 922–2FUN; www.pennslanding corp.com.
- **Sunoco Welcome America! Celebration** (July), (800) 770–5883; www.americasbirthday.com.
- **Daily News Presents "Yo! Philadelphia"** (Labor Day weekend), (215) 636–1666.

There's even a page called "Family Attractions." The Web site of the Philadelphia Convention and Visitors Bureau is www.pcvb.org. For travel and lodgings try http://philadelphia.citytravelguide.com. Another worthwhile site is http://philadelphia.about.com. You can take a virtual tour of City Hall at www.geocities.com. City Hall has its own Web site (www.ajaxelectric.com/city hall), too, as do many museums and attractions listed in this guide.

Another helpful resource is the *Philadelphia's Playground Map,* which came out in early 2002. This colorful map, designed by an artist, captures the distinct character of Philadelphia's neighborhoods.

If you're visiting Philly for several days, we recommend the CityPass, which gets you into six attractions for one price and with no ticket lines. You can save about 50 percent off the combined box-office prices for The Franklin Institute; Philadelphia City Trolley Tour; the Philadelphia Zoo; The Academy of Natural Sciences; Independence Seaport Museum and Historic Ships; and in New Jersey, the New Jersey State Aquarium and Camden Children's Garden. Tickets are valid for nine days from first date of use. Admission to all six sites is $28.50 for adults, $25.00 for seniors sixty-five and over, and $17.00 for children ages three to eleven. You can purchase CityPass at any participating attraction, the Independence Visitor Center, or in advance at www.citypass.com.

Philadelphia is a great walking city. Most attractions are an easy jaunt from hotels and from each other. And when the feet get sore or the kids get cranky, you can always hop on the purple PHLASH bus, which travels in a loop from Penn's Landing to the Art Museum. To get to some of the attractions in the outskirts of the city, a car can be handy, but the one-way streets in Center City and cost of parking can be frustrating. Public transportation or walking is your best bet.

Sometimes when traveling with small children, or just to get the lay of the land, an organized tour is a good idea. There are lots of companies that offer tours of Philadelphia, on everything from a reproduction of an old-time trolley or a horse and buggy to a streamlined coach. Here are some companies to

Amazing Philadelphia Facts

"Most Honest" City According to FBI statistics, Philadelphia is the safest of the nation's twelve largest cities. It is also one of the cleanest and, according to *Condé Nast Traveler,* America's "most honest" city.

contact: American Trolley Tours/Choo-Choo Trolley, (215) 333–2119; Philadelphia Carriage Co., (215) 922–6840; '76 Carriage Co., (215) 923–8516 (tours begin at Independence National Park); Riverboat Queen Fleet, (215) 629–1131 (cruises leave from Penn's Landing); Philadelphia Trolley Works, (215) 925–TOUR; PHLASH bus, (215) 4–PHLASH.

Historic Philadelphia

When most people think of Philadelphia, they think of its place in U.S. history. You'll hear the word *first* a lot while touring this historic city. In fact, the area that makes up Independence National Historic Park (from Second to Sixth Street along Walnut Street) is called "America's most historic square mile." Here, you'll meander the streets walked by Benjamin Franklin, Thomas Jefferson, Betsy Ross, George Washington, Dolley Madison, John Adams . . . the list goes on and on.

INDEPENDENCE NATIONAL HISTORICAL PARK (all ages)

www.nps.gov/inde

Forty-five acres in Center City, comprising more than forty different historic buildings, make up Independence National Historical Park, including the Liberty Bell Pavilion, Independence Hall, Congress Hall, Old City Hall, Second Bank of the United States, Carpenters' Hall, New Hall Military Museum (formerly the Army-Navy Museum and Marine Corps Museum), Franklin Court, Christ Church, Bishop White House, Todd House, and Declaration House. For a preview you can see photos of the park online at www.rushyoung.com/philadelphia/indepen. Another site to check is http://usparks.about.com.

INDEPENDENCE VISITOR CENTER (all ages)

Sixth and Market Streets; (215) 597–8974; www.independencevisitorcenter.com. Most park buildings are open 9:00 A.M. to 5:00 P.M. daily. These hours are subject to some change, and in summer some buildings are open into the evening. Admission is **Free**.

The brand-new Independence Visitor Center is not just a spectacular new building; it's the perfect introduction to Philadelphia and the surrounding region.

Start by parking your car in the underground Autopark at Independence Mall. Inside the visitors center, make sure you visit its state-of-the-art theater for a brief video that gets you oriented. A second theater shows the excellent film *Independence!* directed by John Huston. Then, you can make reservations for restaurants in the area, purchase tickets, or sign up for a Philadelphia heritage tour. You can even print out your own itinerary in visitor computer stations. You can get a snack at the Old Capital Coffee Bar or browse through the gift and book shop.

Be sure to pick up a copy of the *Historic Philadelphia Gazette,* a free newspaper that lists events, demonstrations, and current hours for many sites in Philadelphia. (At home, check www.HistoricPhiladelphia.org.)

Most buildings within the park are free and open to the public, but a guide is required to tour some, and for others, such as the Todd House and the Bishop White House, tickets are required. There is an admission fee ($) for persons aged sixteen and older to enter the Second Bank of the United States, as well as for the House Tour that includes the Bishop White and Todd Houses. The urban park rangers of the National Park Service obviously love their jobs, and they'll make history come alive with their stories of colonial Philadelphia.

Also making history come alive are the Town Criers and other actors in period costumes that help transport visitors back in time. A special-events list distributed by the Town Criers gives a schedule of presentations, such as General Washington's Call to Arms. Families are encouraged not only to watch these events, but also to participate. Most events take place on weekends, with daily performances in summer. For more information call (800) 76-HISTORY or (215) 629-5801.

SECOND BANK OF THE UNITED STATES and CARPENTERS' HALL (ages 10 and up)

Second Bank is located on Chestnut Street between Fourth and Fifth Streets; (215) 597–8974; open daily 9:00 A.M. to 5:00 P.M. Admission $ for 16 and older. Carpenters' Hall is open Tuesday through Sunday 10:00 A.M. to 4:00 P.M.; closed Tuesday in January and February. Admission is **Free**. *Carpenters' Hall information, (215) 925–0167.*

The Second Bank of the United States and Carpenters' Hall, where the First Continental Congress met in 1774, are worth noting. Perhaps with kids you'd like to see the exterior only. Today Carpenters' Hall displays early carpenter's tools and chairs. The Second Bank houses the park's portrait gallery, featuring portraits of many Revolutionary War heroes. For information call the visitors center at (215) 597-8974.

NEW HALL MILITARY MUSEUM (ages 6 and up)

Carpenter's Court between Third and Fourth Streets on the south side of Chestnut Street; call the visitor center (215–597–8974) for information. Open daily 10:00 A.M. to 2:00 P.M., but hours may change seasonally. Admission is **Free**.

The Army-Navy Museum and Marine Corps Museum have been combined to form the New Hall Military Museum, which offers a treasure trove for military buffs. On display are uniforms, dioramas, weapons, ship models, battle flags, and other memorabilia of the U.S. armed forces, going back to the Revolution. The museum features a gun deck preserved from an eighteenth-century naval ship, as well as interactive displays such as one that allows visitors to control a ship's sails and rudder, and an honor roll of Marines who gave their lives in battle.

 ### BISHOP WHITE HOUSE and TODD HOUSE (ages 8 and up)

Walnut Street between Third and Fourth Streets; (215) 597–8974. The Todd House and Bishop White House are open daily from 9:00 A.M. to 4:30 P.M. Tickets are $ for adults over 16 and may be purchased at the Independence National Historic Park Visitor Center.

The Bishop White House and Todd House present an interesting opportunity to compare and contrast two different early American lifestyles.

Bishop White was the first Episcopal bishop of Pennsylvania and chaplain of the Continental Congress and of the new U.S. Senate, and this elegant home was built for him and his family in 1786. Children will enjoy the boys' and girls' bedrooms, where initials were carved into the wood more than 200 years ago.

The Todd House, on the other hand, represents a middle-class Quaker home from the same period. Although well-to-do, this family lived more simply. After the death of John Todd, Dolley Todd married James Madison and became one of the most famous U.S. First Ladies.

 ### INDEPENDENCE HALL (ages 6 and up)

Chestnut Street between Fifth and Sixth Streets; (215) 597–8974. Open by tour only. Admission is **Free**.

It goes without saying that Independence Hall is a must-see for all ages. This building was originally known as the Pennsylvania State House, but in 1824 when General Lafayette returned to Philadelphia, he called it "the hall of independence," and the name stuck. The Declaration of Independence was adopted here, and the U.S. Constitution was written here. The Assembly Room has been restored to look exactly as it did in 1776.

Between 1790 and 1800, when Philadelphia was the capital of the United States, the Congress met in Congress Hall next door. On the other side of Independence Hall is Old City Hall, where the U.S. Supreme Court met from 1791 to 1800. Unlike many historic buildings, Old City Hall is handicapped accessible.

LIBERTY BELL (all ages)

Sixth and Market Streets; (215) 597–8974. The Liberty Bell Pavilion is open from 9:00 A.M. to 5:00 P.M., with extended hours in summer. Admission is Free. *Handicapped accessible.*

The Liberty Bell is currently located in the park across the street from Independence Hall. Young and old will want to see and touch this emblem of freedom and democracy for people all over the world. In winter 2002, the Bell will move to a new Liberty Bell center near Sixth and Chestnut Streets. The new complex will include a Bell Chamber, exhibits concerning the Bell, and a queuing area.

Contrary to popular belief, the Liberty Bell's famous crack was not the result of overzealous ringing on July 4, 1776. In 1846, a thin crack was detected. It was repaired but cracked again when rung on George Washington's birthday. It has not rung since. To read the whole story, check www.ushistory.org/libertybell/.

HISTORIC REENACTMENTS IN AND AROUND INDEPENDENCE NATIONAL HISTORICAL PARK (all ages)

Schedules are available in the visitors center. Or call (215) 629-5801 or visit the Web site http://historic.philly.com.

Be inducted into the Continental Army. Hear strolling singers perform colonial ditties. The colonial actors from Historic Philadelphia, Inc. bring the past to life at selected sites in the historic district.

Amazing Philadelphia Facts

Philadelphia is the largest city in Pennsylvania, the second largest on the East Coast (New York is first, but you knew that), and the fifth largest city in the United States.

NATIONAL CONSTITUTION CENTER (ages 8 and up)

Arch Street, between Fifth and Sixth Streets; www.constitutioncenter.org.

The National Constitution Center, due to open July 4, 2003, is the first-ever museum honoring and explaining the U.S. Constitution, its history, and its relevance to our daily lives. The center will be located on Independence Mall, along with Independence Hall and the Liberty Bell. Watch for more details about this new center, which is expected to include interactive exhibits and activities. Although the center is not yet open, its Web site is already up and running and well worth checking out.

DECLARATION HOUSE (GRAFF HOUSE) (ages 8 and up)

Seventh and Market Streets; (215) 597–8974. Declaration House is open daily 9:00 A.M. to 1:00 P.M. Hours may change seasonally, so call ahead for information. Admission is **Free***. Handicapped accessible.*

A couple of blocks away from the Liberty Bell is Declaration House (or Graff House), also part of the National Historic Park. In 1776 the Virginia delegate (Thomas Jefferson) to the Second Continental Congress rented rooms in this building, and it was in these rooms that he wrote a little document called the Declaration of Independence. School-age kids will be especially interested to see the exact place where the Declaration of Independence was penned.

On the same block, but not part of the park, are two unusual museums: the Atwater Kent Museum and the Balch Institute of Ethnic Studies.

ATWATER KENT MUSEUM (ages 6 and up)

15 South Seventh Street; (215) 922–3031; www.philadelphiahistory.org. Open Tuesday through Saturday 10:00 A.M. to 4:00 P.M. Closed on major holidays. Admission is $. Handicapped accessible. **Free** *admission on Saturday.*

The Atwater Kent Museum tells the history of Philadelphia, a city whose story parallels that of our nation as a whole. Children under twelve enjoy the low-tech, hands-on approach. Special family programs include hat making or a visit from the "candy man," as well as exhibitions such as the annual Toys of Holidays Past, Trains and Trolleys, and Children Turning the Centuries.

BALCH INSTITUTE OF ETHNIC STUDIES (ages 6 and up)

18 South Seventh Street; call (215) 925–8090 for information. Both the museum and library are open Tuesday through Saturday from 10:00 A.M. to 4:00 P.M. Admission is $.

Walking Tour of Independence National Historic Park Area

There's no way a family can see all the sites in this neighborhood in one day, but here's a walking tour that will give you an idea where things are. Some of these destinations are not within easy walking distance for young children, but older ones should do fine.

Park your car at the underground Autopark under the Independence Visitor Center at Sixth and Market Streets. Although most people head right for the Liberty Bell or Independence Hall, it's a good idea to start your visit with a stop at the new Independence Visitor Center. If you wish to see Todd House or the Bishop White House, this is where you get your tickets. Here, you can also pick up maps, make up an itinerary, or get tickets for the historical sites. The new visitors center is very conveniently located and the best place to start your walking tour.

From the visitors center it's only a block to the corner of Market and Seventh, where you can see Declaration House. On the same block, but not part of the National Historical Park, are the Atwater Kent Museum and the Balch Institute of Ethnic Studies. Farther north on Seventh Street is the African-American Museum. Or, if you start at the visitors center and go the opposite direction, you're only a few steps from the current location of the Liberty Bell. (In winter 2002–2003, it is due to move to Sixth and Chestnut, also not far from the visitors center.)

Independence Hall is located on Chestnut Street between Fifth and Sixth. Walking east on Arch Street, you'll pass the Free Quaker Meeting House Museum and Christ Church Burial Ground (Fifth and Arch), where many colonial and Revolutionary heroes are buried. For good luck, toss a penny at Ben Franklin's grave.

Between Second and Third on Arch Street is the Betsy Ross House, administered independently. From here, walk down Arch Street toward Second Street, turn left on Second, and then make a right down a little street called Elfreth's Alley. Take your time enjoying this lovely spot. Fireman's Hall is right around the corner. You're only a couple of blocks from the City Tavern if you'd like to take a break.

Walking on Second Street, stop in at Christ Church, between Arch and Market Streets. From Christ Church walk toward Market Street, turn left, and go 2 blocks to Franklin Court and the National Liberty Museum.

The Balch Institute of Ethnic Studies is a museum of memorabilia illustrating the history of the many ethnic groups that immigrated to Philadelphia and housing an extensive genealogical research library. The Balch Institute has recently announced an unusual agreement with The Historical Society of Pennsylvania: In 2002 the Balch Institute will close at its current location, and the collection and library will relocate to the historical society building at Thirteenth and Locust Streets. Its programs will gradually resume there. For more information call (215) 732-6200 or visit the historical society's Web site, www.hsp.org.

LIGHTS OF LIBERTY (ages 6 and up)

Shows depart from PECO Energy Liberty Center, Sixth and Chestnut Streets, and take place throughout Independence National Historic Park. Tuesday through Sunday dusk to 11:15 P.M., up to six shows per hour, May through October. Additional shows may be added during holiday seasons. Purchase tickets ($$$) at the PECO Energy Liberty Center, or reserve in advance by calling (215) LIBERTY or (877) GO–2–1776.

Your family can be a part of the Revolution! Lights of Liberty, the world's first walking sound and light show, uses the latest technology to immerse you in the Revolution as it happened and where it happened. Walking along these historic streets, you'll see five-story projections on historic buildings. Wireless headsets equipped with 3-D sound make you feel as if you're a member of the crowd surrounding Independence Hall as the Declaration is read. Headsets are available in a children's version, as well as several different languages. Since each person gets an individual headset, everyone can choose the version that's most appropriate. This is an excellent introduction to the city's historic district. There is some walking on cobblestone streets, which may be difficult for toddlers and strollers.

U.S. MINT (ages 8 and up)

Fifth and Arch Streets; (215) 408–0114; www.usmint.gov. January through April, open 9:00 A.M. to 4:30 P.M. Monday through Friday; May through June, open Monday through Saturday; July and August, open Monday through Sunday; September through December, open Monday through Friday. Closed major holidays. Admission is **Free**.

The U.S. Mint is the world's largest coinage operation. Visitors can take a forty-five-minute self-guided audiovisual tour and watch money in the making from a glass-enclosed gallery.

AFRICAN-AMERICAN MUSEUM IN PHILADELPHIA (all ages)

701 Arch Street; (215) 574–0380; www.aampmuseum.org. Open Tuesday through Saturday 10:00 A.M. to 5:00 P.M. and Sunday noon to 5:00 P.M. Admission is $$ for adults, $ for seniors, students, and the physically challenged.

Celebrating its twenty-fifth anniversary in 2002, the African-American Museum houses 500,000 objects, images, and documents, including fine arts, folk art, photography, and more. Call for information about current exhibitions.

Amazing Philadelphia Facts

Philadelphia is America's number-one city for African-American tourism.

BETSY ROSS HOUSE (ages 6 and up)

239 Arch Street; (215) 686–1252; www.ushistory.org/betsy. March through October, open daily 10:00 A.M. to 5:00 P.M.; November through February, closed on Monday except holidays. Suggested donation: $.

Just 2 blocks away from the U.S. Mint, on Arch between Second and Third Streets, is the Betsy Ross House. Yes, Betsy Ross really lived here at 239 Arch Street. And yes, she really did sew flags for the Continental Congress, although nobody is certain how active a role she played in the design of the American flag. Her renovated house is an excellent example of a colonial artisan's home. Greeters are in colonial garb, and tours are self-guided, with kid-friendly signs. The tour itself is brief, but there is continuous family-friendly entertainment on the stage in the courtyard. For example, you might meet Betsy Ross, Ben Franklin, or an eighteenth-century magician.

ELFRETH'S ALLEY (all ages)

Between Arch and Race Streets on Second Street in Old City; (215) 574–0560. Mantua Maker's House Museum and Windsor Chairmaker's House are open Tuesday through Saturday 10:00 A.M. to 4:00 P.M. and Sunday noon to 4:00 P.M. Admission is $ for adults and children 5 to 18; kids under 5 are **Free**. *Maximum admission per family, $$.*

To get an idea of what Philadelphia may have looked like in the 1700s, take a walk down Elfreth's Alley, the oldest residential street in

America. Families still inhabit this cobblestone alley tucked between Arch and Race Streets on Second Street in Old City. Walking down this charming street, you can imagine what life must have been like when these thirty houses were built between 1728 and 1836, when carpenters and other artisans lived here.

Number 126, the 1762 Mantua Maker's House Museum, and Number 124, the Windsor Chairmaker's House, are open to the public. (A mantua was a type of gown made by the house's first residents, a pair of seamstresses.) A guide will show you around. Other houses are open during special open house events. On weekends in summer there are demonstrations of traditional crafts, such as basket weaving, broom making, needlework, and candle dipping. In June, the Elfreth's Alley Association hosts Fete Days, when many of the houses and gardens are opened to the public, and colonial crafts are demonstrated. On the second Friday of December, the alley hosts "Deck the Alley," a candlelight open house tour. The garden and Windsor Chairmaker's House are handicapped accessible. People still live in these houses, so remind your children to use their manners.

 MUM PUPPET THEATRE (all ages)
115 Arch Street; (215) 925–8686; e-mail: mum@libertynet.org. Productions run from October through April. Admission varies with productions.

The remarkable Mum Puppet Theatre has built a reputation for fun and innovative puppet performances. Some productions are aimed at younger children, others are more sophisticated. Call ahead for specifics.

 FIREMAN'S HALL (all ages)
147 North Second Street; (215) 923–1438. Open Tuesday through Saturday 9:00 A.M. to 5:00 P.M. Admission is **Free**.

Just about every family has somebody who wants to be a firefighter when he or she grows up. Fireman's Hall will fascinate that somebody. Ever since Benjamin Franklin founded the city's first fire department in 1736, Philadelphia has had fire equipment and firefighters. You'll see old-fashioned leather buckets, hand pumpers, three fire wagons that date from 1730, a spider hose reel from 1804, fire helmets from around the world, and a memorial wall for firefighters who died in the line of duty. Aspiring firefighters can try out the re-created living quarters of real firefighters or take the helm of a fireboat. Fireman's Hall is in the historic district, half a block from Elfreth's Alley.

Amazing Philadelphia Facts

Fairmount Park is the nation's largest landscaped city park.

CHRIST CHURCH (ages 8 and up)

Second Street between Arch and Market Streets; call (215) 922–1695 to check winter hours and for group reservations. The church is open to the public from 9:00 A.M. to 5:00 P.M. Monday through Saturday and from 1:00 to 5:00 P.M. on Sunday.

At Christ Church you can find the pews formerly occupied by George Washington, Benjamin Franklin, Betsy Ross, and other characters out of your history books. Kids will be interested to learn that this is also the birthplace of a character from a children's book: Amos, the mouse who befriended Ben Franklin in the classic *Ben and Me.* "The Nation's Church" is now celebrating 300 years as an active Episcopal parish, with Sunday morning services at 9:00 and 11:00 and communion services on Wednesday at noon. All are welcome to attend.

NATIONAL LIBERTY MUSEUM (ages 6 and up)

321 Chestnut Street; (215) 925–2800; www.libertymuseum.org. Open daily 10:00 A.M. to 5:00 P.M. Closed on Monday in the winter. Admission is $$ for adults and $ for seniors and students.

Brand new in 2000, the National Liberty Museum was created to celebrate our nation's history of freedom and the wonderfully diverse society it has produced. After your family has seen the places where our liberty was born, bring them here to learn what we all must do to preserve our liberty.

Using artwork, dioramas, displays, and hands-on experiences, visitors are encouraged to think about the responsibilities we all share. Visitors can "vote" on real contemporary issues and learn about more than 350 modern-day heroes of all backgrounds. They can see a model of Nelson Mandela's cell or Anne Frank's attic. (For parents of younger children, it is easy to bypass the more disturbing images.) First, view the introductory film, and then go up to the third floor and work your way down. Doing this, you'll end your experience at the shredder machine, where kids are encouraged to write down "mean words" they've heard or used and put them into the shredder, where they are ripped into colorful shards. A walk across the "Bridge of Forgiveness" completes the experience.

Highlighted in the museum are many beautiful glass sculptures. Glass is used as a metaphor for, and illustration of, liberty because once broken, it cannot be put back together the same way. This is an inspiring trip, especially for older children who are beginning to be aware of social issues.

FRANKLIN COURT (ages 6 and up)

Market Street between Third and Fourth Streets; (215) 597–8974. Open Monday through Friday 10:00 A.M. to 4:00 P.M., Saturday and Sunday 10:00 A.M. to 5:00 P.M.

Benjamin Franklin's home no longer stands at this site, but you can still see its foundation, as well as several other houses that Franklin owned. This area has been transformed into Franklin Court, an interactive learning experience aimed at school-age kids that's like meeting the great man himself.

Kids can listen to the voices of such notable historic figures as John Adams, Ralph Waldo Emerson, Thomas Jefferson, Harry S. Truman, Mark Twain, Lord Byron, and General Lafayette, all offering their opinions of Franklin. A series of dioramas illustrates Franklin's career, and the movie *Portrait of a Family* tells about his family life.

To enter Franklin Court, enter the archway between Market and Chestnut, in the middle of the block between Third and Fourth Streets. You can also use the walkway on Orianna Street from Chestnut Street.

"BEN FRANKLIN" (all ages)

For details contact "Ben Franklin" at P.O. Box 40178, Philadelphia 19106; call (215) 238–0871; or fax (215) 238–9102. **Free.**

When Franklin returned to Philadelphia from Paris in 1785, he used to sit under the mulberry tree at Franklin Court—and there you can find him still, daily Memorial Day through Labor Day, 10:00 A.M. to noon. An especially wonderful treat for young children, "Ben Franklin" himself invites kids to gather around and listen to stories of his life.

CITY TAVERN (ages 6 and up)

138 South Second Street; (215) 413–1443.

Now that you're completely steeped in history, why not eat a historic meal? Don't make the mistake of assuming City Tavern is just a restaurant with a colonial theme. Dining here gives a real feeling of the past.

This historic gathering place, now part of the Independence National Historic Park, was opened in 1774. Paul Revere came here in May of that year to announce that the Port of Boston was closed. General Washington set up headquarters here, and Benedict Arnold slept here. John Adams called it "the most genteel tavern in America."

The building was rebuilt in 1975 to look exactly as it did in colonial times. The tavern serves Thomas Jefferson Ale, brewed exclusively by the Dock Street Brewing Company, along with colonial specialties such as turkey-thigh stew and beef and pork pie. More tame entrees are also available, but this is not the place to bring picky eaters.

City Tavern is in the heart of the Historic District, a short walk from Elfreth's Alley.

ALSO IN THE HISTORIC DISTRICT

Other sites within the Historic District include **Congregation Mikveh Israel** and the **National Museum of American Jewish History,** at 55 North Fifth Street, which tells the story of the American-Jewish experience. Open daily except Saturday and Jewish holidays. Admission is $. Call (215) 923–3811 for more information.

The Waterfront/Penn's Landing

New things are happening all over Philadelphia, and the site that once hosted William Penn's arrival in 1682 bustles with new activity. A new Hyatt Regency hotel has just opened, as well as a state-of-the-art amphitheater with new festival space encompassing the area from Walnut to Market Streets along Columbus Boulevard.

On the Philadelphia side of the river, you can enjoy RiverRink (in season), the Independence Seaport Museum, Dave & Buster's, and lots of shops. A new Family Entertainment Center is under construction.

If you take the RiverLink ferry across the river to Camden, New Jersey, you can see the Camden Aquarium and Children's Garden or attend a concert at the Tweeter Center. To find out more about these attractions, check the Web site www.pennslandingcorp.com.

The Spirit of Philadelphia cruises leave from Penn's Landing at Lombard Circle, near the Chart House Restaurant. For information call (215) 923–1419 or check www.spiritofphiladelphia.com.

INDEPENDENCE SEAPORT MUSEUM AND HISTORIC SHIPS (all ages)

211 Columbus Boulevard at Walnut Street; (215) 925–5439; http://seaport. philly.com. Open daily 10:00 A.M. to 5:00 P.M. Admission to the Museum and Historic Ship Zone (Olympia and Becuna) is $$ for adults; $ for children ages 5 to 12. Children under 5 enter **Free**. *The museum offers* **Free** *admission on Sunday mornings from 10:00 A.M. to noon.*

Start your visit to Penn's Landing with the Independence Seaport Museum, which uses exciting family-oriented interactive exhibits to tell the story of four centuries of maritime history. The collection of nautical artifacts and ship models that were formerly housed in the old Philadelphia Maritime Museum have been incorporated into a panorama and are enlivened at every turn by audiovisuals and multimedia computers. Kids can try out an immigrant's steerage bunk or a rowing machine, or learn about the history of underwater exploration. This is a great place for any folks with a taste for the nautical.

In exhibits like Home Port Philadelphia, children can chart a course for Penn's Landing and navigate underneath the three-story replica of the Benjamin Franklin Bridge. Protecting the Nation features the bridge of the guided-missile destroyer USS *Lawrence,* most recently used in the Persian Gulf Conflict. Divers of the Deep explores the development of diving technologies such as helmets and scuba gear.

The Independence Seaport Museum also includes Historic Ship Zone, where you can see two real vessels: the *Olympia* and the *Becuna* (319 Delaware Avenue, at Spruce Street; 215-922-1898). Step aboard the *Olympia,* flagship of Admiral Dewey's Asiatic fleet, and see the bronze impressions of the admiral's feet in the exact spot where he stood in 1898 and said, "You may fire when you are ready, Gridley." Then take the kids aboard the *Becuna,* a guppy-class submarine from World War II, where sixty-six men shared the tight living quarters.

If you purchase a RiverPass, it includes round-trip fare on the River Link ferry from Penn's Landing to Camden, New Jersey, plus admission to both the New Jersey State Aquarium and the Independence Seaport Museum. The aquarium is worth a visit, especially if you have school-age kids. They can even pet a shark (a small, harmless one, of course). A Children's Garden is adjacent to the aquarium.

DAVE & BUSTER'S (ages 6 and up before 10:00 P.M.)

Pier 19 North, 325 North Columbus Boulevard (formerly Delaware Avenue); (215) 413–1951. Open to children 11:30 A.M. to 10:00 P.M.

Older children or young adults will probably enjoy Dave & Buster's. This unusual attraction bills itself as a family entertainment center with something for everyone. New attractions include Virtual World and Eyework, a turbo-ride theater.

Parents should be aware, however, that not all activities are appropriate for all ages. For example, many of the video games have violent content. There are also bars here. Dave & Buster's has taken over all 70,000 square feet of Pier 19 on the Philadelphia waterfront and filled it with skee-ball, hoop toss, video games, a variety of bars and restaurants for different tastes, music, and virtual-reality games. You can even play golf on a virtual golf course. There are billiards, shuffleboard, and an outdoor deck with a view of the Ben Franklin Bridge.

All games are activated by a "power card." The only additional charges are for food, beverages, billiards, and the turbo-ride. No one under twenty-one is permitted unless accompanied by a parent. Clean and neat clothing required; no tank tops. No more than three children to one guardian over twenty-five years of age.

Parkway Attractions

Philadelphia has a tradition of excellence in museums. On Benjamin Franklin Parkway, sometimes called "Philadelphia's Champs-Elysées," there's something for everyone—from toddlers to teenagers. We've found that for most of the museums on the parkway, it's best to beat the crowd by arriving in the morning right when the museum opens.

Amazing Philadelphia Facts

Founded in 1812, Philadelphia's Academy of Natural Sciences is the oldest scientific research institution in the Western Hemisphere.

ACADEMY OF NATURAL SCIENCES (all ages)

Nineteenth Street and Ben Franklin Parkway; (215) 299–1000. Open Monday through Friday 10:00 A.M. to 4:30 P.M., weekends and selected holidays 10:00 A.M. to 5:00 P.M. Admission is $$; under 3, **free***. Handicapped accessible.*

You really should not miss the butterfly exhibit, which can only be described as "magical." Last time we were here, our six-year-old insisted on walking through *twice!* On the third floor Outside In is a hands-on exhibit for children twelve and under. Kids can touch mice, snakes, "legless lizards" (skinks), frogs, turtles, and enormous cockroaches from Madagascar. Enthusiastic and well-informed volunteers are available to answer questions. Near Outside In is a robotic dinosaur not to be missed. It roars! (Very little children may be frightened.)

The Academy of Natural Sciences is the oldest continuously operating natural-history institution in the Western Hemisphere, but to our kids, it will always be "the dinosaur museum." Dinosaur Hall features *Tyrannosaurus rex* and *Gigantosaurus,* one of the largest meat-eating dinosaurs ever discovered. In The Dig, visitors can be paleontologists and dig for real fossils with real tools.

Make sure you check the schedule when you arrive at the academy, because there are live animal shows and films at regular intervals. Wheelchair accessible. Family memberships are available.

FRANKLIN INSTITUTE (ages 5 and up)

Twentieth Street and Benjamin Franklin Parkway; (215) 448–1200; www.fi.edu. The Science Center is open daily 9:30 A.M. to 5:00 P.M. The Mandell Center and Tuttleman Imax Theater are open Monday through Thursday 9:30 A.M. to 5:00 P.M., Friday and Saturday 9:30 A.M. to 9:00 P.M., and Sunday 9:30 A.M. to 6:00 P.M. Call for prices and Imax and planetarium show times. Admission starts at $$ for children 4 to 11, $$$ for adults.

If you visited the Franklin Institute as a child, as we did in 1969, you'll probably remember walking through the model of the human heart, following the path that the blood vessels take, hearing the sound of the heartbeat. Or maybe for you the highlight was climbing up on the real 1926 Baldwin locomotive or sitting in the cockpit of an airplane. If you have fond memories of these exhibits, don't worry—they're still here, still delighting children. But today there's a lot more, too.

The Franklin Institute was founded in 1824, and exhibits such as the heart pioneered the idea of hands-on museum displays. The museum has continued its tradition of forward-looking exhibits. Several new exhibits were added in 2000 and 2001. The Sports Challenge uses interactive devices and virtual-reality technology to teach kids about the physics, physiology, and material science behind their favorite sports. In Kidscience, children ages five to eight can explore a cave, turn the crank of a water wheel, and have a lot of fun

*S*eeing Independence National Historic Park with Limited Time

If you have only time for a half-day visit, use your time wisely. Don't miss these highlights:

- Visitors center
- Independence Hall and Congress Hall
- Liberty Bell Pavilion
- Franklin Court

If you have a little more time, we recommend these sites:

- Declaration House
- Bishop White House
- Todd House

while learning basic science concepts. In The Tram Factory, you can visit the Franklin Institute's beloved Baldwin steam locomotive in its new home, as the centerpiece of a brand-new Railroad Hall.

Be sure to also check out the Science Center, which includes exhibits about flight, optical illusions, and the Fels Planetarium.

The Tuttleman Imax Theater showcases very special movie experiences on its huge screen, giving a 180-degree field of view. Check to see what movie is currently playing, but the short feature *Philadelphia Symphony,* which usually precedes the main show, presents an excellent introduction to Philly.

The gift shops offer an unusual assortment of educational and scientifically oriented toys, books, posters, and so forth.

 PLEASE TOUCH MUSEUM (ages 2 to 8)

210 North Twenty-first Street. For details call (215) 963–0666. Hours are 9:00 A.M. to 4:30 P.M. daily, 9:00 A.M. to 5:30 P.M. from July 1 to Labor Day. Admission is $$ for ages 1 and over; children under 1 are Free. *In late 2004, the museum is expected to move to a new location on Penn's Landing.*

The Franklin Institute may be best for older kids, but the Please Touch Museum is designed especially for children eight and under. Your child can visit again and again, always discovering something new.

Sendak presents an ingenious landscape of settings and characters from the beloved books of Maurice Sendak, including *Where the Wild Things Are* and *In the Night Kitchen*. Kids can climb onto Max's 10-foot-by-6-foot bed as the walls actually turn into a jungle filled with "Wild Things."

There are seven other major exhibit areas. In The Supermarket, kids push kid-size shopping carts through a fully-stocked supermarket complete with cash registers. Me on TV is a child-size TV studio in which kids can create sound effects and see themselves on TV. This area has recently been upgraded to include more cameras, more monitors, a news desk, and a weather station. There is even a special area for the youngest visitors, ages three and under.

The Please Touch Museum also offers many great annual events. Every President's Day weekend (in February), there's Junior Jazz. In October the museum celebrates Halloween, and on the day after Thanksgiving, there's The Gift of Reading and The Enchanted Colonial Village. On December 31, there's a Countdown to Noon for those too young to stay up for New Year's.

Recognized by *USA Today* as one of the top children's museums in the country, the Please Touch Museum has also been named one of the best children's museums in the world, according to *The Observer* of London.

Adult supervision is required, and the museum specifies that no more than three children can accompany one adult. The signs posted give helpful suggestions to parents. Wheelchair accessible. Strollers not permitted on gallery floor. Membership available.

A Paulsen Family Adventure

It was obvious from the moment we entered the main floor of the Please Touch Museum for the first time, with three-year-old Judah and infant Seth, that this was a pretty stimulating place.

The large open space had been divided into different environments to attract young visitors. There were children building with blocks, playing with puppets, trying on costumes, petting a rabbit, and climbing in and out of the cab of a SEPTA bus. The voices of play surrounded us.

We looked down and Judah was missing. We checked all the exciting places that we thought he'd gravitate toward. No Judah.

We finally found him in the reading corner curled up with a book.

SCIENCE PARK (all ages)

Twenty-first Street, between Winter and Race Streets. Admission through Please Touch Museum or Franklin Institute. Open May through October only.

The Franklin Institute teamed up with the Please Touch Museum to build the Science Park, a family-centered outdoor learning area including more than twenty elements, such as miniature golf, a radar detector, and more. Admission is **Free** with admission to either museum.

 ### FREE LIBRARY OF PHILADELPHIA (all ages)

Nineteenth and Vine Streets. Call (215) 686–5322 for hours. Admission is **Free**.

The Free Library of Philadelphia stands across Logan Square from the Franklin Institute and the Academy of Natural Sciences and down the parkway from the Art Museum and Rodin Museum. It houses more than six million books, magazines, newspapers, and other printed items and frequently hosts special events and exhibits. The library is open daily in winter, closed Sunday in summer. On Sunday there are tours of its remarkable rare books department.

 ### RODIN MUSEUM (ages 6 and up)

Twenty-second Street and Benjamin Franklin Parkway; (215) 684–7500; www. rodinmuseum.org. Open Tuesday through Sunday 10:00 A.M. to 5:00 P.M. A per-person contribution ($) is suggested. **Free** *guided tours are available. Call (215) 763–8100 for days and times.*

Everybody knows Rodin's *Thinker*. You can see this popular sculpture at the Rodin Museum, along with the most complete collection of Auguste Rodin's work outside Paris. This museum is administered by the Philadelphia Museum of Art, down the parkway.

 ### PHILADELPHIA MUSEUM OF ART (ages 6 and up)

Located at the end of Benjamin Franklin Parkway at Twenty-sixth Street; (215) 684–7500; www.philamuseum.org. Open Tuesday through Sunday 10:00 A.M.to 5:00 P.M., on Wednesday until 8:45 P.M. Admission is $$ for adults and students age 13 and up; children to age 12, **Free**. *Special admission is charged on Sunday, when the rule is "Pay what you wish, all day."* **Free** *guided tours are conducted hourly between 11:00 A.M. and 3:00 P.M. Tours are also available in foreign languages (215–684–7923) and sign language (215–684–7601). The Museum Restaurant is open for lunch Tuesday through Sunday 11:30 A.M. to 2:30 P.M. and for dinner Wednesday 5:00 P.M. to 7:30 P.M. Sunday brunch is available*

from 11:00 A.M. TO 3:30 P.M. The cafeteria is open 10:00 A.M. to 4:30 P.M. Handicapped accessible.

At the far end of the parkway, on the other side of Eakins Oval, are some steps that many people will recognize. Who can forget that memorable scene from *Rocky* when the boxer runs up all these steps? But the collection inside the Philadelphia Museum of Art is even more memorable—with a permanent collection of some 300,000 works, including one of the largest and most important collections of European art in the United States. The art museum takes a somewhat unusual approach, juxtaposing the painting, sculpture, furniture, ceramics, textiles, and architectural elements from the same period to convey a sense of that time. The museum is also known for its outstanding collection of rural Pennsylvania crafts and works by Thomas Eakins. We know a seven-year-old boy who could spend all day in the Arms and Armor collection.

The art museum's neoclassical facade stands at the end of Benjamin Franklin Parkway at Twenty-sixth Street, within walking distance (unless your children's legs are very short) of the Franklin Institute, Free Library of Philadelphia, Please Touch Museum, Logan Circle, and other parkway sites.

"Something every Sunday" is how the museum describes its family activities. Different programs are offered, usually on a walk-in basis, for families with children ages three to thirteen. Most of the programs take place on Sunday at 11:30 A.M. or 1:30 P.M. Programs range from storytelling to hands-on art activities, with titles like Tales and Treasures, Try a Technique, and Gallery Games. Many of these programs are free, and the rest are $. Accompanying adults are **Free**. Children especially like the Japanese teahouse, Chinese palace hall, and the thirteenth-century French cloister. Every day of the week you can pick up a family-oriented, self-guided tour brochure at the West Information Desk. The museum's automated information line is (215) 684–7500. For information about family activities and children's art classes, call (215) 684–7605. Handicapped accessible, with changing tables in the rest rooms.

 ## EASTERN STATE PENITENTIARY (ages 7 and up)

Fairmount Avenue at Twenty-second Street, 5 blocks from the Philadelphia Museum of Art and the parkway; (215) 236–3300; www.EasternState.org. Open 10:00 A.M. to 5:00 P.M. on selected days May through October: in May, Saturday and Sunday; in June, July, and August, Wednesday through Sunday; in September

and October, Saturday and Sunday. Guided tours are available every hour from 10:00 A.M. to 4:00 P.M. Children under 7 are not admitted. Admission: adults, students, and seniors $$, children ages 7 to 17 $.

When Charles Dickens visited the United States in 1842, there were two sights he didn't want to miss: Niagara Falls and the Eastern State Penitentiary. It has been called the most influential prison in the world, because its design was grounded on the nineteenth century's most modern ideas about civic responsibility and criminal behavior. Instead of using physical punishment, this prison was designed to encourage solitude and penitence.

A nationally broadcast special on the History Channel and a full-page spread in the *New York Times* have focused on the prison, and the number of visitors has tripled in recent years.

Al Capone did time here, as did the "gentleman bandit" Willie Sutton. An operating prison for more than 140 years, until 1971, the building has been reopened as the Eastern State Penitentiary Historic Site Society makes plans for its future. At present there are special art exhibits here, and sometimes dramatic productions.

The building has been made safe for tours but has otherwise been left "as is." Visitors must wear hard hats and stay with tour groups. Most people won't have to be reminded; the decaying plaster, dampness, and remnants of prison life make this a pretty eerie place—great for teenagers! The Halloween Ghost Tours are very popular; call (215) 763-NITE. The gift shop offers T-shirts, posters, and books with a prison theme.

Fairmount Park

At 8,700 acres, Philadelphia's Fairmount Park is one of the world's largest city parks and an amazing source of activities. The park includes: Andorra Natural Area, Bartram's Gardens, Boathouse Row, Japanese House and Garden, Smith Playground and Playhouse, and the Philadelphia Zoo. Of lesser interest to families with children are the following sites: Historic Fairmount Waterworks, Horticultural Center, Memorial Hall, Ryerss Library and Museum, and the ten colonial mansions of Fairmount Park. Although the Philadelphia Museum of Art is technically part of Fairmount Park as well, we have included it in our discussion of "Parkway Attractions."

The Fairmount Park Information Center is located at Memorial Hall, North Concourse Drive near Forty-second Street and Parkside Avenue; (215) 685-0000 (yes, those zeroes are correct). For a guided tour of the mansions, please contact Mansions of Fairmount Park, Park House Guides Office, Philadelphia

Museum of Art, or call (215) 684–7926. There are also trolleys that circulate around the park, stopping at all the historic mansions so that you may tour the houses on your own. For information about these trolleys (and also Philadelphia City Trolley Tours), please call (215) 925–TOUR.

Amazing Philadelphia Facts

More Revolutionary War battles were fought within a 50-mile radius of Philadelphia than in all the New England states combined. It was also the capital during the Revolution, except for nine months when it was occupied by the British. It then served as the nation's capital from 1790 to 1800.

ANDORRA NATURAL AREA (all ages)

Between Ridge and Germantown Pikes on Northwestern Avenue; (215) 685–9285. The park is open daily dawn to dusk. The visitors center is usually open on weekends noon to 4:00 P.M. **Free***; some educational programs have fees.*

Andorra Natural Area offers many wonderful programs for children including nature trails, exhibits, and special events. Most activities begin at Treehouse Visitor Center, a one hundred-year-old home where you can explore a touch table and other exhibits. Even when the visitors center is closed, there are maps, activity sheets, program calendars, and other information available.

Two annual festivals emphasize hands-on participation. In October you can pick apples and make them into apple butter at the Harvest Festival, and in February you can tap a tree at the Maple Sugar Festival.

HISTORIC BARTRAM'S GARDEN (gardens: all ages; house: ages 8 and up)

Fifty-fourth Street and Lindbergh Boulevard; (215) 729–5281; www.libertynet. org/bartram. The garden is open daily from dawn to dusk; admission is **Free***. The home is open Tuesday through Sunday noon to 4:00 P.M. There is a charge ($) for the house tour.*

The oldest surviving botanical garden in the country includes the pre-Revolutionary home of botanist John Bartram, as well as forty-four acres of gardens.

BOATHOUSE ROW (all ages)

A lovely place for a stroll along the Schuylkill River, Boathouse Row consists of twelve nineteenth-century buildings where Philadelphia's rowing clubs keep their boats. The outline of each boathouse is trimmed with lights to create a luminous view of the boathouses from across the river at night.

JAPANESE HOUSE AND GARDEN (ages 5 and up)

Near the Horticultural Center, at Belmont and Montgomery Avenues; (215) 878–5097; www.shofuso.org. Open May 1 through October, Tuesday through Sunday 10:00 A.M. to 4:00 P.M. Admission is $; children under 6 enter **Free**.

The Japanese House and Garden offers many events that your family might enjoy, including a Japanese tea ceremony presented in the Japanese House. At the annual Children's Festival, held in May, kids can learn about origami, kimonos, Japanese crafts, dolls, and armor. They can also see a traditional tea ceremony, hear traditional music and stories, and try Japanese food. This event is modeled after the Japanese celebrations of Boys' Day and Girls' Day. At the Summer Festival in June, kids can participate in the beautiful custom of launching lantern boats.

SMITH MEMORIAL PLAYGROUND AND PLAYHOUSE (ages 2 to 12)

Kelly Drive; (215) 765–4325. Enter the park at the statue of Ulysses S. Grant on Kelly Drive and follow the signs to the playground. The playhouse is open year-round Monday through Saturday 10:00 A.M. to 3:30 P.M. Available on Sunday for birthday parties. The playground is open 9:00 A.M. to 4:45 P.M. daily. It closes one hour earlier in winter. The playhouse is open to children ages 5 and under, and the playground is open to ages 12 and under. Admission is **Free**.

If you haven't heard about Smith Memorial Playground and Playhouse, you're in for a treat. This attraction in Fairmount Park hosts an average of 1,000 children daily during the summer and celebrated its one-hundredth birthday in 1999. On one recent weekend, an 86-year-old woman and three generations of her family all slid down the Giant Slide (built in 1908) together, all reliving their own childhood memories.

Inside the playhouse there are three floors of activities for preschoolers. The train on the first floor was donated by the group Boyz II Men, whose members played here as children. The foam-block room has been expanded, and a reading room with books, cozy corners, and a puppet stage has been added. In Smithville (on the basement level), little kids climb into the kid-size cars and "drive" on kid-size roads, with delightful details like traffic lights and parking meters.

During the summer months, there is an outside carousel for preschoolers, two swimming pools (including a wading pool for little ones), and a concession stand. Adjacent to Smith Memorial, on its property is the only Frisbee golf course in the city, **Free** and open to all ages.

Winner of several "Best of Philly" awards for birthday parties and the Giant Slide and dubbed "Best Playground for Children," Smith's is partially handicapped accessible. There are rest rooms in the house, and a concession stand is open seasonally. There is also plenty of free parking.

A Paulsen Family Adventure

Typical first-time parents, we doted on everything Judah did. At the Smith Memorial Playground, we coaxed our three-year-old up the ladder to the slide. Every rung was greeted with cheers. We applauded him as he cautiously shuffled across the catwalk and slid down the slide.

We were so busy encouraging Judah we didn't pay any attention to seven-month-old Seth, who crawled up the ladder and across the catwalk and slid down the slide all by himself!

THE PHILADELPHIA ZOO (all ages)

3400 West Girard Avenue; (215) 243–1100; www.philadelphiazoo.org. Open daily 9:30 A.M. to 5:00 P.M. Admission: adults $$$, seniors and children ages 2 to 11 $$, members and children under 2 **Free**.

The Philadelphia Zoo has some exciting additions. In June 1998 the renovated Reptile House opened, featuring a replica of an Everglades thunderstorm and Indiana Jones Temple of Doom, with not one, but two, king cobras.

In July 1999 the Primate Reserve opened, featuring great apes, monkeys, lemurs, and more.

A new annual feature is not to be missed. From April to October, weather permitting, the Birds of Australia exhibit is open. Even bigger kids are wide-eyed with wonder when these colorful birds drink nectar from the children's hands.

The zoo offers a treat for all ages—a chance to meet more than 1,800 animals housed in naturalistic settings, all surrounded by beautiful trees and plantings. Other highlights include the white lions, tigers, elephants, rhinos, bears, and more.

Amazing Philadelphia Facts

Museums There are more than one hundred museums in Philadelphia alone.

The Rest of Center City

Former Philadelphia mayor Edward G. Rendell realized the importance of tourism to his city. One of his first actions upon taking office was to start renovating the amazing City Hall (at the intersection of Broad and Market Streets, the dead center of William Penn's original plan for the city) and open it for **Free** tours.

 CITY HALL (observation deck, all ages; tour, ages 8 and up)
Broad and Market Streets; (215) 686–2840. Tours available daily at 12:30 P.M. Tours are **Free***, but donations are welcome. The observation deck is open daily 9:30 A.M. to 4:15 P.M.*

Philadelphia's City Hall celebrated its one hundredth birthday in 2001. See the courtroom where the film *Philadelphia* was made and the 548-foot-tall tower that is topped by a statue of William Penn. When the Phillies became the National League champions in 1994, maintenance workers placed a baseball cap on Penn's head. The observation deck (at William Penn's feet) affords a spectacular view of the city.

CLAES OLDENBURG'S CLOTHESPIN (all ages)
Located in Centre Square Plaza at Fifteenth and Walnut Streets.

Either you love it or you hate it. Either way, Claes Oldenburg's public sculpture of a giant clothespin is one you're not likely to forget.

ROBERT INDIANA'S PHILADELPHIA *LOVE* (all ages)
Located at Kennedy Plaza, Fifteenth Street and JFK.

This public sculpture became famous in the 1960s and 1970s. It has been cleaned and looks better than ever.

PENNSYLVANIA ACADEMY OF THE FINE ARTS (ages 8 and up)

118 North Broad Street at Cherry; (215) 972–7600. The museum is open Tuesday through Saturday 10:00 A.M. to 5:00 P.M. and on Sunday 11:00 A.M. to 5:00 P.M.; closed New Year's Day, Thanksgiving, and Christmas. Admission is $$ for adults, seniors, and students with ID; $ for children under 5 to 12; and Free *to members and children under 5.*

Walking up Broad Street near Cherry, 1 block from City Hall and the Convention Center, you can't miss the graceful facade of the Pennsylvania Academy of the Fine Arts, home of the nation's first art museum and its first art school, the Academy School. The building, with its Gothic arches and lacy ironwork, is a masterpiece of High Victorian Gothic architecture. The museum collection includes works by Benjamin West, Charles Willson Peale (one of the academy's founders), Thomas Eakins (who served as the academy's director during the 1880s), Mary Cassatt, Winslow Homer, Horace Pippin, Andrew Wyeth, Alexander Calder, Louise Nevelson, and many others.

You can make your visit more lively with Family Inform, an audioguide system. Look around the galleries to find numbers that you key into the audio machine's keypad, and you can hear messages about the works of art.

Avenue of the Arts Broad Street south of City Hall has been renamed the Avenue of the Arts. Already home to the Academy of Music, Kimmel Center, the Merriam Theater, and the University of the Arts, several new theaters are planned for the street.

ACADEMY OF MUSIC (ages 10 and up)

Broad and Locust Streets; call (215) 893–1935 for information or to make reservations.

That spectacular opera house seen in the movie *The Age of Innocence* is Philadelphia's own Academy of Music. You can see the landmark if you attend a concert by the Philadelphia Orchestra or a performance by the Opera Company of Philadelphia. But by reservation only, you can take a one-hour afternoon tour of this beloved building on Broad and Locust Streets, including a peek backstage and into the artists' dressing rooms.

THE KIMMEL CENTER FOR THE PERFORMING ARTS (ages 3 and up)

260 South Broad Street on the Avenue of the Arts; (215) 790-5800; www.rpac.org.

The Kimmel Center, opened in December 2001, joins the Academy of Music to become one of the nation's largest performing arts complexes. The Kimmel Center and Academy of Music are home to eight of Philadelphia's premier ensembles: The Philadelphia Orchestra, The Opera Company of Philadelphia, the Pennsylvania Ballet, American Theater Arts for Youth, The Chamber Orchestra of Philadelphia, PHILADANCO, The Philadelphia Chamber Music Society, and Peter Nero and the Philly Pops.

Tickets for all Philadelphia Orchestra and Kimmel Center presentations are available through one source, PhilaTix, which includes some 700 performances annually.

The Philadelphia Orchestra offers outstanding children's concerts at reasonable prices. The Sound All Around series is aimed at three- to five-year-olds, and the Family Concert series is for ages six to twelve.

READING TERMINAL MARKET (all ages)

Twelfth and Arch Streets; (215) 922–2317. Open Monday through Saturday 8:00 A.M. to 6:00 P.M. year-round.

If you're hungry and you don't know what to eat, or if you're planning a picnic, stop by the Reading Terminal Market, where farmers and merchants from around the Philadelphia area (many of them Amish) sell very fresh produce, cheese, fish, meats, baked goods, and much more. There are hundreds of stalls to browse through, so each member of the family is sure to find something delicious.

While you're in the area, head across the street and up the stairs to the old **Reading Terminal,** which has been converted as part of the Pennsylvania Convention Center. This cavernous hall was at one time the main train station in downtown Philadelphia.

CHINATOWN (all ages)

Between Arch and Vine Streets, Eleventh to Eighth Streets. For information about Chinatown call (215) 922–2156.

Go 1 block east of the Reading Terminal, and you're in the heart of Philadelphia's Chinatown. Stop here for authentic Chinese cuisine and products.

EDGAR ALLAN POE NATIONAL MEMORIAL (ages 10 and up)

532 North Seventh Street; (215) 597–8780; www.nps.gov/edal. Open November through May, Wednesday through Sunday 9:00 A.M. to 5:00 P.M.; June through October, daily 9:00 A.M. to 5:00 P.M. Closed Thanksgiving, Christmas, and New Year's Day. Admission is Free.

A couple of long blocks north of Chinatown is the house where Edgar Allan Poe lived with his wife and mother-in-law in 1843–44. There is a brief slide presentation about the author's life.

 ROSENBACH MUSEUM AND LIBRARY (ages 10 and up)

2010 Delancey Place, on Rittenhouse Square; (215) 732–1600; www.libertynet. com/rosenbl. Open Tuesday through Sunday 11:00 A.M. to 4:00 P.M. (last tour, 2:45 P.M.). Closed Monday, national holidays, and the period from August 1 to the second Tuesday after Labor Day. Admission is $$; seniors and students (including children) $.

To get a feeling of a traditional, stately Philadelphia neighborhood, stroll around the blocks surrounding Rittenhouse Square. On Rittenhouse Square, the Rosenbach Museum and Library houses an astounding collection of rare books, manuscripts, antique furniture, silver, porcelain, and works of art in the beautiful home of the Rosenbach brothers, who lived here from 1948 until their deaths in 1952 and 1953. This wonderful museum is more suited to older children and literary folks, although occasionally there are special exhibits of illustrated books that may appeal to youngsters.

Among the more than 30,000 rare books and 300,000 manuscripts are letters penned by George Washington, Thomas Jefferson, Benjamin Franklin, and Abraham Lincoln. You may also see Lewis Carroll's own copy of *Alice's Adventures in Wonderland,* the manuscript for James Joyce's *Ulysses,* and the notes for Bram Stoker's *Dracula.* The museum also owns more than 3,000 original drawings by Maurice Sendak, noted author of classic children's books.

For information about handicapped accessibility, call (215) 732–1600, ext. 25 or e-mail maw-rml@libertynet.org.

 CIVIL WAR LIBRARY AND MUSEUM (ages 10 and up)

1805 Pine Street; (215) 735–8196. Open Thursday through Saturday 11:00 A.M. to 4:30 P.M. Admission: $$ for adults, $ for seniors and students with ID.

A couple of blocks away from the Rosenbach Museum, the Civil War Library and Museum houses artifacts from that tumultuous era in our history.

North Philadelphia

Philadelphia is home to a huge number of colleges and universities. Besides adding to the rich cultural diversity of the city, these institutions offer some unusual museums.

TEMPLE UNIVERSITY DENTAL MUSEUM (ages 8 and up)

Broad Street and Allegheny Avenue; (215) 707–2816. Open by appointment only.

The Victorian dental office, on the thrid floor of the dental school, is open full time, no appointment necessary. By appointment only, you can also tour an unusual collection of dental memorabilia going back to the 1700s. Its best-known piece is the first dental chair in the United States, dating from the 1790s.

WAGNER FREE INSTITUTE OF SCIENCE (ages 8 and up)

1700 West Montgomery Avenue; (215) 763–6529; www.wagnerfreeinstitute.org. Open Tuesday through Friday 9:00 A.M. to 4:00 P.M. for self-guided tours. Occasional Saturday openings; call for schedule. Admission is **Free**.

The Wagner Free Institute of Science presents an unusual opportunity to visit a science museum that looks pretty much the way it did in about 1890. This is a great place for amateur naturalists and paleontologists.

Amateur scientist William Wagner founded the institute in 1855 to provide free science education to all, regardless of race, gender, or financial resources. He used his personal collections to illustrate the lectures, and these objects now form the core of the museum's exhibits, which were given their present arrangement after Wagner's death in 1885.

More than 100,000 specimens, including fossils, minerals, shells, mounted animals, skeletons, and insects, are displayed in the Victorian cherrywood cases. (Very young children may have difficulty seeing into some of the cases.) All children under eighteen must be accompanied by an adult. The institute also offers evening and Saturday-morning science classes (off-site) for ages twelve and up.

SHOE MUSEUM (ages 10 and up)

Eighth and Race Streets, at the Temple University School of Podiatric Medicine. **Free** *tours must be arranged in advance by calling (215) 625–5243.*

A unique diversion, the Shoe Museum at the Temple University School of Podiatric Medicine displays footwear belonging to celebrities such as Ringo Starr, Julius Erving, Lucille Ball, Mamie Eisenhower, and Ronald and Nancy Reagan. There are also shoes from around the world, tiny Chinese shoes for bound feet, huge shoes for circus giants, tap shoes, ballet slippers, and many more.

UNIVERSITY OF PENNSYLVANIA MUSEUM (ages 8 and up)

Thirty-third and Spruce Streets; (215) 898–4000; www.upenn.edu/museum. Open Tuesday through Saturday 10:00 A.M. to 4:30 P.M. and Sunday 1:00 to 5:00 P.M. Closed Sunday in summer. Admission is a donation of $$ for adults, $ for students and children; children under 6 are **Free**. *For information on Family Fun Days, call (215) 898–4890. For children's workshops call (215) 898–4015.*

The University of Pennsylvania Museum is a treasure trove for your budding archaeologist or anyone interested in sphinxes, mummies, African sculpture, or ancient Mayan, Greek, or Polynesian culture. The three floors of this museum are loaded with a wealth of artifacts unearthed by the University of Pennsylvania Museum's own world-renowned archaeological and ethnographic expeditions.

Kids will be awe-struck by the genuine Sphinx of Ramesses II, weighing in at twelve tons of solid granite. They will be mystified, and perhaps a little unnerved, by the real mummies. The huge Chinese crystal ball is a favorite with our kids. Other ongoing exhibits include Raven's Journey: World of Alaska's Native People.

The annual Chinese New Year celebration and the Celebration of African Cultures, both popular family events, are held in the winter. Please note that while the large marble halls keep pretty cool, the building is only partially air-conditioned. The Cafe offers a kid-friendly menu, especially on weekends. The Pyramid Gift Shop has educational and inexpensive items for children. Handicapped accessible, with diapering facilities in some bathrooms.

MUTTER MUSEUM AND COLLEGE GALLERY OF THE COLLEGE OF PHYSICIANS OF PHILADELPHIA (ages 10 and up)

19 South Twenty-second Street, between Chestnut and Market Streets; (215) 563–3737; www.collphyphil.org. The Mutter Museum and College Gallery are open Monday through Saturday 10:00 A.M. to 4:00 P.M. Admission is $$ for adults, seniors, students, and children 6 to 18; children under 6 enter **Free**.

For years the College of Physicians of Philadelphia (not an educational institution, but the nation's oldest private medical society) has maintained the Mutter Museum of medical anomalies. Begun as a teaching collection for medical students in a time when students had little access to clinical situations, it has become known for its wall of more than one hundred skulls, the tumor removed from President Cleveland's jaw, and the preserved body of an eighteenth-century woman.

The college's exhibits, however, are now moving into the twenty-first century by taking on some of the hottest issues in current medicine. The new College Gallery features temporary exhibits that examine important issues. For example, a recent exhibit studied the dilemma posed "When the President is the Patient." The new C. Everett Koop Community Medical Information Center (CHIC) is a **Free** library on health, with books, CD-ROMs, Internet access, and videos.

ALSO IN THE AREA

Also on the Penn campus, kids might enjoy a look at **College Hall,** one of two Philadelphia structures reputed to be a model for the *Addams Family* house. (Charles Addams went to Penn and was well acquainted with this building. The other candidate is the Ebeneezer Maxwell Mansion in Chestnut Hill.) There are also some interesting sculptures on this campus, such as Claes Oldenburg's oversized button and the statue of Benjamin Franklin.

Philadelphia Sports Philadelphia has a number of professional sports teams whose games provide terrific family outings.

The Phillies play National League baseball at Veterans Stadium in South Philadelphia. They are expected to move to a new stadium in April 2004. For tickets call (215) 463–1000.

The Eagles also currently play at Veterans Stadium and expect to move to a new stadium in 2003. For Eagles tickets call (215) 463–5500.

The First Union Complex now includes the new First Union Center, home to the Philadelphia Flyers (NHL), Sixers (NBA), and Wings (MILL); and the Comcast First Union Spectrum, home of the Phantoms (AHL) and Kixx (NPSL). The box office at (215) 339–7600 serves both.

Veterans Stadium and the First Union Complex are located across the street from each other in South Philadelphia, at Broad Street and Pattison Avenue.

South Philadelphia

South Philadelphia is home to many of the city's ethnic neighborhoods, as well as the world's largest outdoor market, the Italian Market.

ITALIAN MARKET (all ages)

Ninth Street, between Warton and Christian Streets; (215) 922–5557.

    The Italian Market is a great place to find unusual cheeses, fresh fruits and vegetables, homemade pasta, exotic spices, and unusual kitchen wares.

MUMMERS MUSEUM (ages 8 and up)

1100 South Second Street; (215) 336–3050; www.mummers.com. Open Tuesday through Saturday from 9:30 A.M. to 4:30 P.M., and Sunday from noon to 4:30 P.M. It is closed on Monday, and on Sunday in July and August. Admission is $; guided tours are available by reservation.

    No Philadelphian can hear the tune of "Golden Slippers" without picturing the sequined costumes, the feathers, and, of course, the distinctive strut of the mummers. But non-Philadelphians may need a word of explanation.

    Philadelphians have created a mummers tradition all their own in the annual Philadelphia New Year's Day Parade, when the string bands, fancy brigades, and clowns strut up Broad Street. The Mummers Museum surrounds you with the spangles, the colors, the history, and the music of the mummers. You can see videos of past parades, learn how the costumes are made, and practice your "Mummers' Strut." In nice weather, the string bands appear for concerts on selected Tuesday evenings at 8:00 P.M.

FORT MIFFLIN ON THE DELAWARE (ages 8 and up)

*Fort Mifflin Road; (215) 492–1881; www.spiritof76.net. Open April through November, Wednesday through Sunday 10:00 A.M. to 4:00 P.M. During the off-season prebooked tours may be available. Admission is $$ for adults, $ for seniors and children 2 to 12, and **Free** for children under 2.*

    Fort Mifflin played a strategic role in the Revolutionary War. In 1777, more than 200 British warships sailed up the Delaware River with needed supplies for British troops occupying Philadelphia. For seven weeks the little fort held back the mightiest navy in the world.

Although it was almost completely destroyed in the process, Fort Mifflin never surrendered.

On Sunday afternoons, in addition to tours, there are militia-guard drills. A blacksmith also demonstrates how weapons were made in this period.

Manayunk and Chestnut Hill

Although located within Philadelphia's city limits, the Manayunk and Chestnut Hill sections feel more like small towns than urban neighborhoods. Manayunk, one of the country's oldest villages, has a reputation as an artists' community. Main Street in Manayunk is lined with art galleries, boutiques, and unusual shops. Chestnut Hill has a different atmosphere, with its beautiful old homes and elegant shops. Both offer wonderful restaurants (see the Where to Eat section of this chapter).

EBENEEZER MAXWELL MANSION (ages 8 and up)

Greene and Tulpehocken Streets, Chestnut Hill; (215) 438–1861. Open Friday through Sunday 1:00 to 4:00 P.M.

Rumor has it that the Ebeneezer Maxwell Mansion is the model for the *Addams Family* house, as depicted by Philadelphia's own Charles Addams. It is unclear how much the cartoonist Charles Addams was influenced by the Victorian buildings he saw, but it is known that he was familiar with both College Hall (on the Penn campus) and the Ebeneezer Maxwell Mansion, and both may have shaped the architecture of the *Addams Family* house. This eighteen-room Victorian mansion in the Chestnut Hill section was built in 1859. Young children will love the children's bedroom, filled with games and toys of the period. The gadgets are also wonderful, including an apple corer and a sausage stuffer. The gardens include a grape arbor and a small lake. At Christmas there's a Dickensian Christmas celebration and in fall a ghost walk.

MORRIS ARBORETUM (all ages)

Germantown Pike at 100 Northwestern Avenue, Chestnut Hill; (215) 247–5777; www.upenn.edu/morris. Open Monday through Friday 10:00 A.M. to 4:00 P.M., Saturday and Sunday from November through March 10:00 A.M. to 4:00 P.M., and April through October 10:00 A.M. to 5:00 P.M. Guided tours are given Saturday and Sunday at 2:00 P.M. Admission: adults $$, students $, and children under 6 **Free**.

The Morris Arboretum, the botanical garden of the University of Pennsylvania, is filled with exotic plants and picturesque vistas. The arboretum fills ninety-two acres in Chestnut Hill, including Japanese gardens, rose gardens, the only Victorian fernery in the United States, and a charming pond complete with swans.

For kids, the real highlight of the Morris Arboretum is definitely the new Garden Railway, open from mid-June until early October. This delightful G-scale model railroad has six trains and three trolley lines, operating on a layout of thirty-four miniature buildings including Independence Hall, Betsy Ross House, and many more. The buildings are replicated to scale and constructed out of acorns, moss, bark, twigs, leaves, seeds, and honeysuckle. The ten bridges and trestles are made of logs and railroad ties. There's even a waterfall.

In season, the Garden Railway display is open daily 10:00 A.M. to 4:00 P.M. and until 8:00 P.M. on Thursday. It is handicapped accessible.

A Paulsen Family Adventure On a beautiful summer day some years ago, we took six-year-old Judah, three-year-old Seth, and a friend, Patrick, to the Morris Aboretum. In the Rose Garden, I arranged the boys beside a fountain for a photo. When I snapped the picture, all three boys were smiling. But by the time I put my camera down and looked up, the only part of Seth I could see was his legs. He'd fallen head-first into the water. I pulled Seth up, expecting him to be frightened, but he grinned and said, "I go scuba diving!"

Northeast Philadelphia

INSECTARIUM (all ages)

8046 Frankford Avenue in Northeast Philadelphia; (215) 335–9500. Open 10:00 A.M. to 4:00 P.M. Monday through Saturday. Admission is $$ per person. It is **Free** *for anyone younger than 2 with a paying adult.*

Named "Philly's Best Kid's Attraction, Repulsive" in 2001, the Insectarium has been featured in *Life* magazine. Steve's Bug-Off Exterminating Co. has assembled the Insectarium, a collection of live insects in naturalized settings, mounted specimens, and interactive displays. This one-of-a-kind museum is designed to teach the importance of insects as part of the diversity of nature—but mostly it's a lot of fun. You won't be able to forget the "cockroach kitchen," the "glow-in-the-dark" scorpion, the live termite tunnel, or the tarantulas (no matter how hard you try). A new outdoor Learning Garden will open in spring 2003, including a butterfly tent.

JOHN HEINZ NATIONAL WILDLIFE REFUGE (all ages)

8601 Lindbergh Boulevard, in the Tinicum section; call (215) 365–3118 for information; http://heinz.fws.gov. The programs, facility, and grounds are **Free***. The Cusano Environmental Education Center (CEEC) is open 8:30 A.M. to 4:00 P.M. daily. The trails are open 8:00 A.M. to sundown daily.*

The 1,200-acre John Heinz National Wildlife Refuge is managed by the U.S. Fish and Wildlife Service for conservation of habitat and promotion of environmental education. The refuge is alive with 281 species of birds and healthy populations of mammals, reptiles, and amphibians. Ten miles of hiking and biking trails meander along the Tinicum Marsh and Darby Creek. Don't forget your binoculars to enhance the view from the Observation Tower.

The Cusano Environmental Education Center (CEEC) was built using sustainable design techniques. The building includes a resource center, classrooms, Tinicum Treasures Bookstore, and a "living marsh machine." The center houses many interactive exhibits and displays highlighting wetlands and wildlife.

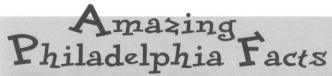

Amazing Philadelphia Facts

The Benjamin Franklin Parkway has been called "Philadelphia's Champs-Elysées."

Where to Eat

IN PHILADELPHIA

City Tavern, *138 South Second Street; (215) 413–1443; www.citytavern.com.* Children's menu, booster seats. In the heart of the Historic District.

Italian Market, *Ninth Street between Christian and Dickinson; (215) 922–5557.*

Katmandu, *417 North Columbus Boulevard; (215) 629–7400.* High chairs, booster seats, children's menu. Great view of the Ben Franklin Bridge.

Magnolia Cafe, *1602 Locust Street; (215) 546–4180.* Cajun/Creole food. Booster seats, children's menu.

Marabella, *1700 Benjamin Franklin Parkway; (215) 981–5555.* Italian food. High chairs and booster seats, children's menu, crayons, and balloons.

Mulberry Market, *236 Arch Street; (215) 592–8022.* Deli-style food, sandwiches, hoagies. Across the street from the Betsy Ross House.

Pizzeria Uno, *509–511 South Second Street; (215) 592–0400.* Located in South Street area. High chairs, booster seats, children's coloring menu with crayons.

Reading Terminal Market, *Twelfth and Arch Streets; (215) 922–2317.*

IN MANAYUNK

Le Bus, *4266 Main Street; (215) 487–2663.* Children's menu, high chairs, casual atmosphere.

Sonoma, *4411 Main Street; (215) 483–9400.* "Italifornia" food. High chairs, booster seats; babies and toddlers welcome.

Where to Stay

IN PHILADELPHIA

Best Western Center City Hotel, *501 North Twenty-second Street; (215) 568–8300 or (800) 528–1234.* Convenient to major museums and other attractions. Restaurant, outdoor pool.

Holiday Inn–Center City, *1800 Market Street; (215) 561–7500 or (800) HOLIDAY.*

Holiday Inn–Express Midtown, *Thirteenth and Walnut; (215) 735–9300 or (800) 5–MIDTOWN.*

Holiday Inn–Independence Mall, *(Historic Area), 400 Arch Street; (215) 923–8660 or (800) HOLIDAY.* Seasonal outdoor rooftop pool.

Sheraton Society Hill, *1 Dock Street; (215) 238–6000.*

For More Information

Greater Philadelphia Tourism Marketing Corp., *(888) 999–3790; www.gophila.com.*

Philadelphia Convention and Visitors Bureau, *(800) 537–7676 or (215) 636–1666; www.pcvb.org.*

Amazing Philadelphia Facts

Philadelphia is known for its distinctive foods, including cheese steaks, scrapple, snapper soup, and soft pretzels with mustard.

Philadelphia Countryside

Imagine a rainbow of giant crayons and enormous glass walls you're not only allowed but *supposed* to color on! The Crayola Factory is the perfect place to let your imagination run wild. And that's just one of the exciting things happening in the Philadelphia Countryside.

Sesame Place's Vapor Trail, its first-ever roller coaster, is designed to include all members of the family. Dorney Park has Steel Force, the tallest, longest, and fastest steel roller coaster on the East Coast. Norristown's Elmwood Park Zoo has expanded and improved, with its new Conservation Playground.

A three-day Revolutionary War Driving Tour, which begins with the Battle of Brandywine in September 1777, traces the Continental Army's struggles against the British through the Paoli Massacre, the Battle of Germantown, Whitemarsh Encampment, and the Battle of Old Gulph Road to Valley Forge. It

Faith & Emily's
Favorite Philadelphia Countryside Attractions

1. Sesame Place, Langhorne
2. Crayola Factory, Easton
3. Colonial Pennsylvania Plantation, Media
4. Valley Forge National Historical Park, Valley Forge
5. Mercer Museum, Doylestown
6. Dorney Park and Wildwater Kingdom, Allentown
7. Tubing at Point Pleasant
8. Elmwood Park Zoo, Norristown

Nazareth

Delaware River

Easton

Claussville
Schnecksville
Bethlehem
Allentown
Hellertown
Breinigsville
Alburtis

Point Pleasant

New
Hope

Lahaska
Washington
Hilltown
Doylestown
Crossing
Chalfont
Schwenksville

Worcester
Morrisville
Elverson
Churchville
Langhorne
Phoenixville
Audubon
Glenside
Valley Forge
Norristown
Chester
Merion
Springs
Paoli
Philadelphia
West Chester
Media
Swarthmore
Chadds Ford
Delaware River

PHILADELPHIA COUNTRYSIDE

includes a narrative of the events, along with driving instructions to eleven historic sites in Montgomery, Chester, Delaware, and Berks Counties, and in Philadelphia. For information call the Valley Forge Convention and Visitors Bureau at (610) 834-1550 or (888) VISIT-VF, or log onto www.valleyforge.org.

The area surrounding Philadelphia offers many other opportunities for family adventure. Living-history sites such as Hopewell Furnace, Colonial Pennsylvania Plantation, and Peter Wentz Farmstead bring kids face-to-face with the past. The Barnes Foundation's collection of Impressionist art is dazzling, and its building has been recently restored. The streets of New Hope teem with art galleries, craft shops, and restaurants. Historic parks such as the Brandywine Battlefield, Washington Crossing, and Valley Forge offer a great combination of history and outdoor fun, all in the beautiful Pennsylvania countryside.

Faith & Emily's
Favorite Philadelphia Countryside Events

- **Mercer Museum FolkFest** (May); (215) 345-0210.

- **Pennsylvania Fair,** Bensalem (May); (215) 633-0404 or (215) 639-9000; www.pennsylvaniafair.com.

- **Devon Horse Show** (ten days surrounding Memorial Day weekend); (610) 964-0550.

- **Musikfest,** Bethlehem (August); (610) 861-0678; www.musikfest.org.

- **Time of Thanksgiving,** Lenni Lenape Museum (autumn); (610) 797-2121.

- **Great Allentown Fair** (starts on the Tuesday before Labor Day); (610) 435-7469; www.allentownfairpa.org.

- **Philadelphia Folk Festival** (weekend before Labor Day); (215) 242-0150, (215) 247-1300, or (800) 556-FOLK; www.folkfest.org.

- **Scarecrow Festival Weekend** at Peddler's Village (September); (215) 794-4000; www.peddlersvilage.com.

- **Great Pumpkin Carve and Show** in Chadds Ford (October); (610) 338-7376; www.voicenet.com/ncfhs/.

- **Longwood Gardens Christmas Display** (November to January 1); (610) 388-6741.

The following Web sites introduce you to this area:

- Bucks County Conference and Visitors Bureau, Inc.: www.buckscountycvb.org

- Valley Forge: www.valleyforge.org/

- Lehigh Valley Convention and Visitors Bureau: www.lehighvalleypa.org

- Chester County Conference and Visitors Bureau: www.brandywinevalley.com

- Delaware County: www.delcocub.org/

- Montgomery County: www.montcopa.org

Brandywine Valley

For a trip that includes historic homes and battlefields, art, and gardens, all within easy distance of one another, contact the Chester County Tourist Bureau (800–228–9933). You may wish to make a weekend visit to the towns of Kennett Square and Chadds Ford. The Web site for the Chadds Ford Historical Society is www.voicenet.com/~cfhs/.

The fields, mills, and farms of rural Pennsylvania have found their way into the art of Chadds Ford's most famous artist, Andrew Wyeth. Here you're surrounded by Wyeth's landscapes and his art. You can visit the historic Brandywine Battlefield, eat lunch in a historic inn, shop, and take a walk along the Brandywine River.

 LONGWOOD GARDENS (all ages)

Route 1 in Kennett Square; (610) 388–1000; www.longwoodgardens.org. The outdoor gardens and conservatory open at 9:00 and 10:00 A.M., respectively, every day of the year. Both close at 5:00 P.M. from November through March and at 6:00 P.M. from April through October, although both are frequently open later for special events and holiday displays. Call ahead for a complete schedule. Admission is $$$ for adults ($$ on Tuesday), $$ for youths ages 16 to 20, $ for children 6 to 15, and Free under age 6. Prices subject to change.

Longwood Gardens is a place to enjoy the variety of nature, both indoors and out. In a four-acre conservatory, Longwood's visitors can see orchids, roses, bonsai, exotic jungle plants, and waterfalls, even on the coldest winter days. And on warmer days, you can tour the outside gardens and the fountains. No matter what the weather, don't miss the annual holiday display.

Longwood Gardens is currently redesigning its indoor Children's Garden. In the meantime, there are outdoor areas for youngsters. The

Kids Corner is open in the summer and early fall with a sunflower house, A-Z garden, weather station, and root-view box. Check the schedule for special children's events. Also check out the Web site, which has a great children's map of the gardens. The Terrace Restaurant includes both a cafeteria and a sit-down dining room. Reservations are recommended for the dining room.

BRANDYWINE RIVER MUSEUM (ages 6 and up)

Route 1; (610) 388–2700; www.brandywinemuseum.org. Open daily 9:30 A.M. to 4:30 P.M. Admission is $$ for adults, $ for senior citizens, students with ID, and children 6 to 12; ₣ree *for children under 6. N. C. Wyeth House and Studio open April through November; $ additional admission.*

Andrew Wyeth came from a family of distinguished artists. The Brandywine River Museum, in a converted gristmill on Route 1 in Chadds Ford, has the world's largest collection of Andrew Wyeth's work, as well as that of his father, N. C. Wyeth; his son, Jamie Wyeth; and other family members.

Children especially go for Jamie Wyeth's painting *Portrait of Pig* and the life-size animal sculptures along the riverbank. Many visitors will recognize the illustrations of N. C. Wyeth for such swashbuckling classics as *Treasure Island* and *Kidnapped.* The Brandywine River Museum has just introduced a new audio tour of its permanent collection as well as selected exhibitions. This lively tour answers questions such as, "How did Jamie Wyeth convince a pig to pose for a painting?" Works by other artists from the Brandywine region hang near still-life paintings, landscapes, and an unparalleled collection of American illustration.

Surrounding the museum are stands of wildflowers, trees, and shrubs indigenous to the Greater Brandywine Valley. For an additional fee, visitors may tour the N. C. Wyeth House and Studio.

JOHN CHADS HOUSE (ages 8 and up)

Route 100; (610) 388–7376. Open May through September, Saturday and Sunday from noon to 5:00 P.M. Admission is $$ for adults, $ for children. Combination ticket to both John Chads House and Barns-Brinton House is $$ for adults and $ for children.

Often you can watch bread being baked in the beehive oven. On the weekend after Labor Day, the Chadds-Ford Historical Society, which administers both John Chads House and Barns-Brinton House, hosts the annual Chadds Ford Days. The event features pony rides, music,

Brandywine Valley art, games, and crafts. People often come for the sausage sandwich.

CHADDS FORD VILLAGE (ages 6 and up)

Route 1; (610) 388–7361. **Free**.

Chadds Ford Village is a charming place to browse in craft shops or to enjoy a meal at the Chadds Ford Inn, which has been serving travelers since 1736.

BARNS-BRINTON HOUSE (ages 8 and up)

Route 1; (610) 388–7376. Same hours and admission fees as the John Chads House.

At the Barns-Brinton House, guides in period costume demonstrate colonial crafts and give tours of this eighteenth-century home and tavern. Just past the herb garden, you'll find the Chaddsford Winery.

BRANDYWINE BATTLEFIELD PARK (ages 8 and up)

Route 1; (610) 459–3342. The battlefield park grounds are open, **Free***, year-round Tuesday through Saturday 9:00 A.M. to 5:00 P.M. and Sunday noon to 5:00 P.M. The visitors center is open Tuesday through Saturday 9:00 A.M. to 5:00 P.M. and Sunday noon to 5:00 P.M. Closed Monday. Admission for house tour only: $. A family rate ($$) is available.*

After retreating at the Battle of Brandywine, George Washington's troops moved on to camp at Valley Forge. At Brandywine Battlefield Park you can tour the house where Washington set up his headquarters. The visitors center offers an audiovisual introduction to the park, along with maps for a self-guided driving tour that includes twenty-eight historic points of interest. A reenactment of the battle is held every September. There is a museum shop, and picnic areas are available.

Elverson

HOPEWELL FURNACE (ages 8 and up)

2 Mark Bird Lane; (610) 582–8773, TDD 582–2093; www.nps.gov/hofu/. Open daily 9:00 A.M. to 5:00 P.M., except New Year's Day, Martin Luther King Jr. Day, Presidents' Day, Veterans Day, Thanksgiving, and Christmas. Entrance fee is $ per person. For living-history events an additional fee ($) per person is charged. Annual passes, family passes, and senior passes are available.

Watch a real blacksmith hammer a shape from white-hot iron. Visit a cast house where iron weapons were made for the Continental Army. Learn how colonists prepared food and clothing. Hopewell Furnace National Historic Site gives you a chance to see what life was like in a colonial iron-making town. As you take your self-guided walking tour, taped messages give you a first-hand feeling for the experiences of the people who lived and worked here. Although open year-round, the site is most active in summer, when authentically costumed artisans demonstrate their crafts. Mother's Day is sheep-shearing day. The visitors center and rest rooms are wheelchair-accessible. Some of the historic structures are accessible. Call for more details about handicapped accessibility.

ALSO IN THE AREA

Nearby, **French Creek State Park** offers outdoor family adventures such as hiking, fishing, swimming, and camping, as well as winter sports. You may wish to have lunch or do some shopping in **Victorian St. Peter's Village.**

Chester Springs

Where nature brought forth yellow water with medicinal properties, man has brought forth *The Blob*. Some would say Chester Springs's attractions have run "from the sublime to the ridiculous."

 HISTORIC YELLOW SPRINGS (ages 8 and up)
Art School Road; (610) 827–7414. Open for self-guided tours Monday through Friday 9:00 A.M. to 4:00 P.M., weekends by reservation. Closed major holidays. A donation is suggested.

For centuries, starting with indigenous peoples and, later, colonial settlers, presidents, and entertainers, people have come to Yellow Springs in hopes of finding a cure for their illnesses. In 1722 there was a health spa here. From 1916 to 1952 the Pennsylvania Academy of Fine Arts ran a landscape school on these beautiful grounds. And later still, Valley Forge Films made movies here, including the 1958 Steve McQueen classic *The Blob* and *4-D Man*.

At present this site is operated as Historic Yellow Springs, Inc. Visitors may take a self-guided tour of the grounds and eighteenth- and nineteenth-century buildings, but it's most fun to come during a special event such as art shows, classes, and workshops or to attend annual events such as the Frolicks.

West Chester

QVC STUDIO TOURS (ages 6 and up)

1200 Wilson Drive; (800) 600–9900; www.qvctours.com. Tours are conducted daily, every hour on the hour, 10:00 A.M. to 4:00 P.M. Reservations are not required. Not recommended for children under 6.

The QVC cable home-shopping channel conducts a tour of its large studio complex. If you're a fan of QVC, this tour is a must. If you're not a QVC shopper, the tour offers an interesting look behind the scenes of TV production. The guided tour follows the path of a QVC product from sourcing, testing, and TV presentation to home delivery.

Valley Forge

VALLEY FORGE NATIONAL HISTORICAL PARK (all ages)

Visitors center at State Route 23 and North Gulph Road; (610) 783–1077; www.nps.gov/vafo. Park buildings are open daily except Christmas from 9:00 A.M. until 5:00 P.M. Admission is $ for Washington's Headquarters. Children 16 and under are **Free***. Park grounds are open to the public* **Free***.*

The nice thing about Valley Forge National Historical Park is its mixture of history and outdoor fun.

After viewing the eighteen-minute introductory film and exhibits at the visitors center, you can get information about touring the park. The visitors center also displays various exhibits and artifacts that help you get more out of your visit.

There are so many different ways to enjoy Valley Forge that you can choose the one that's just right for your family. From June to October tour buses take a regular route, allowing visitors to get off when a particular site sparks their interest and then catch the next bus. A map allows families to take a self-guided driving tour accompanied by a narrated audiotape, if desired.

Trails are available for visitors who prefer to see the park by bike, on foot, or on horseback. Pick up a brochure at the visitors center for more information about the trails. There are fields perfect for kite flying and three different picnic areas.

No matter how you go, your kids will not want to miss the re-created encampment where Washington's troops spent the winter of

1777–78. And it may be sexist to say so, but boys are especially interested in the Artillery Park, reconstructed fortifications, and the Grand Parade Grounds, where the troops trained for battle. General Washington set up his temporary headquarters in Isaac Potts's House (also known as Washington's Headquarters), now restored to look as it did during that famous winter. Costumed interpreters appear at the Muhlenberg Brigade daily from June through August, 10:00 A.M. to 4:00 P.M., weekends year-round in good weather.

The **Washington Memorial Chapel,** privately operated, commemorates the Revolutionary War and the armed forces. Also privately operated, the **Valley Forge Historical Society Museum** on Route 23 (610-783-0535; www.valleyforgemuseum.org) exhibits a collection of Revolutionary War memorabilia.

The self-guided driving tour is open all year from 6:00 A.M. to 10:00 P.M. The visitors center is completely handicapped accessible; most of the historic buildings are not. The park hosts special events on Washington's Birthday, the anniversary of the march into Valley Forge (December 19), French Alliance Day (first weekend in May), and the anniversary of the march out (June 19).

ALSO IN THE AREA

For another kind of family adventure in the Valley Forge area, contact **United States Hot Air Balloon Team,** P.O. Box 490, Hopewell Road, St. Peters 10470; (610) 469-0782 or (800) 763-5987.

The nation's second largest shopping mall, the **Plaza and Court of King of Prussia,** is only minutes from Valley Forge Park, on Route 202.

Amazing Pennsylvania Facts

Valley Forge Battered by defeats throughout the fall of 1777, Gen. George Washington and his troops retreated to Valley Forge for the winter. By February 1778 he had lost nearly half his men to death, disease, and desertion.

Audubon

Although John James Audubon lived at Mill Grove for only three years, it was his first home in America (he arrived here in 1803), and the perfect place to inspire his career as a painter of birds.

MILL GROVE (house, ages 6 and up; grounds, all ages)

Audubon and Pawlings Roads; (610) 666–5593. Open Tuesday through Saturday 10:00 A.M. to 4:00 P.M.; Sunday 1:00 to 4:00 P.M.; **Free**.

One hundred and seventy-five acres of greenery, 175 species of birds, and 400 species of flowering plants surround the house, built in 1762. This is a lovely spot to stroll in the woods or enjoy a peaceful view of Perkiomen Creek. Inside the home you may tour eleven rooms filled with Audubon's collection of paintings, stuffed birds, and birds' eggs. The museum also owns a complete set of Audubon's greatest work, *The Birds of America,* with each bird painted in actual size. Call for a calendar of events and programs.

Paoli

What is it about the Philadelphia area that seems to breed unforgettable characters? Doylestown has Henry Mercer, Merion has Albert Barnes, and Paoli has Wharton Esherick.

WHARTON ESHERICK STUDIO (ages 8 and up)

Horseshoe Trail Road. For directions and reservations call (610) 644–5822 or log onto www.levins.com/esherick.html. Reservations are required for one-hour tours of Esherick's home and studio. Tours are available March through December, Saturday 10:00 A.M. to 5:00 P.M. and Sunday 1:00 to 5:00 P.M. Admission is $$ for adults, $ for children under 12.

Wharton Esherick started out as a painter, but after moving in 1913 to a stone farmhouse near Paoli, he became fascinated with wood. The Wharton Esherick Studio reflects this fascination. Everywhere you look, you discover some whimsical wooden object: wooden sculptures, wooden picture frames, wooden furniture.

Esherick was also entranced by what is now called "found objects." The handrail of his astounding double-spiral staircase is a real mastodon tusk! The artist created chairs out of hammer handles or wagon wheels.

Phoenixville

WATER WORLD (all ages)

On Route 724 in Phoenixville; (610) 935–1290. Open daily May through September noon to 9:00 P.M. Admission is $$ per person. Access to water slides is $$.

Water World is a relaxing place to cool off on a sticky summer day, with two water slides, a rope swing, a large pool, and a wading pool for the little ones. There is a small snack bar and picnicking facilities.

Norristown

ELMWOOD PARK ZOO (all ages)

Harding Boulevard, Norristown; (610) 277–DUCK; www.elmwoodparkzoo.com. Open daily 10:00 A.M. to 5:00 P.M. (gates close at 4:00 P.M.). Call for current admission rates.

Exciting things have been happening at Elmwood Park Zoo, always a favorite for younger children. Enter the aviary, and you are surrounded by a naturalistic wetland environment filled with waterfowl, beaver, and two fun-loving river otters. The murky Bayou Building houses alligators, snakes, and armadillos. The new Tom Kimmel Conservation King-

Amazing Pennsylvania Facts

William Penn Although he founded Pennsylvania, William Penn lived here for only a total of four years.

dom is an imaginative playground that teaches kids about conservation while they have fun. And in late 2002, the new Oberkircher Discovery Center is due to open. In all there are more than 200 animals representing forty species, including jaguars, cougars, timber wolves, and a peregine falcon.

The youngest children still love feeding the ducks in the duck pond and petting the sheep and goats in the Petting Barn (open seasonally). There is also a snack shop, a gift shop, and pony rides. Handicapped accessible, with diapering facilities in the rest rooms.

51

Media

Media is the home of Ridley Creek State Park, where you can see the Colonial Pennsylvania Plantation.

 COLONIAL PENNSYLVANIA PLANTATION (ages 6 and up)

Located in Ridley Creek State Park; (610) 566–1725; www.de.psu.edu/cpp/. Open weekends, April to November, 10:00 A.M. to 4:00 P.M. Usually closed for rain.

On an eighteenth-century farm, animals were left to graze freely, not penned up as they are today. In the root cellar the farmer's family stored carrots, onions, and potatoes; in the springhouse, flowing water cooled milk and eggs. The clothing was made by hand, spun of natural fibers. All these details are meticulously re-created at Colonial Pennsylvania Plantation.

This is actually a working farm where 120 acres of crops are grown, using methods that date back more than 200 years. Here you can observe the staff demonstrating cooking, spinning, weaving, sheep shearing, planting, and harvesting. Even the clothing worn by inter-preters is authentic—right down to the fibers. School groups get a chance to dip candles or cut firewood in the authentic manner.

Also in the park, the adjacent Tyler Arboretum has an extensive col-lection of native and non-native plants. Highlights include a giant sequoia with a circumference of 9 feet and a unique fragrant garden designed specifically for the visually impaired. The arboretum is open daily at no charge, 8:00 A.M. until dusk. Call (610) 566-5431.

Swarthmore

 SCOTT ARBORETUM (all ages)

Swarthmore College campus; (610) 328–8025; www.libertynet.org/gardens. Open daily from dawn to dusk; Free.

One hundred and ten acres surrounding Swarthmore College con-stitute the college's Scott Arboretum. Come here for a quiet stroll through collections of flowering cherries, roses, conifers, daffodils, dogwoods, lilacs, hollies, rhododendrons, and more. Specialty gardens include the Theresa Long Garden of Fragrance, the Dean Bond Rose Garden, and the Winter Garden, which provides longed-for colors in the gray of winter.

Merion

THE BARNES FOUNDATION (ages 8 and up)

300 North Latches Lane; (610) 667–0290. Open Friday, Saturday, and Sunday 9:30 A.M. to 5:00 P.M., September through June, by advance reservation only. During the months of July and August, the galleries are open Wednesday through Sunday 9:30 A.M. to 5:00 P.M. Admission: $$ per person. Audio tour: $$ per person.

The art lovers in our family have always been awe-struck by the paintings at The Barnes Foundation, one of the nation's most amazing private collections of Impressionist and Post-Impressionist art. This collection remained one of the art world's best-kept secrets until a national tour took many of its masterpieces to several major museums.

The Barnes Foundation has undergone some changes lately, including a complete restoration, the addition of a gallery shop, and new audio tours. If you use the audio tour and take time to talk about the art with your children, this can be a wonderful learning experience.

Dr. Albert C. Barnes was a physician and businessman by vocation, but art and education were his great loves, and he held very definite opinions about them. He collected more than 180 Renoirs, seventy Cézannes, and many Matisses, including a mural specifically commissioned for the gallery. The wall ensembles explore light, line, color, and space in an amazing multicultural array that includes works by van Gogh, Picasso, El Greco, Soutine, and Glackens, as well as Greek, Roman, Egyptian, and Native American artists.

Handicapped accessible, with diapering facilities in the ladies' bathroom. The Barnes is within fifteen minutes of Suburban Square, Ardmore, for shopping or a bite to eat at Ruby's Diner.

Amazing Pennsylvania Facts

Henri Matisse In 1930 Dr. Albert Barnes commissioned the artist Henri Matisse to paint a mural for The Barnes Foundation in Merion. However, the measurements for the wall space were incorrectly translated from inches to centimeters, so when the mural arrived from France, it was 5 feet too short! Although he had spent more than a year on the first version, Matisse started all over again. The second version now decorates three arches above the main gallery in The Barnes Foundation.

Glenside

KESWICK THEATER (ages 6 and up)

Easton Road and Keswick Avenue; (215) 572–7650.

The Keswick Theater offers concerts, plays, and other productions year-round. Ticket prices vary.

Churchville

CHURCHVILLE NATURE CENTER (ages 6 and up)

501 Churchville Lane; (215) 357–4005. The nature center is open Tuesday through Sunday 9:00 A.M. to 5:00 P.M. The grounds are open dawn to dusk. Admission is **Free**.

Trails at the Churchville Nature Center are open from sunup to sundown daily. Inside the nature center you can view dioramas depicting local wildlife. There are also children's programs, such as nature crafts, junior naturalist hikes, and activities centered on the Lenape Native Americans.

Langhorne

SESAME PLACE (all ages)

100 Sesame Road, Route 1 to Oxford Valley exit; (215) 752–7070; www. sesameplace.com. Operating days and hours vary, with the park opening in May for weekends only; starting in mid-May daily 10:00 A.M. to 5:00 P.M.; staying open later after Memorial Day and returning to weekend-only hours after Labor Day until mid-October, when it closes for the season. Single-day admission (ages 3 to 54) costs $$$$. Discounts are available for families of four or more or during late-afternoon hours. Holders of Passport tickets receive unlimited admission for the season, plus special benefits.

Just about any kid will have fun at Sesame Place. We've found that even kids too grown up for Cookie Monster can't help but enjoy many of the water rides and physical play environments. Recent additions include "Pet Pals," a live animal show featuring animals rescued from shelters. Another crowd-pleaser is Vapor Trail, Sesame Place's first roller coaster.

You can walk down Sesame Street, a full-size replica of the thoroughfare seen on the popular TV show, and take pictures of your kids in front of Bert and Ernie's house. You'll love the Rock Around the Block parade and "Elmo's World Live!" starring *Sesame Street* characters. There are more than fifty kid-powered physical play elements, such as Nets and Climbs and Ernie's Bed Bounce.

Amazing Pennsylvania Facts

The New York Times recently included Sesame Place on its list of best water parks in the United States.

The park has fifteen water attractions, and most will appeal to all members of your family. Big Bird's Rambling River is a winding, relaxing circular tube ride your kids can go around and around all afternoon. Even very young children have no fear on Teeny Tiny Tidal Waves and the Rubber Duckie Lake. Sky Splash is filled with giant-size water adventures including an 8-foot-tall rubber duckie and huge tinker toys that spray water.

Sesame Place is located in Langhorne about thirty minutes from Philadelphia at exit 29A on I-95 North. Most areas are accessible to the disabled, and special events include some designed for disabled children. Bathing suits are required for all water attractions.

A Paulsen Family Adventure In the summer of 1994, we visited Sesame Place and decided to go on "Big Bird's Rambling River." We climbed into our tubes, my younger son, Seth, with me and my older son, Judah, on his own. But, I forgot to take off Judah's glasses.

Being a kid, Judah paddled straight for the nearest jet of water, got doused, and lost his glasses ten seconds into the ride. We had not brought his spares.

We reported the loss at the Guest Services office, but we didn't hold out much hope of finding them. We were told that it took around thirty minutes for the water to circulate through the system and all drains were checked periodically. We checked back at the desk a little later and, sure enough, there were Judah's glasses.

Morrisville

PENNSBURY MANOR (ages 6 and up)

*400 Pennsbury Memorial Road; (215) 946–0400; www.pennsburymanor.org.
Open Tuesday through Saturday 9:00 A.M. to 5:00 P.M. and Sunday noon to 5:00
P.M. Last tour begins 3:30 P.M. Admission is $$ for adults and $ for seniors and
children 5 to 12; children under 5 enter* Free. *Family rate $$$.*

Pennsylvania was William Penn's "holy experiment," a colony
founded on Quaker moral principles. Although he only lived here for a
total of about four years, Pennsbury Manor was never far from his
thoughts. Today his home has been restored, complete with icehouse,
stable, smokehouse, garden, and livestock. The boathouse contains a
replica of the vessel Penn used to commute to Philadelphia. The oven in
the bake-and-brew house can bake up to thirty loaves of bread at a time.

On Sunday afternoons from April to October, Pennsbury Manor
offers living history just for families. It has an activity room and a
worker's cottage where kids can try seventeenth-century skills, such as
writing with a quill pen. Geese, peacocks, sheep, and Red Devon cattle—
authentic breeds wherever possible—populate the farm.

ALSO IN THE AREA

When William Penn was living at Pennsbury Manor, he attended Quaker Meeting at Falls Meeting in Fallsington, a town built around its meetinghouses.
Guided tours start at the Gillingham Store and include several restored historic buildings: Moon-Williamson House; Burges-Lippincott House; and the
Stage Coach Tavern. Fallsington is located on Route 13 off I–95. For details
contact Historic Fallsington, Inc. at (215) 295–6567.

Washington Crossing

We picture "Washington's crossing" as in the famous painting by Emanuel
Leutz, with George Washington standing heroically in the small boat as his
troops row across the Delaware to surprise the Hessians on Christmas Day.
The German artist had never seen Washington Crossing when he painted it in
the nineteenth century. It may not be safe to stand up in a small boat, but the
image depicts an artist's impression of a historic event. In the Memorial Building at Washington Crossing National Historic Park, you can see a copy of the

painting (the original is owned by the Washington's Crossing Foundation). It's larger than life in more ways than one—the painting is 20 feet long, 12 feet tall.

 ### WASHINGTON CROSSING NATIONAL HISTORIC PARK (ages 8 and up)

State Routes 32 and 532, 3 miles north of I–95 exit 31; (215) 493–4076; www.spiritof76.net. The visitors center and historic buildings are open Monday through Saturday 9:00 A.M. to 5:00 P.M. and on Sunday noon to 5:00 P.M. There is a fee for the buildings ($). The park grounds, however, are open at no charge from 8:00 A.M. until sunset. **Free.**

A thirty-minute film at the visitors center describes the events of December 25, 1776, which led to the turning point of the Revolution. Washington planned his surprise attack from his headquarters in the Thompson-Neely House, and he ate dinner before the crossing at the Old Ferry Inn. In the Durham Boat House, you can see the boats that were actually used for the crossing.

Every year on Christmas Day the park hosts a reenactment of Washington's crossing. Other special events here include Gingerbread Days, Tavern Nights, and special activities in honor of Washington's birthday. Gazebo Games, another special event, lets kids try out the games and toys enjoyed by eighteenth-century children.

 ### BOWMAN'S HILL TOWER and BOWMAN'S HILL WILDFLOWER PRESERVE (all ages)

Located on the grounds of Washington Crossing National Historic Park; (215) 862–2924 or (215) 862–3166. Open daily from 8:00 A.M. until sunset; **Free.**

During the Revolution sentries were posted in Bowman's Hill Tower, which has now been restored. Surrounding the tower you'll see breathtaking varieties of wildflowers. You can pick up a self-guided tour map that also includes a list of flowers currently in bloom.

New Hope

In summer the streets of New Hope bustle with people drawn to the more than 200 art galleries, craft shops, restaurants, and history this town offers. But New Hope welcomes visitors any time of the year. You can get more information about bed-and-breakfasts in New Hope by stopping by the New Hope

Information Center, 1 West Mechanic Street. For brochures about New Hope, call (215) 862–5880. To talk to a staff member about New Hope, call (215) 862–5030.

CORYELL'S FERRY HISTORIC BOAT RIDES (all ages)

Ferries leave Coryell's Ferry at Gerenser's Exotic Ice Cream, 22 South Main Street (215–862–2050; www.spiritof76.net), April through October starting at 11:00 A.M.

Artists began settling in New Hope in the late 1800s, but the town started out as Coryell's Ferry, which began carrying passengers across the Delaware in canoes in 1733. Ferries still operate here for half-hour tours; only now they use more commodious paddleboats. The longest ride on the river, aboard a 65-foot Mississippi riverboat, leaves at 11:00 A.M. daily, in season. Call for details or to find out about special kids' days on the ferry.

COLONIAL NEW HOPE WALKING TOURS (ages 6 and up)

Gerenser's Exotic Ice Cream, 22 South Main Street; (215) 862–2050; www. spiritof76.net. Tours of New Hope are available April through October, starting at noon.

General Washington visited New Hope at least four times. To learn more about the history of this town, you can take a walking tour. Tickets and schedules for walking tours of New Hope are available here.

NEW HOPE MULE BARGES (all ages)

New Street; (215) 862–2842 or (800) 59–BARGE. Open April through November. Boat fares $$ for adults, $ for children.

You can take a ride on a mule barge, sailing past eighteenth-century homes, gardens, and workshops. Many barges are equipped with folk singers or historians. The Delaware Canal became operational in 1840, and, at its height, mules hauled thousands of barges, carrying loads of coal and limestone. The canal includes 25 lift locks, 9 aqueducts, and 106 bridges.

BOAT RIDES AT WELLS FERRY (all ages)

At the end of Ferry Street on River; (215) 862–5965. Open May through October 11:00 A.M. to 6:00 P.M. Admission: adults $$, children $.

The *Star of New Hope* carries thirty-six passengers at a time on a guided tour. Tour guides offer a little history, as well as a glimpse at New Hope's varied architecture. Some tour guides play guitar music as well.

NEW HOPE AND IVYLAND RAILROAD (all ages)

Station at Bridge and Stockton Streets; (215) 862–2332; www.newhoperailroad. com. Trains run daily April to November, weekends only January until March. In December, special Santa Claus rides are offered. Tickets are $$$ for adults, $$ for seniors and kids 2 to 11, and $ for children under 2. The train operates seasonally.

The New Hope and Ivyland Railroad, built in 1889, eventually made the canal obsolete. If you take this train on its forty-five-minute narrated trip to Lahaska, you will notice a curved trestle bridge. If this bridge looks like something right out of *The Perils of Pauline,* that's because this actually was the bridge that was used in those movies.

ALSO IN THE AREA

The **Bucks County Playhouse** offers a series of plays for children on Friday and Saturday, at reasonable prices. Call (215) 862-2041 for a schedule, or check the Web site www.buckscountyplayhouse.com.

If you wish to take any kind of ride or tour, including walking tours, check at **Gerenser's Exotic Ice Cream** at 22 South Main Street, where tickets and schedules are available. You can purchase tickets for a **colonial walking tour** (215-862-2050). This is also where you get tickets for **Coryell's Ferry** (see page 58). Have some ice cream while you're here. To find out about **Ghost Tours,** call (215) 357-5637 or (215) 957-9988. You can also find out about different tours and boat rides by checking out the Web site http://bctc.org/. We especially enjoy just strolling along the canal, watching the barges go by. Some of the restaurants here have views of the canal.

Lahaska

While in Peddler's Village, take a look at some of the unusual shops and restaurants.

GIGGLEBERRY FAIR (all ages)

Peddler's Village, Routes 202 and 263; (215) 794–8960; www.giggleberryfair. com. Open Sunday through Tuesday 10:00 a.m. to 6:00 p.m., Wednesday and Thursday 10:00 A.M. to 8:00 P.M., and Friday and Saturday 10:00 A.M. to 10:00 P.M. Discovery Land/Giggleberry Mountain Combination Pass $$ per person. Individual tickets for specific attractions are also available.

Giggleberry Fair opened its doors in June 2001 "to provide a wholesome, quality experience for children to be both educated and entertained." Comprising four children's attractions, Giggleberry Fair is

10,000 square feet of family fun.

Peddler's Village has recently restored its wonderful Grand Carousel, built in 1922 by the famous Philadelphia Toboggan Company. The carousel has been joined by Giggleberry Mountain, Discovery Land, and the Painted Pony Café to create Giggleberry Fair.

Giggleberry Mountain is the area's largest and most attractive indoor obstacle course, challenging for both children and adults. The colorful, two-story, six-level structure is filled with tens of thousands of soft foam "berries." Kids fill tote bags with as many berries as they can grab and climb up through netting mazes to different levels where they can "blast" berries at their friends or reach the top of two different slides. Even adults get right in there with their kids. It's loud, but it's a happy loudness.

In Discovery Land, kids can explore a variety of calmer play environments. There's a pretend farm and orchard, a mini climbing wall, a rubber-duck waterway, and plenty of games. All games are rated "green"—suitable for all ages—by the Coin-Operated Video Game Parental Advisory System.

The Painted Pony Café offers pizza, hot dogs, a salad bar, and other kid-friendly choices.

Point Pleasant

The signers of the Declaration of Independence had to sweat it out in the notorious Philadelphia humidity, but you don't have to. Point Pleasant, north of Lahaska and New Hope, offers some great ways to cool off in its inviting, kid-friendly rapids. Bucks County River Country rents canoes, tubes, and rafts from April through October. To make reservations (which are required) or to find out about prices and special Pedal and Paddle trips, call Bucks County River Country (215-297-5000).

BUCKS COUNTY RIVER COUNTRY (ages 6 and up)

Route 32, Upper Black Eddy; (215) 297–5000. Call for days, hours, prices, and river conditions.

Our kids spent a carefree summer afternoon riding the current in tubes, occasionally dunking each other or taking time to see how deep the water was (not very). To protect your feet, remember to wear old sneakers that can get wet, and don't forget the sunscreen. Bucks County River Country also presents other events in the woods, such as the nation's largest haunted-woods hayride.

Our Tubing Trip —by Seth Paulsen-Sacks, at age 10

We had to wait in a line and tell the people how much we weighed. Then they gave us the inner tubes. All the kids in my group tied their tubes together with a camp counselor. The current was strong. We had to paddle so the current wouldn't pull us away. Luke and Paul fell off their tubes so the counselor got off, held onto our tubes, and waited for them to get back on. When we were waiting, it felt like we were still moving because of the current.

We saw a hot dog guy on a motorboat with big balloons on a string. You could buy hot dogs from him if you had money.

When we got back we found little frogs the size of ants and I caught three.

Doylestown

A wonderful choice for a day trip, Doylestown will charm you with its cast-iron lampposts, neat nineteenth-century houses, and unusual shops and galleries. You can walk to the Mercer Museum and James A. Michener Museum. Also within walking distance is the County Theater, showing art and vintage, as well as first-run, movies; the picturesque Doylestown Inn; as well as many other restaurants and shops. A short drive out of town, you may also wish to visit Fonthill and the Moravian Pottery and Tileworks. For information about Historic Doylestown, call (215) 345-0788.

MERCER MUSEUM (ages 6 and up)

84 South Pine Street, near Ashland; (215) 345–0210; www.mercermuseum.org. Open Monday through Saturday 10:00 A.M. to 5:00 P.M., Sunday noon to 5:00 P.M. On Tuesday, the museum closes at 9:00 P.M. Closed New Year's Day, Thanksgiving, and Christmas. Admission is $$ for adults, $ for youth ages 6 to 17; children under 6 enter Free.

On Pine Street in the charming town of Doylestown stands what can only be described as a castle, not of stone but of poured concrete, brainchild of Henry Chapman Mercer (1856-1930).

In 1916 Mercer built what is now the Mercer Museum, with its turrets and parapets, to house his collection of more than 50,000 artifacts and tools of more than sixty different American trades. Entering the central court of the museum, you find yourself surrounded by odds and ends hanging over your head: a Conestoga wagon; a whaling skiff; wooden buckets. Then, take the elevator up to the top floor and walk down, working your way through the implements left behind by shoe-makers, bakers, candlemakers, milliners, and farmers of America's past. Several new features are of special interest to families. Look for the new "Go for the Green" tags that mark exhibits designed for kids to touch, to build things, to pull the reins, and more. Bright paw prints indicate clues on a family scavenger hunt around the collection, and the new audio guides feature a channel just for kids. The museum also offers family events such as sleepovers, "Summer Boredom Busters," and "Under the Stars" movies.

Our kids felt that the highlight of the collection was the vampire-killing kit. They also enjoyed hunting for the footprints left in the concrete by Mercer's pet dog. The museum is unheated, so bring a sweater. There are special children's programs, as well as FolkFest in May.

 ## JAMES A. MICHENER ART MUSEUM (all ages)

138 South Pine Street; (215) 340–9800; www.michenerartmuseum.org. Open Tuesday through Friday 10:00 A.M. to 4:30 P.M., Saturday and Sunday 10:00 A.M. to 5:00 P.M. Open until 9:00 P.M. on Wednesday. Admission is $$ for adults, $ for students; children under 12 are **Free.**

The James A. Michener Art Museum, across the street from the Mercer Museum, offers the finest collection of Pennsylvania Impressionist paintings, as well as other important examples of regional contemporary and figurative art. Housed in a renovated historic site that formerly served as the Bucks County Jail from 1884–1985, the museum also includes a multimedia interactive exhibition, "Creative Bucks County: A Celebration of Art and Artists" and a permanent exhibit on James Michener himself. The family education center provides puzzles and discovery boxes for children to explore. Light snacks are available at the cafe.

MORAVIAN POTTERY AND TILE WORKS (ages 8 and up)

East Court Street; (215) 345–6722. Open daily, except major holidays, 10:00 A.M. to 4:45 P.M. Tours leave every thirty minutes, with the last tour departing at 4:00 P.M. Admission is $. The tile shop, open daily 10:00 A.M. to 4:45 P.M., can be entered without admission.

The Moravian Pottery and Tile Works is the legacy of Mercer's effort to preserve an American craft. You can purchase Moravian tiles here or take a tour to see how the tiles are made.

FONTHILL (ages 8 and up)

East Court Street and Route 313; (215) 348–9461. Open Monday through Saturday 10:00 A.M. to 5:00 P.M. and Sunday noon to 5:00 P.M. Reservations are required. Admission for adults is $$, seniors and youth 6 to 17 $. Children under 6 are Free.

Mercer's home, Fonthill, has forty-four rooms, eighteen fireplaces, and thirty-two staircases. Tours have recently been revamped to capture the interests of children. Be sure to check it out.

ALSO IN THE AREA

Gardeners get a breath of fresh air at **Henry Schmieder Arboretum of Delaware Valley College** (on Route 202; 215-345-1500) and the nearby **Inn at Fordhook Farm** (a bed-and-breakfast; call 215-345-1766). The Burpee family (of Burpee Seeds) developed many well-known seed varieties in this area.

Another fun idea: Try ballooning. For information call Color the Sky, Inc. at (215) 340-9966.

Chalfont

BYERS' CHOICE LTD. (ages 6 and up)

4355 County Line Road; (215) 822–0150; www.byerschoice.com. The factory is open at no charge Monday through Saturday, 10:00 A.M. to 5:00 P.M. Understandably, it is closed January (to recover) and major holidays.

At Byers' Choice Ltd. the Byers family and their employees hand-sculpt thousands of delightful Caroler figurines every year, giving a percentage of their profits to charity. They invite visitors to watch the delicate faces molded and painted and to tour their gallery of little carolers in various costumes and settings. Children's eyes grow wide when they see these tiny landscapes filled with doll-like figures, each one unique, each one singing a Christmas carol. There is also a gift shop and a short movie about the history of the company.

ALSO IN THE AREA

At **Malmark, Inc. Bellcraftsmen** (Bell Crest Park, Route 611, in Plumsteadville), the world's largest manufacturer of tuned handbells offers tours of its factory by appointment only. Call (215) 766-7200 for an appointment.

Amazing Pennsylvania Facts

Bucks County's fertile soil has nourished Broadway luminaries like George S. Kaufman, Moss Hart, Oscar Hammerstein II; writers like James Michener and Pearl S. Buck; and artists such as George Nakashima and Edward Hicks.

Hilltown

 GREEN HILLS FARM (PEARL BUCK HOUSE) (ages 10 and up)

520 Dublin Road, 1 mile southwest of Route 313; (215) 249–0100, ext. 170 or (800) 220–BUCK. Guided tours are available March through December, Tuesday through Saturday, at 11:00 A.M., 1:00 P.M., and 2:00 P.M. On Sunday, tours leave at 1:00 P.M. and 2:00 P.M. only. Admission is $$ for adults, seniors, and students, ₣ree for children under 6.

Perhaps you or your kids have read *The Good Earth* or other books by Pearl S. Buck. The author settled in this farmhouse at Green Hills Farm. In her office here she wrote more than one hundred novels. Buck was not only a writer but also a humanitarian. An early supporter of human rights, civil rights, and women's rights, her home still houses the offices of Pearl S. Buck International, "bringing hope to children worldwide."

The oldest section of the house was built in 1740, with sections added in 1825 and 1935. The furniture, artifacts, and contemporary artwork represent a true blending of East and West.

Worcester

 PETER WENTZ FARMSTEAD (ages 6 and up)

Off Route 73 at Schearer Road; (610) 584–5104. Open year-round Tuesday to Saturday 10:00 A.M. to 4:00 P.M. and Sunday 1:00 to 4:00 P.M.; closed Monday and major holidays. Admission is ₣ree. Donations are accepted.

The historians at Peter Wentz Farmstead have done an exceptional job researching and restoring this farm to its appearance in 1777, when General Washington occupied the house before and after the Battle of Germantown.

If you thought colonial farms were painted in subdued tones, you'll be amazed at the paint colors and wild patterns on the walls: dots, zig-zags, stripes, and more.

Special events are scheduled throughout the year, when you can watch costumed volunteers demonstrate colonial crafts using authentic techniques. You can watch spinning, weaving, candle making, and cook-ing, as well as unusual arts such as *scherenschnitte,* the German art of paper cutting. The kids especially like the farm animals. Annual events include a Market Day with Revolutionary War activities on the first Sat-urday in June, the Colonial Craft Festival on the first Saturday in Octo-ber, and Candlelight House Tours on the first Saturday in December.

ALSO IN THE AREA

Only a few blocks away, on Weikel Road, you can see the **Morgan Log House,** built in 1695 and more than 90 percent intact. The Morgans, who lived here, had ten children, one of whom grew up to become the mother of Daniel Boone. Open April to November weekends only, noon to 5:00 P.M., or by appointment. Call (610) 368-2480.

Schwenksville

PENNYPACKER MILLS (ages 8 and up)

Route 73 and Haldeman Road; (610) 287–9349; www.montcopa.org/ historicsites. Open Free *of charge Tuesday through Saturday 10:00 A.M. to 4:00 P.M. and on Sunday 1:00 to 4:00 P.M. Last daily tour begins at 3:30 P.M. Closed Monday and major holidays.*

Seven miles down Skippack Pike (Route 73) from the Peter Wentz Farmstead, you can see an excellent example of Colonial Revival archi-tecture. Pennypacker Mills was owned by the Pennypacker family as early as 1747. In 1900 Samuel W. Pennypacker purchased it and added onto the home, making a turn-of-the-twentieth-century mansion. The mansion retains original furnishings. Pennypacker was governor of Penn-sylvania from 1903 to 1907, as well as a respected historian, collector, and farmer. The home is surrounded by fifteen acres of gardens land-scaped in the English "natural" style. At present the site is preserved by Montgomery County as a turn-of-the-twentieth-century country gentle-man's estate.

Pennypacker Mills hosts special events for children, including a Hal-loween celebration with hayrides. Special children's events re-create the neighborhood parties once held by the Pennypacker daughters. There are also living-history events including a Civil War re-enactment and Christmas holiday celebrations. Call for details about these events and others for adults, families, and young children.

ALSO IN THE AREA

The **Philadelphia Folk Festival,** which celebrated its fortieth birthday in 2001, is one of the oldest and best folk festivals in the country. The folk festival brings music, crafts, dancing, and thousands of people to Old Pool farm in Schwenksville every August. For information call (800) 556–FOLK or check out the Web site, www.folkfest.org.

Alburtis

The anthracite iron industry played an important role in the development of this area, beginning in 1839.

LOCK RIDGE FURNACE MUSEUM (ages 6 and up)

Franklin Street; (610) 435–4664. Open weekends May through September 1:00 to 4:00 P.M. Admission is **Free**.

Lock Ridge Furnace Museum operated as a furnace until 1914 and is now one of the sites administered by the Lehigh County Historical Society.

Breinigsville

TERRY HILL WATERPARK (all ages)

On Route 222 in Breinigsville; (610) 395–0222; www.terryhill.com. Open noon to 6:00 P.M. daily beginning in June. In July and August, open to 7:00 P.M. weekdays and noon to 8:00 P.M. weekends. Admission is $$$.

Terry Hill Waterpark has three pools, nine water slides, refreshments, and more. The Kiddie Play Area and two child-size slides have recently been expanded.

Allentown

On the waterfront in Allentown, long-quiet historic transportation and industrial buildings are being transformed into Lehigh Landing. The eleven-acre project will eventually include a visitors center for the region, playground, baseball field, riverfront walk, and more.

Lehigh Landing will be located immediately north of the Hamilton Street Bridge, a short walk east of downtown Allentown. Keep up-to-date on new developments by checking the Web site at www.americaonwheels.org.

Also in the planning stage is Bethlehem Works, a large entertainment complex to be built on the grounds of the former Bethlehem Steel. It is expected to include the National Museum of Industrial History as well as an ice skating rink, swimming pool, hotels, restaurants, and shopping.

AMERICA ON WHEELS (all ages)

718 Hamilton Street; (610) 432–4200; www.americaonwheels.org.

Due to open at Allentown's Lehigh Landing in 2003, America On Wheels will include highly interactive exhibits focusing on the past, present, and future of transportation, from carriages, wagons, and bicycles to motorcycles, cars, and trucks. Current plans include a 40-foot-high entrance hall with a 35-foot combination lift and turntable platform to display a featured vehicle. The first-floor east gallery will tell the story of American trucking, featuring Mack truck vehicles and artifacts. The museum grounds will be used for outdoor exhibits, including Safety Square, a 2,000-foot area focused on adult and child safety.

MUSEUM OF INDIAN CULTURE AND LENI LENAPE HISTORICAL SOCIETY (ages 5 and up)

 2825 Fish Hatchery Road; (610) 797–2121. Open Thursday through Sunday noon to 3:00 P.M. Admission is $; special group rates are available. Wheelchair accessible.

As the saying goes, you can't understand another person until you've walked a mile in his moccasins. The Museum of Indian Culture and Leni Lenape Historical Society gives kids just this kind of opportunity. Children will enjoy the many hands-on exhibits that illuminate Native American culture, as well as the exhibits of tools, baskets, and crafts. Three ceremonies are held annually: Corn Planting in May; Roasting Ears of Corn in August; and Time of Thanksgiving in October. There are also picnic facilities, two nature trails, and a fish hatchery.

ALLENTOWN ART MUSEUM (ages 5 and up)

Fifth and Court Streets; (610) 432–4333; www.allentownartmuseum.org. Open Tuesday through Saturday 11:00 A.M. to 5:00 P.M. and Sunday noon until 5:00

P.M. *Admission is $;* **Free** *for kids under 12. Admission is also* **Free** *on Sunday if you enter between noon and 1:00 P.M.*

The Max Hess Junior Gallery at the Allentown Art Museum offers hands-on art activities and touchable sculpture for children. The museum also shows family-oriented films.

HAINES MILL (ages 8 and up)

3600 Haines Mill Road; (610) 435–9601. Open weekends from May until September, 1:00 to 4:00 P.M. Admission is **Free***.*

The mill was built in 1760 and operated until 1956, after having been renovated in 1909 with a water-turbine power source.

LEHIGH COUNTY HISTORICAL MUSEUM (ages 10 and up)

Fifth and Hamilton Streets; (610) 435–9601; www.voicnet.com/~lchs. The museum and library are open 10:00 A.M. to 4:00 P.M. Monday through Saturday. The museum is also open Sunday 1:00 to 4:00 P.M. Admission is **Free***.*

Housed in Allentown's Old Courthouse, the Lehigh County Historical Museum displays artifacts from the earliest inhabitants of the Lehigh Valley, the Lenni Lenape, as well as from the Pennsylvania Germans and other settlers who came to this area. The museum also includes the Scott Andrew Trexler II Memorial Library, an extensive collection of county and genealogical records.

LIBERTY BELL SHRINE (ages 8 and up)

Zion Church at 622 Hamilton Mall; (610) 435–4664; www.geocities.com/ Athens/Ithaca/1760. Open May through October Monday through Saturday noon to 4:00 P.M. In November, December, February, March, and April open Thursday through Saturday noon to 4:00 P.M. Admission is **Free***.*

Did you know that during the Revolutionary War, when the British occupied Philadelphia, all the bells in the city were removed so that the British would not be able to melt them down for ammunition? From September 1777 to June 1778, the Liberty Bell was hidden under the floor of Allentown's Zion Church at 622 Hamilton Mall, 1 block away from the Lehigh County Historical Museum. At present the Liberty Bell Shrine includes an exact replica of the famous bell, as well as flags, maps, weapons, uniforms, and a 46-foot mural showing scenes from the Revolution.

Amazing Pennsylvania Facts

Liberty Bell During the Revolutionary War, when the British occupied Philadelphia, all the bells in the city were removed so that the British would not be able to melt them down for ammunition. So from September 1777 to June 1778, the Liberty Bell was hidden under the floor of Allentown's Zion Church.

DORNEY PARK and WILDWATER KINGDOM (all ages)

*Near exit 16 on Route 309 South, at 3700 Hamilton Boulevard. For more information call (610) 395–3724. Hours for both parks vary according to season. Dorney Park is open weekends only in May and September, then daily from Memorial Day to Labor Day. Wildwater Kingdom is open mid-May to Labor Day and selected weekends in September. At the height of the season, tickets cost $$$$ for anyone 48 inches or taller, $$$ for anyone under 47 inches and seniors, and are **Free** for children under 3. These prices include admission to both parks. There is a parking fee ($$).*

Dorney Park's latest attraction is "Dominator," a three-story tower structure featuring two rides. One tower blasts riders sixteen stories into the air before it unceremoniously drops them. The other tower lifts riders slowly up 175 feet, then sends them downward at "faster-than-free-fall" speed.

Steel Force, the tallest, longest, and fastest steel roller coaster on the East Coast, lifts willing passengers (some would call them victims) up 200 feet in the air, hurls them 205 feet to the ground, and then races them through a 120-foot tunnel and up a hill 161 feet high, all before speeding through a maze of twists, turns, camelbacks, and a second tunnel.

Dorney Park also has three other world-class roller coasters, and Wildwater Kingdom has eleven water slides. Younger children will love meeting the Berenstain Bears, playing in the TotSpot, and cooling off in two water park areas specifically for small fry. Our kids could have spent the whole day in the giant wave pool.

In the fall, Dorney Park combines its rides with the frightening fun of Halloween to create Halloweekends.

ALSO IN THE AREA

The Lehigh County Historical Society administers a number of sites, including the Lehigh County Museum and several historic homes. **Trout Hall** (414 Walnut Street; 610–435–9601) is Allentown's oldest home, built in 1770 by the son of the city's founder, William Allen. The **Troxell-Steckel House** in nearby Egypt (4229 Reliance Street; 610–435–9601) is an excellent example of a rural German-style farmhouse. Its barn contains a collection of old buggies and wagons. Trout Hall is open April through November, Tuesday through Saturday noon to 3:00 P.M. and on Sunday from 1:00 to 4:00 P.M. The Troxell-Steckel House is open weekends only 1:00 to 4:00 P.M.

Frank Buchman, founder of the worldwide Moral Rearmament Movement, who was nominated for two Nobel prizes, lived at 117 North Eleventh Street in Allentown. The **Frank Buchman House** displays some of Buchman's souvenirs from an extraordinary life. The house is open for tours weekends only 1:00 to 4:00 P.M.

Schnecksville

GAME PRESERVE (all ages)

5150 Game Preserve Road; (610) 799–4171; www.gamepreserve.org. Open April through October, 10:00 A.M. to 5:00 P.M., last admission at 4:00 P.M. Admission: adults 13 to 64, $$; seniors 65 and older and children 2 to 12, $.

The Game Preserve is actually a zoo featuring a wide variety of wildlife in naturalistic habitats. There's a butterfly garden, pony rides, animal contact area, a birds of prey exhibit, and the zoo's newest residents: Arctic wolves. Stay tuned for exciting renovations in upcoming years.

Claussville

CLAUSSVILLE ONE-ROOM SCHOOLHOUSE (ages 6 and up)

Route 100; (610) 435–9601. Open on weekends from May through September 1:00 to 4:00 P.M. Admission is $ for adults; members and children Free.

Children can picture what school must have been like in the Claussville One-Room Schoolhouse, in which children learned from 1893 until 1956. They can imagine kids sitting at these very desks, reading the very books displayed there. The schoolhouse is one of the Lehigh County Historical Society sites.

Hellertown

If your kids are fascinated by crystal formations, rocks, minerals, and stalagmites and stalactites, don't miss Lost River Caverns, located in Hellertown.

LOST RIVER CAVERNS (ages 6 and up)
726 Durham Street, south of Bethlehem on Route 412, off I–78 exit 21; (610) 838–8767; fax (610) 838–2961; www.lostcave.com or www.lostrivercaverns. com. Open year-round. From Memorial Day to Labor Day, open 9:00 A.M. to 6:00 P.M.; the rest of the year, 9:00 A.M. to 5:00 P.M. Closed major holidays. Admission is $$ for adults and $ for children 3 to 12; children under 3 are Free.

Yes, there is an actual lost river at Lost River Caverns. The clear water flows into the cavern from an unknown source, and then disappears just as mysteriously. Take an underground tour of a natural limestone cavern with crystal formations and a crystal chapel. There is also a museum, gift shop, and picnic grove.

Bethlehem

The Star of Bethlehem shines on Star Mountain every night of the year, watching over this city founded by Moravian settlers and named "Bethlehem" on Christmas Eve, 1741. You may wish to visit during Christkindlmarkt, in December, when lanterns are lit, or in August, when Musikfest is held. But no matter when you visit, start out at the visitors center, where you can see a film and multimedia presentation about the city. You can pick up a schedule of events and walking-tour map, or you can schedule a guided tour. The visitors center is in the Historic District, off Route 378, at 52 West Broad Street. Call (610) 868-1513, (610) 867-0173, or (800) 360-8687.

GEMEIN HAUS (all ages)
66 West Church Street; (610) 867–0450. Open Tuesday through Sunday noon to 4:00 P.M. Closed in January. Admission: $$ for adults, $$ for children 6 to 12, Free *for children under 6.*

A log cabin five stories tall, built entirely without nails, Gemein Haus served as the Moravians' church when they first came to Bethlehem. It was also their sleeping quarters and workshop. Now it serves as a museum of Moravian history, exhibiting Moravian furniture, needlework, toys, and art.

COLONIAL INDUSTRIAL QUARTER (ages 6 and up)

459 Old York Road; (610) 691–0603. Open for self-guided tours, Free, *daily from dawn to dusk.*

There is a self-guided walking tour of the quarter. Pick up a walking-tour brochure at the Luckenback Mill. Groups can call ahead to arrange a tour of the buildings. On selected Saturdays and Sundays in summer, and for other special events, costumed interpreters host your visit.

KEMERER MUSEUM OF DECORATIVE ARTS (ages 8 and up)

427 North New Street; (610) 868–6868; www.historicbethlehem.org. Open Tuesday through Sunday noon to 5:00 P.M. Admission: $$ for adults, $ for children 6 to 12, Free *for children under 6.*

The Kemerer Museum features eighteenth- and nineteenth-century decorative arts such as furniture, folk art, textiles, paintings, and toys. Call for a schedule of changing exhibits.

BURNSIDE PLANTATION (all ages)

1461 Schoernersville Road, next to the Bethlehem Racquet Club; (610) 868–5044; www.historicbethlehem.org. Open for Free *self-guided tours Monday through Sunday 8:30 A.M. to 5:00 P.M.*

Seven acres of James Burnside's original farm developed as a living-history museum to interpret farming between 1748 and 1848. You can see the restored farmhouse, 1841 bank barn, summer kitchen, and kitchen garden. The new 2-mile walking trail, the Monocacy Way, has recently opened. The Monocacy Way actually starts at Illick's Mill Park, crosses Burnside Plantation, and continues through the Colonial Industrial Quarter. The plantation hosts an annual Blueberry Festival on the last weekend in July.

THE DISCOVERY CENTER OF SCIENCE AND TECHNOLOGY (all ages)

511 East Third Street; (610) 865–5010; www.discovery-center.org. Open Tuesday through Saturday 9:30 A.M. to 4:30 P.M., Sunday noon to 4:30 P.M. Admission is $. Children under 3 enter Free. *There are additional fees for the Laser Theater shows and for selected special exhibits and shows.*

"Discover the fun of learning" is the slogan of the Discovery Center, where more than ninety hands-on interactive exhibits cover many science and technology topics. WaterWorks demonstrates water distribution, the water cycle, and natural water filters. The Tunnel challenges kids to navigate a 76-foot-long tunnel using only the senses of touch, smell, and hearing. There's also a Science Playground, Workbench, and more. The center offers educational programs, scout badge days, summer camp, birthday parties, and other activities. Fully wheelchair accessible.

BANANA FACTORY (ages 5 and up)

25 West Third Street; (610) 332–1300; www.bananafactory.org. Open Monday through Thursday 8:30 A.M. to 9:00 P.M., Friday 8:30 A.M. to 7:00 P.M., and Sunday 9:00 A.M. to 5:00 P.M. Admission is **Free**.

The mission of the Banana Factory is "to kindle, support, and celebrate the artistic, cultural, and creative spirit of the Lehigh Valley." Located in a former warehouse for bananas, the Banana Factory offers classes for children and adults, as well as art exhibits. There are twenty-three artists' studios in the building, which is also home to the Pennsylvania Youth Theater and the Bethlehem Musikfest Association.

ALSO IN THE AREA

For ten days every August, the streets, plazas, and historic places of Bethlehem vibrate with music from all over the world. Bethlehem's Musikfest attracts hundreds of musicians and music lovers to performances at thirteen outdoor and six indoor venues. Specially for the children, clowns, jugglers, and magicians roam the streets. There is also an interactive theater for kids and parents. Hands-on crafts, an outdoor art studio call "Muralplatz," and both regional and international foods, plus a fireworks display, complete the festivities.

Nazareth

Like Bethlehem, Nazareth was founded in the 1700s by Moravian settlers. At present Nazareth is also the home of Martin Guitars.

MARTIN GUITAR FACTORY (ages 8 and up)

510 Sycamore Street; (610) 759–2837 or (800) 633–2060; www.martinguitar. com. Guided tours Monday through Friday at 10:00 A.M. For groups of ten or more, reservations are required and a per-person fee ($) is charged.

A small museum displays limited-edition guitars made for people like Gene Autry and Johnny Cash. The **Free** tour takes about an hour and brings you close-up to the craftspeople who create the instruments.

ALSO IN THE AREA

Other sites in Nazareth include **Moravian Historical Society** (214 East Center Street; 610–759–5057; www.moravianhistoricalsociety.org), **Whitefield** (pronounced wit-field) **House Museum** (214 East Center Street; 610–759–5070), and **Nazareth Speedway** (located on Highway 191 in Nazareth; call 610–759–8000 for tickets).

Easton

Did you know that the average child in the United States will wear down 730 crayons by his tenth birthday? Your children won't want to miss out on the Crayola Factory at Two Rivers Landing, 30 Centre Square.

CRAYOLA FACTORY (all ages)

30 Centre Square; (610) 515–8000; www.crayola.com. Open Tuesday through Saturday 9:30 A.M. to 5:00 P.M. and Sunday noon to 5:00 P.M. Longer hours from Memorial Day through Labor Day, 9:00 A.M. to 6:00 P.M. on weekdays, 11:00 A.M. to 6:00 P.M. on Sunday. Closed on Monday except for the following holidays: Martin Luther King Jr. Day, Presidents' Day, Memorial Day, Labor Day, Columbus Day, and the Monday after Christmas. Closed New Year's Day, Easter, Thanksgiving, Christmas Eve, and Christmas Day. Admission price includes access to the Crayola Factory and the National Canal Museum. Admission: $$ for adults and children, children under 2 are admitted **Free**.

In July 1996 something new and colorful came to Easton: the Crayola Factory, a 20,000-square-foot family discovery center filled with dozens of hands-on activities designed to get kids to "think outside the lines." More than 1.5 million visitors of all ages have seen the brightly colored liquid wax molded into crayons, expressed their creativity with markers on giant glass walls, made rubbings and transfers, and mixed colors of light.

In The Factory Floor exhibit, an expert crayon maker mixes the hot wax and pigments to mold your own souvenir four-pack of crayons. You can also see how Crayola markers are made and take home a souvenir marker. Learn about the history of Binney & Smith in the Crayola Hall of Fame, where you can see the sweater that TV's "Mr. Rogers" wore when he molded the one hundred-billionth Crayola crayon. And remember those eight colors that were retired in 1990? They're here, too. In The Creative Studio, you can decorate a sidewalk with chalk and literally write on the walls. In Easton Press & Bindery, kids can explore traditional and nontraditional print-making techniques.

The Crayola Factory is housed on the second floor of the Two Rivers Landing cultural center in downtown Easton. The National Canal Museum is on the third and fourth floors, and one admission gets you into both. The National Heritage Corridor Visitors Center, on the first floor, is open to the public **Free** of charge. There's also a McDonald's in the building!

NATIONAL CANAL MUSEUM (ages 8 and up)

30 Centre Square; reservations and information (610) 515–8000, office (610) 559–6613. Open year-round Tuesday through Saturday 9:30 A.M. to 5:00 P.M., Sunday noon to 5:00 P.M. Closed Monday except for the following holidays: Martin Luther King Jr. Day, Presidents' Day, Memorial Day, Labor Day, and Columbus Day. Admission to the National Canal Museum and the Crayola Factory is $$; children under age 2 are **Free**.

The Delaware Canal runs from Easton to Bristol, and its area has recently become a National Heritage Corridor. There are opportunities to learn about the canal's place in history in Bristol, New Hope, and other towns.

Here at the National Canal Museum, interactive exhibits allow you to operate a lock model or pilot your boat through the lock. Artifacts, photomurals, and life-size figures create a sense of "being there" as a canal boatman recounts tales of canal life interspersed with traditional canal songs.

THE ANATOMY ACADEMY AT THE WELLER CENTER (all ages)

325 Northampton Street; (610) 258–8500; www.wellercenter.org. Admission: $$ per person.

The Carl and Emily Weller Center for Health Education has for some years served school groups only. In October 1999 the Weller Center opened its doors to the general public, becoming the first interactive museum in the United States to focus on health education. Kids can walk through a giant model of the human brain. There's also a giant nose that actually sneezes. ("Oooh, gross!" they'll say, but they'll love it.) Other exhibits focus on nutrition, human growth and development, and drug abuse. Located adjacent to the Crayola Factory and the National Canal Museum, the Weller Center also has a very nice gift shop.

JOSIAH WHITE II CANAL BOAT RIDES and HUGH MOORE PARK (all ages)

Hugh Moore Park (look for CANAL BOAT signs); (610) 559–6613. Rides available first Saturday in May to mid-June: Tuesday through Friday 9:45 A.M. to 2:20 P.M., Saturday, Sunday, and Memorial Day 1:30 to 4:30 P.M. From mid-June to Labor Day: Monday through Saturday 10:30 A.M. to 5:00 P.M., Sunday 12:45 to 5:00 P.M. Weekends in September: Saturday, Sunday, and Labor Day 1:30 to 4:00 P.M. Fares: adults, $$; children 3 to 15, $.

A costumed interpreter takes you on a forty-minute ride on a mule-drawn canal boat. Special evening rides with dinner and music are available, as are charter rides for groups.

While in Hugh Moore Park, you may wish to take advantage of the park's trails, pavilions, picnic areas, and playground. The Locktender's House Museum re-creates the life of a locktender and his family.

Where to Stay

IN BUCKS COUNTY

Best Western New Hope Inn, *6426 Lower York Road, New Hope; (215) 862–5221 or (800) HOPE–202.* Country setting, pool, restaurant.

Holiday Inn Select–Bucks County, *4700 Street Road, PA Turnpike, exit 28, Trevose; (215) 364–2000 or (800) HOLI-DAY.* Indoor pool. Sesame Place packages available.

The Warrington, *Routes 611 and 132, Warrington; (800) 333–1827.* Pool, playground, restaurant.

IN MONTGOMERY COUNTY

Doubletree Guest Suites, *Plymouth Meeting, 640 West Germantown Pike, Plymouth Meeting; (610) 834–8300 or (800) 222–TREE.* Suite accommodations, restaurant, indoor pool.

The Inn at King of Prussia By Best Western, *127 South Gulph Road, King of Prussia; (610) 265–4500.* Convenient to Valley Forge National Historic Park as well as King of Prussia shopping. Outdoor pool.

McIntosh Inn, *260 North Gulph Road, King of Prussia; (800) 444–2775.* Next to King of Prussia mall. Great rates for families.

McIntosh Inn, *Route 1 and Route 352 South, Media; (800) 444–2775.* Convenient to Brandywine River Museum, Brandywine Battlefield, Chadds Ford, etc.

The Philadelphia Marriott West, *111 Crawford Avenue, West Conshahacken; (610) 941–5600.* Convenient to Valley Forge, Philadelphia, Main Line, and Manayunk.

For More Information

Bucks County, *(800) 836–2825; www. bctc.org.*

Bucks County Tourist Commission, Inc., *(800) 836–BUCKS or (215) 345–4552; www.bctc.org.*

Chester County Tourist Bureau, Inc., *(800) 228–9933 or (610) 344–6365; www.brandywinevalley.com.*

Delaware County Convention and Visitors Bureau, Inc., *(800) 343–3983 or (610) 565–3679.*

Lehigh Valley Convention and Visitors Bureau, Inc., *(800) 747–0561 or (610) 882–9200.*

Montgomery County Historic Sites, *www.montcopa.org.*

Nazareth Area Visitor Center, *201 North Main Street, Nazareth 18064; (610) 759–9174.*

New Hope—Village of New Hope, Greater New Hope Chamber of Commerce, *P.O. Box 633, New Hope 18938; (215) 862–3730.*

Valley Forge Convention and Visitors Bureau, *(888) VISIT–VF or (610) 834–1550; www.valleyforge.org.*

New Hope Information Center, *1 West Mechanic Street, New Hope 18938; (215) 862–5880.*

Hershey–Pennsylvania Dutch Country

ershey–Pennsylvania Dutch Country beckons with amusement parks, historical sites, Pennsylvania Dutch arts and crafts, and lots of train rides. This is the Keystone State's classic countryside, with Amish farms and roadside markets. It was also the site of the Battle of Gettysburg, where more American lives were lost than in any other single battle in U.S. history.

Harrisburg, the state capital on the shores of the Susquehanna, is in the midst of a renaissance. City Island, once abandoned, has been transformed into a family-entertainment spot, with miniature golf, the *Pride of the Susquehanna* riverboat, Class AA baseball, a children's railroad, and more.

Kids delight in Hershey, Chocolate-Town USA, with its streetlights shaped like chocolate kisses and its triple helping

*F*aith & *E*mily's
Favorite Hershey–Pennsylvania Dutch Country Attractions

1. Hersheypark, Hershey

2. Strasburg Rail Road, Strasburg

3. Railroad Museum of Pennsylvania, Strasburg

4. Whitaker Center for Science and the Arts, Harrisburg

5. State Museum of Pennsylvania, Harrisburg

6. *Pride of the Susquehanna* riverboat, Harrisburg

7. Fishing on the Yellow Breeches River, Boiling Springs

8. Herr Foods, Inc., Nottingham

9. Gettysburg National Military Park, Gettysburg

10. Middletown and Hummelstown Railroad, Middletown

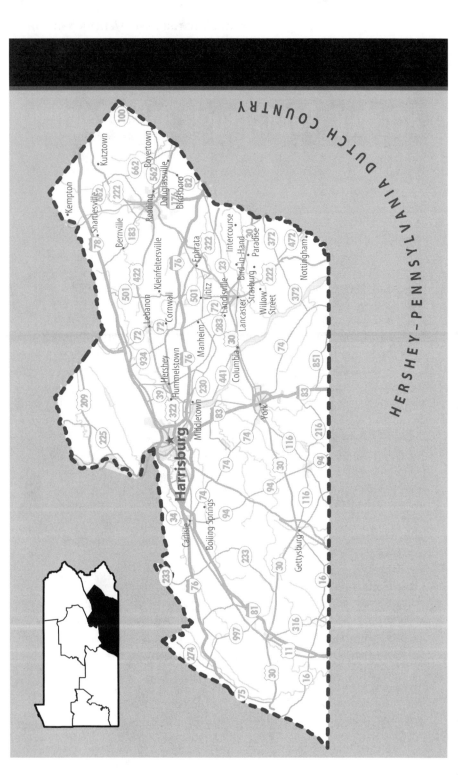

of kid-friendly attractions—Hersheypark, ZooAmerica, and Chocolate World.

Some 70,000 Plain People live in Lancaster County, members of communities such as the Amish, Brethren, and Mennonites. Plain People appreciate it when tourists respect their privacy and dislike of cameras. Visits to The People's Place, the Amish Farm, and "The Amish Experience" will present important opportunities to teach your children sensitivity.

Families who visit Pennsylvania Dutch Country often comment on the food: It's abundant and inexpensive. Family-style restaurants abound, with diners seated at large tables and delicious, simple food passed around in large bowls.

A reader recently asked about driving on country roads in Lancaster County. If you take Route 772 starting in Intercourse and continuing toward Columbia, this well-marked road loops through the county, past Amish and Mennonite farms. You can stop at a farm stand and buy vegetables or preserves from an Amish child. You'll poke through little towns like Lititz, stumble upon quilt and craft shops, and admire scenic overlooks. The staff at the Pennsylvania Dutch Convention and Visitors Bureau can help you map out your own route, taking into consideration your own interests and the season.

Faith & Emily's
Favorite Hershey–Pennsylvania Dutch Country Events

- **Greater Harrisburg Arts Festival** (Memorial Day weekend); (717) 238–5180.
- **Civil War Reenactments at Gettysburg National Military Park** (July); (717) 338–1525; www.gettysburgreenactment.com.
- **Kutztown Pennsylvania German Festival,** Kutztown Fairgrounds, Kutztown (nine days surrounding July 4); (888) 674–6136; www.kutztownfestival.com.
- **Pennsylvania Renaissance Faire** (late summer to early fall); (717) 665–7021.
- **Fort Hunter Day** (September); (717) 599–5751.
- **Hersheypark Creatures of the Night** (October); (717) 534–3860 or (800) HERSHEY.
- **Charles Dickens Victorian Christmas** (November through December); (717) 665–7021.
- **Hersheypark Christmas Candylane** (November through December); (717) 534–3860 or (800) HERSHEY.

The Pennsylvania Dutch area is a great place for a farm vacation. For more information on a vacation of any type in Pennsylvania Dutch Country, call the Pennsylvania Dutch Convention and Visitors Bureau at (717) 299–8901. To learn about farm vacations, write to the Pennsylvania Farm Vacation Association, Pennsylvania Department of Agriculture, Marketing Department, 2301 North Cameron Street, Harrisburg 17110–9408. A list of farm B&Bs is included in this chapter.

Here are some useful contacts:

- **Gettysburg Convention and Visitors Bureau** (Adams County); (800) 337–5015 or (717) 334–6274; www.gettysburg.com.
- **PA Capital Regions Vacation Bureau, Inc.** (Cumberland, Dauphin, Franklin, Lebanon, and Perry Counties); (800) 995–0969 or (717) 249–4801; www.pacapitalregions.com.
- **Pennsylvania Dutch Convention and Visitors Bureau** (Lancaster County); (800) PA DUTCH or (717) 299–8901; www.padutchcountry.com.
- **Reading and Berks County Visitors Bureau;** (800) 443–6610 or (610) 299–4085; www.readingberkspa.com.
- **York County Convention and Visitors Bureau;** (888) 858–YORK or (717) 848–4000; www.yorkpa.org.
- **The Pennsylvania Dutch Country Welcome Center;** www.800padutch.com.

Kempton

HAWK MOUNTAIN SANCTUARY (ages 8 and up)

Five miles east of Route 61, north of Hamburg, off Route 895; (610) 756–6000; www.hawkmountain.org. The visitors center is open daily year-round 9:00 A.M. to 5:00 P.M.; extended hours in fall. Admission is $$ for adults, $ for seniors and children 6 to 12.

Hawk Mountain Sanctuary's twin missions are conservation and education. This nature-observation area attracts bird-watchers from up and down the East Coast to Berks County to watch the many species of hawks and eagles that pass through the area on their annual migrations. Some trails are rocky, so younger children may not be able to keep up.

Children should be reminded that noise may frighten the birds. At the height of migration, North Lookout becomes almost like a theater with a crowd of onlookers, so children should be instructed to keep their voices low. Parents should use their best judgment; if your child won't be able to be quiet, wait a few years. Bring binoculars, wear a jacket, and check the Web site or call ahead for a brochure that gives timetables of migration. Spring and summer are great times for family outings at Hawk Mountain.

WK&S RAILROAD LINE (all ages)

Take Route 143N or 737N into Kempton and follow signs to WK&S Railroad. For schedules and more information, call (610) 756–6469 or log onto www.wknsrr. com. The steam train runs on Sunday from May through October and on Saturday during June, July, August, and October. The diesel train runs on Saturday in June and August. Fares are $$ for adults, $ for children ages 3 to 11. Children under 3 ride **Free**.

The train ride on the Wanamaker, Kempton, and Southern is about 6 miles round-trip and takes about forty minutes. Pack a picnic and have the train drop you off at a trackside grove. You can ride all day if you like. A Santa Claus Special rides the rails in December; in October, it's time for the Harvest Moon Special. Please note that although the train is sometimes known as the Hawk Mountain Line, it does not actually go to Hawk Mountain.

Kutztown

CRYSTAL CAVE (ages 8 and up)

Situated between Allentown and Reading off Route 222 at Crystal Cave and Valley Roads. For information and the schedule of guided tours, call (610) 683–6765; www.crystalcavepa.com. Admission: $$ for adults, $ for children ages 4 to 11.

Crystal Cave, discovered in 1871, is the oldest operating cave in Pennsylvania. Just use your imagination and you can see the ice-cream cone, the crystal ballroom, the giant's tooth, and the prairie dogs inside the geological formations here. After your underground adventure, try some of the **Free** activities such as the nature trail, picnic area, and Amish buggy display.

This cave is probably less strenuous than some, with railings and walkways. No strollers are permitted in the cave, so put the baby in a backpack, if possible. The Main Inn has a large rest room and lounge, but no changing table. Picnic tables are available, some covered. You can eat at the Pennsylvania Dutch Fast Food Restaurant, Sugar Shack, and ice-cream shop, open seasonally. Miniature golf is also available for a fee ($ per person).

Reading

There is a lot going on in Reading. In 2002 OINK!, an interactive children's museum, is coming to Reading, and a few other new attractions are already up and running.

In 2001 the Reading Phillies opened their new Reading Phillies Pool Pavilion at GPU Stadium. Now, a day of AA baseball is even more fun for families and groups, with picnic tables, swimming, and cascading waterfalls. Water cannons erupt from the pool whenever the Phillies score a run. For details check www.readingphillies.com or call (610) 375-8469.

Also new in 2001, the Sovereign Center opened, as well as the newly renovated Sovereign Center for the Performing Arts (formerly the Rajah Theater). The Sovereign Center hosts many concerts and ice shows, and is also home to the newly franchised Reading Royals Ice Hockey team. For information check www.sovereigncenter.com or www.royalshockey.com.

The Reading Public Museum (610-371-5850, www.berks.net/museum) boasts an impressive collection of both art and science exhibits.

OINK! CHILDREN'S VILLAGE (ages 12 and under)

Routes 176 and 724; (610) 898–OINK or (610) 898–6465; www.apollo-pools.com. Hours and admission prices to be announced.

Due to open in 2002, OINK! is described as "a very noisy, active, multidimensional space that will stimulate the twelve-and-under visitor to think outside the box and to color beyond the lines." OINK! will focus on our heritage, from the Native Americans to agriculture to industry, exploring the basics of economics, information technology, and even values and government, using the latest ideas in interactive learning.

Shartlesville

ROADSIDE AMERICA

109 Roadside Drive, near exit 23 off I–78/US22; (610) 488–6241; www.roadsideamericainc.com. Summer (July through Labor Day): Open daily 9:00 A.M. to 6:30 P.M., weekends 9:00 A.M. to 7:00 P.M. Winter (September through June): Open daily 10:00 A.M. to 5:00 P.M., weekends 10:00 A.M. to 6:00 P.M. Admission is $. Children 5 and under enter **Free***. Group rates available.*

One of our readers recently wrote us a letter suggesting that we include a favorite destination of her family, Roadside America. This unique indoor miniature village is a wonderful piece of Americana. One man, Laurence Gieringer, created this scale model during more than sixty years of meticulous work. There are trains chugging through tunnels and over bridges, a gristmill, a trolley, and even a tiny fountain in the miniature zoo.

Young children may have to be lifted up to see some of the displays, but they'll love it anyhow.

Boyertown

 BOYERTOWN MUSEUM OF HISTORIC VEHICLES (all ages)
85 South Walnut; (610) 367–2090; www.boyertownmuseum.org; e-mail: museum@enter.net. Open Tuesday through Sunday 9:30 A.M. to 4:00 P.M. Admission is $. Children under 6 enter **Free**. *Reservations are required for groups.*

The Boyertown Museum of Historic Vehicles has recently moved to a larger building where it can offer an expanded exhibition space, expanded gift shops (including one for kids), and a theater. The museum is devoted to exploring the history of the early vehicle industry in southeastern Pennsylvania. You can see horse-drawn carriages, rare automobiles, early trucks, graceful sleighs, sturdy wagons, and high-wheel bicycles.

Douglassville

 MARY MERRITT DOLL MUSEUM and **MERRITT'S MUSEUM OF EARLY CHILDHOOD (ages 10 and up)**
Located between Pottstown and Reading on Route 422. Call (610) 385–3809 for the doll museum and (610) 385–3408 (www.merritts.com) for the museum of early childhood. Open Monday and Wednesday through Saturday 10:00 A.M. to 4:30 P.M.; Sunday and holidays 1:00 to 5:00 P.M. Combination admission to both museums is $.

At the doll museum, your children can see thousands of antique dolls, the oldest dating from the 1660s. More than fifty dollhouses are on display. Just stroll around the toy trains, toy boats, rag dolls, pull toys, baby dolls, hobby horses, and paper dolls. We recommend that parents consider their children's maturity level; very little children might be frustrated that they can't touch the displays.

The museum of early childhood was designed to give other family members something to do while the doll enthusiasts were in the doll museum. It includes Colonial and Victorian antiques. Each museum has its own gift shop. Handicapped accessible.

Birdsboro

DANIEL BOONE HOMESTEAD (all ages)

400 Daniel Boone Road; (610) 582–4900. Open Tuesday through Saturday 9:00 A.M. to 5:00 P.M., Sunday noon to 5:00 P.M. year-round. Admission is $. Family rate $$$.

Daniel Boone was born and grew up in a log cabin at Daniel Boone Homestead. Only the foundation of the original cabin remains, but the oldest section of the log cabin that stands here now was built in 1750, around the time the Boones moved away. Here you can see a blacksmith's shop, smokehouse, bake oven, and sawmill. Children especially enjoy the horses and sheep. There are facilities available for picnicking and camping. The second floor of the house is not handicapped accessible, but disabled visitors may view a video of it.

Bernville

KOZIAR'S CHRISTMAS VILLAGE (all ages)

782 Christmas Village Road, 7 miles past the Reading Airport in Bernville, off Route 183; (610) 488–1110; www.koziarschristmasvillage.com. Open evenings only November through December. Hours vary. Admission is $$ per person; children under 5 enter **free**.

More than fifty years in the making, Koziar's Christmas Village is a holiday tradition—and every year it's new, improved, and all handmade. More than 500,000 lights sparkle on the lakeside house, along with its walkways, trees, and ten outbuildings including Santa's post office and toy shop. There are more than thirty buildings, about eight of which can be entered, but Koziar's is mostly an outdoor experience, so dress accordingly.

Kleinfeltersville

MIDDLE CREEK WILDLIFE MANAGEMENT AREA (ages 8 and up)

Hopeland Road. Visitors center: (717) 733–1512; www.pgc.state.pa.us. Open February 1 to the day before Thanksgiving, Tuesday through Sunday 8:00 A.M. to 4:00 P.M. and Sunday noon to 5:00 P.M. 𝐅𝐫𝐞𝐞.

Bundle up, bring your binoculars, and come to the Middle Creek Wildlife Management Area in February or March and you can see thousands of tundra swans. In spring and fall there are many other species of migrating waterfowl. There are also 6,254 acres of state game land, with seven trails, plus fishing and hunting in designated areas only, including one trout stream that's accessible to the disabled. Picnic areas are available, but you must not feed the birds.

There are a number of annual events at Middle Creek. The first full weekend in August brings the annual art show. During the third full weekend in September, you can see an exhibit of woodcarving including decoys. Also in September is the annual Pennsylvania State Goose-Calling Championship.

Lebanon

THE DANIEL WEAVER COMPANY (ages 8 and up)

Located at the corner of Fifteenth and Weavertown Road, ½ mile off Route 422 in Lebanon. For more information call (717) 274–6100 or (800) WEAVERS. Open Monday through Saturday 9:00 A.M. to 4:00 P.M.; 𝐅𝐫𝐞𝐞 *admission.* 𝐅𝐫𝐞𝐞 *tours also are available.*

Lebanon is the one town where you can see how genuine Lebanon bologna is made. The Daniel Weaver Company, which produces both Weaver's famous Lebanon Bologna and Baum's Bologna, is the oldest commercial manufacturer of Lebanon bologna in the United States. Here you can see the outdoor smokehouses, visit exhibits, enjoy 𝐅𝐫𝐞𝐞 samples, and visit their retail store.

Cornwall

CORNWALL IRON FURNACE (ages 8 and up)

Rexmont Road at Boyd Street, off State Route 419; (717) 272–9711. Open daily Tuesday through Saturday 9:00 A.M. to 5:00 P.M., Sunday noon to 5:00 P.M. (last tour leaves at 4:00 P.M.). Open Memorial Day, Independence Day, and Labor Day. Admission is $.

The most important difference between Cornwall Iron Furnace and Hopewell Furnace (see Philadelphia Countryside, page 46) is that most of Cornwall is original, whereas Hopewell is reconstructed. Cornwall Iron Furnace operated from the 1740s until the 1880s. A guide takes you through the iron-making complex, pointing out the 32-foot-tall furnace itself.

MOUNT HOPE ESTATE, PENNSYLVANIA RENAISSANCE FAIRE (all ages)

Mount Hope Estate. Call (717) 665–7021 or check www.parenaissancefaire.com for details on schedules and admission.

On weekends from August through mid-October, join the raucous revelry of the Pennsylvania Renaissance Faire. Meet sixteenth-century knaves and wenches, jesters, pirates, princesses, and knights who will immerse your family in a spectacle of living theater. Events include jousting, human chess, children's games, crafts, short plays such as *Robin Hood,* and dancing. From the end of October through mid-November, you can be mystified at "Edgar Allan Poe Evermore." ("Edgar Allan Poe Evermore" is macabre and includes direct readings from Poe. It is recommended for older children, from thirteen up.) From Thanksgiving weekend until after Christmas, the estate is decked out quite differently for a festive "Charles Dickens Victorian Christmas," recommended for all ages.

Lititz

JULIUS STURGIS PRETZEL HOUSE (ages 6 and up)

219 East Main Street; (717) 626–4354. Open year-round Saturday 9:30 A.M. to 4:30 P.M. From April 1 to December 1, also open Monday through Saturday 9:30 A.M. to 4:30 P.M. Admission is $.

You can actually twist your own pretzel here at the first pretzel bakery in the country.

Ephrata

Ephrata is an interesting town where you may wish to browse in the art galleries and craft shops. Stop by at **Artworks at Doneckers,** 100 North State Street (717-738-9503).

EPHRATA CLOISTER (ages 10 and up)

632 West Main Street (Routes 272 and 322); (717) 733–6600; www.state.pa. us. Open Monday to Saturday 9:00 A.M. to 5:00 P.M. and Sunday noon to 5:00 P.M. On Monday through Saturday, tours leave at 10:00 and 11:00 A.M., and 1:00, 2:00, 3:00, and 4:00 P.M. Admission is $$ for adults and $ for ages 6 to 12.

Older children may be interested in learning about a true alternative lifestyle at one time practiced in the eighteenth century at Ephrata Cloister. Here you can step into another reality in twelve restored buildings where hymns still seem to echo.

The guided tour starts with a film, *Anticipating Paradise,* and proceeds through three of the twelve buildings. There are two cemeteries, a physician's house, a bakery, and more. Candlelight tours are offered in December.

Intercourse

THE PEOPLE'S PLACE (ages 5 and up)

3510 Old Philadelphia Pike; (800) 390–8436. Open Monday through Saturday 9:30 A.M. to 8:00 P.M. Memorial Day through Labor Day. Off-season the museum is open 9:30 A.M. to 5:00 P.M. Admission to the movie Who Are the Amish? *is $$ for adults and $ for children 5 to 11. Admission to the museum is $$ for adults, $ for children. A combination ticket is $$ for adults, $ for children.*

Kids have lots of questions about the Pennsylvania Dutch. What's it like to dress in Amish clothes? How does it feel to ride in an Amish buggy? And deeper questions: What do the Amish believe? Why do they live differently from most of us? Their questions will be answered here.

After viewing the three-screen, twenty-five-minute feature *Who Are the Amish?,* kids in first through eighth grade can actually try school lessons used by Amish children their age. They can also learn to work the signal indicators on an Amish carriage. Hands-on exhibits and a collection of folk art help build an understanding of the lifestyle chosen by the Amish and Mennonites.

"20 Questions: A Discovery Museum for All Ages" is on the second floor of The People's Place. It answers the twenty most often asked questions about the Amish and Mennonites, both the Old Order and modern groups. Interactive exhibits are on two tracks: one for adults, one for children. Kids love finding Plain Pig, a character who appears throughout the exhibits.

The People's Place Quilt Museum is adjacent. Behind People's Place you'll find the collection of more than thirty craft shops called Kitchen Kettle Village (800-732-3538). You can see fudge being made and Shaker-style furniture being built.

Plain & Fancy Farm Attractions

PLAIN & FANCY FARM

3121 Old Philadelphia Pike on Route 340 between Bird-in-Hand and Intercourse; (717) 768–4400; www.amishnews.com. Open daily. Call ahead for hours.

Easily accessible to Mt. Hope on the opposite side of Route 340 between Bird-in-Hand and Intercourse, you'll find Plain & Fancy Farm with its buggy rides and Pennsylvania Dutch crafts and food. There are a lot of things to do at Plain & Fancy, including buggy rides, "The Amish Experience," and Amish dining. Also at Plain & Fancy, you can visit the Amish Country Homestead (717-768-3600, ext. 10).

You can also take a guided bus tour of Amish country starting at Plain & Fancy Farm. Admission to each attraction may be purchased separately, or you may choose a combination ticket to the theater and homestead, or even a super-saver ticket that includes the theater, homestead, and guided bus tour. While here, pick up a copy of *The Amish County News*.

Amish Country Tours ($$$) depart from the Amish Experience Theater, stopping at roadside stands,

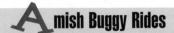

Amish Buggy Rides

- **Abe's Buggy Rides;** (717) 392–1794
- **Ed's Buggy Rides;** (717) 687–0360
- **Aaron and Jessica's Buggy Rides,** at Plain & Fancy Farm; (717) 768–4400

bake shops, and craft shops along the scenic roads of the Amish farmlands. Children receive a worksheet and a small gift to make the tour more fun.

AMISH COUNTRY HOMESTEAD (all ages)

Plain & Fancy Farm, 3121 Old Philadelphia Pike; (717) 768–8400; www. amishnews.com. Hours subject to change seasonally. Admission to the homestead is $$ for adults, $ for children ages 4 to 11. Combination tickets available for homestead, theater, and bus tours.

AARON AND JESSICA'S BUGGY RIDES (all ages)

Plain & Fancy Farm; (717) 768–4400.

Lancaster County offers several opportunities to ride in a Pennsylvania Dutch buggy, but only one ride is owned and operated by an Amish family: Aaron and Jessica's Buggy Rides at Plain & Fancy Farm.

 ### THE AMISH EXPERIENCE (ages 7 and up)

Plain & Fancy Farm; (717) 768–8400 or (717) 768–3600; www.amish experience.com. Hours subject to change seasonally. Admission to theater only is $$ for adults, $ for children 4 to 11. Combination tickets available to homestead, theater, and bus tour.

In a multimedia interactive "experiential theater" that defies labeling, a well-researched, twenty-seven-minute program immerses the audience in the world of the Amish. The unique theater has five different image areas showing different pictures, and special effects. The show *Jacob's Choice* introduces a fictional Amish teenager and his family. Although younger kids will be entertained, children ages seven and up will get the point of what it means to be Amish.

Manheim

 ### KREIDER FARMS

Route 72 (ten minutes from Route 283) at 1461 Lancaster Road; (717) 665–5039. Farm tour hours: Monday, Wednesday, and Friday 9:30 A.M. and 11:30 A.M. by reservation only.

"Daddy, where does milk come from?" Here's a great way to answer this perennial question. At Kreider Farms you can pet young calves, see cows milked on a carousel, and learn how the milk gets from the farm to the supermarket shelf. You can also visit the egg-packaging plant, then top off your visit with lunch or dinner at Kreider Farms restaurant, adjacent to the farm tour. (Kreider Farms also has restaurants at three other locations in the area.)

Where to Eat Amish-Style with Kids

- **Amish Barn Restaurant,** *Route 340 between Bird-In-Hand and Intercourse;* *(717) 768–8886.* Kids eat **Free.**
- **Bird-in-Hand Family Restaurant,** *Old Philadelphia Pike, 5 miles east of Lancaster on Route 340; (717) 768–8266.* Menu-style.
- **Harvest Drive Family Restaurant,** *Intercourse; (717) 768–4510.* Full menu or family-style.
- **Zinn's Diner,** *Route 272, Denver; (717) 336–2500.*
- **Plain & Fancy Farm,** *3121 Old Philadelphia Pike; (717) 768–4400.*

Bird-in-Hand

AMERICANA MUSEUM OF BIRD-IN-HAND (ages 6 and up)
Route 340 East (2709 Old Philadelphia Pike); (717) 391–9780; www.bird-in-hand.com/americanamuseum. Open April through November, Tuesday through Saturday 10:00 A.M. to 5:00 P.M. (Last tour begins at 4:40 P.M.) Admission is $.

The Americana Museum focuses on American life from 1890 to 1930. Touring this indoor complex with a self-guided tour pamphlet, you can stroll through a re-created town of the period including a fully stocked country general store and eight shops common to the era. A children's activity sheet is available.

WEAVERTOWN ONE-ROOM SCHOOLHOUSE (all ages)
Route 340, east of Bird-in-Hand; (717) 768–3976 or (717) 291–1888; www.800paductch.com/wvrtown.html. Open Good Friday through Thanksgiving, starting at 10:00 A.M. Closing time changes seasonally. Hours and days vary seasonally. Admission is $.

Class is in session, with animated figures of a teacher and pupils in the Weavertown One-Room Schoolhouse. The building, desks, and blackboard are original.

ABE'S BUGGY RIDES (all ages)
2596 Old Philadelphia Pike; (717) 392–1794. Open year-round, but closed on Sunday. Admission is $$$ for adults and $$ for children ages 3 to 12; children under 3 are **Free.**

This authentic Amish buggy ride passes by beautiful farmland and farmhouses. The driver tells about the area and answers questions.

Paradise

AMAZING MAIZE MAZE (All ages)

Cherry-Crest Farm; (717) 687–6843; www.amazingmaze.com. Open seasonally. Call ahead for current admission prices.

In 2001 the sixth annual Amazing Maize Maze featured a five-acre cornfield sculpted in the shape of Old MacDonald's Farm. A visit here begins with a staff member who explains it all to get you started. Then, try to find your way out of the maze. As you work your way through, you'll come upon clues, tunnel slides, watering stations, all nine planets, rest areas, the "waters of Neptune," and more. There are two bridges that afford a complete view of the maze. Average time to complete the maze is about an hour. Watch for different designs in coming years. There are also four smaller mazes, a petting zoo, hayride, a "snack shack," and special events. Many people arrive to explore the maze by way of the Strasburg Rail Road.

Strasburg

A reporter for *The New York Times* called the Strasburg area "command central for railroad buffs." Here in the town of Strasburg, transportation enthusiasts can learn about toy trains, real trains, classic cars, and more. It's the perfect place to take little boys who are "into" vehicles.

RAILROAD MUSEUM OF PENNSYLVANIA (all ages)

300 Gap Road, on Route 741 East; (717) 687–8628; www.rrhistorical.com includes this and other railroad museums. Open Monday through Saturday 9:00 A.M. to 5:00 P.M., Sunday noon to 5:00 P.M. Closed Monday from November through April. Admission is $$ for adults and $ for children 6 to 12. A family rate is available.

Renovated to accommodate more trains and a Railway Education Center, the Railroad Museum of Pennsylvania will entrance your junior engineers. It's almost overwhelming to walk into the huge collection of locomotives and rolling stock at this museum, which specializes in railroad trains built or operated in Pennsylvania. Rolling Stock Hall is designed with a balcony and a pit so that you can see the forty-six loco-motives and passenger cars from different angles. Outdoors you can see some thirty-three more cars. The HO-scale layout and education center are open selected hours. There are changing tables in both the men's and women's rest rooms. Handicapped accessible.

STRASBURG RAIL ROAD (all ages)

Route 741 East; (717) 687–7522; www.strasburgrailroad.com. Hours vary sea-sonally. Coach fares are $$ for adults, $ for children 3 to 11. Fares for open-air cars and deluxe lounge cars are $$. Children under 3 ride **Free**.

After you've seen the railroad museum, cross the street for a forty-five-minute ride on the Strasburg Rail Road. Food service is available. The East Strasburg Rail Road Station was built in 1882 and includes railroad gift shops and the Dining Car restaurant. The Strasburg Rail Road is the nation's oldest short-line railroad.

CHOO CHOO BARN (all ages)

Route 741 East; (717) 687–7911; www.choochoobarn.com. Open 10:00 A.M. to 5:00 P.M. daily. Admission is $$ for adults, $ for children 5 to 12. Children under 5 enter **Free**.

The Choo Choo Barn has eighteen miniature trains that chug through 130 animated scenes. If your kids are like ours, you'll want to visit Thomas's Trackside Station, a shop devoted exclusively to Thomas the Tank Engine and his friends from the Island of Sodor. All displays and rest rooms are handicapped accessible, but not all the shops. If you get hungry, there's a picnic area, candy shop, and Isaac's Restaurant and Deli.

NATIONAL TOY TRAIN MUSEUM (all ages)

300 Paradise Lane; (717) 687–8976; www.traincollectors.org. Open daily May through October 10:00 A.M. to 5:00 P.M. Open weekends only in April, Novem-ber, and December. Admission is $.

This museum features metal electric trains and five operating layouts with buttons for the kids to push. There is also a short video, plus dis-play cases full of trains. The museum's theater shows cartoons and comedy films about trains.

ED'S BUGGY RIDES (all ages)

Route 896; (717) 687–0360. Fares: $$ for adults, $ for children 6 to 12.

Now that you've seen trains and cars, you can include horse-drawn vehicles by taking a 3-mile ride at Ed's Buggy Rides.

AMISH VILLAGE (all ages)

Two miles north of Strasburg on Route 896; (717) 687–8511; www.800padutch. com/avillage.html. Hours vary seasonally. Admission is $$ for adults, $ for children 6 to 12.

Tours of the Old Order farmhouse at the Amish Village, which dates back to 1840, emphasize the culture of the Plain People. There's also a one-room school, a windmill, and a blacksmith shop. The smokehouse sells specialty foods like apple butter, candies, and cider. There is a handicapped-accessible rest room with a changing table, but the second floor of the house is not accessible. In December special house tours feature hot mulled cider.

SIGHT & SOUND THEATRES (ages 8 and up)

Route 896; reservations: (717) 687–7800; www.noahonstage.com. Tickets are $$$$ for adults and $$$ for children.

In 1999 the American Bus Association named Sight & Sound Theatres the "Best New Attraction for Groups." The specifically Christian shows at Sight & Sound's two huge theaters will remind you of something from the glory days of Radio City Music Hall. Recent spectacular productions have included *Noah, Behold the Lamb,* and *The Miracle of Christmas. Noah,* for example, featured a four-story ark, 56 actors, 100 live animals, and 125 animatronics (animated figures).

Nottingham

HERR FOODS, INC. (preschool and up)

At intersection of Route 272 and Route 1 in Nottingham. For details and reservations call (800) 284–7488 or (800) 63–SNACK; www.herrs.com. Tours are Free, *but reservations are highly recommended. Open daily 8:00 A.M. to 5:00 P.M. Tours are conducted Monday through Thursday 9:00 A.M. to 3:00 P.M. and Friday 9:00 A.M. to noon.*

You can see how potato chips are made, and then try some chips still warm from the cooker at Herr Foods, Inc. Cutting-edge tour technology uses DVD screens to show you production areas up close. Chipper's Cafe offers hot dogs, chicken nuggets, PB&J, and cookies. Handicapped accessible, with a changing table in the women's room.

Willow Street

 HANS HERR HOUSE (ages 8 and up)

1849 Hans Herr Drive; (717) 464–4438. Open April through December, Monday through Saturday 9:00 A.M. to 4:00 P.M. Open by appointment only in the off-season. Admission is $.

The date 1719 appears on the door lintel of the Hans Herr House. Check with the visitors center first for information about the home, garden, blacksmith's shop, and more. Call for information about special events such as the Hans Herr Heritage Day in August and the Snitz Fest (an apple festival) in October.

Lancaster

Many of the nonprofit museums in the Lancaster area have cooperated in a joint ticketing program. Save your ticket stub from one museum, and when you go to another, you'll get a reduced rate. These museums include the Railroad Museum, Heritage Center Museum of Lancaster County, Ephrata Cloister, Wright's Ferry Mansion, National Association of Watch and Clock Collectors Museum, and many more.

 DUTCH WONDERLAND (ages 3 to 12)

2249 Route 30 East; (717) 291–1888; www.dutchwonderland.com. Open weekends in spring and fall and daily from Memorial Day to Labor Day. Admission includes everything but food and the monorail and is $$$–$$$$. Handicapped accessible.

Dutch Wonderland is still the family-oriented park you remember, although it's had a $1.2 million makeover. The new VR Voyager is a three-axis, computer-controlled motion simulator. A SONY Super Bright digital video compression system and Bose Acoustimass Ten surround-sound system create a virtual-reality experience with more than fifteen different action videos the choose from.

Your six-year-old can drive an old-fashioned motorcar, your twelve-year-old can brave the Sky Princess roller coaster, your family can take a walk in the botanical gardens, and everyone can grab a carpet square and race down the giant slide. There are changing tables in both men's and women's rooms, and food offerings include chicken, pizza, and sandwiches.

Dutch Wonderland is next door to the Discover Lancaster County History Museum and within minutes of the Amish Farm and House, the Weavertown One-Room School, the Old Mill Stream Camping Manor, and a great deal of outlet shopping.

Amazing Hershey–Pennsylvania Dutch Facts Lancaster For exactly one day in 1777, Lancaster served as the U.S. capital.

 NORTH MUSEUM OF NATURAL HISTORY AND SCIENCE (all ages)

400 College Avenue; (717) 291–3941; www.fandm.edu/NorthMuseum. Open Tuesday through Saturday 9:00 A.M. to 5:00 P.M., Sunday 1:30 to 5:00 P.M. Admission is $.

The North Museum, on the campus of Franklin and Marshall College, offers collections of Native American artifacts, birds, fossils, minerals, and a planetarium. Children especially enjoy the Discovery Room and hands-on science and nature exhibits, and the herpetarium with more than forty live reptiles.

 DISCOVER LANCASTER COUNTY HISTORY MUSEUM (all ages)

2249 Route 30 East; (717) 393–3679; www.discoverlancaster.com. From Memorial Day to Labor Day, open 9:00 A.M. to 8:00 P.M. daily. From November through March, open 9:00 A.M. to 5:00 P.M. daily. In September, October, April, and May, open Sunday to Friday 9:00 A.M. to 5:00 P.M., Saturday 9:00 A.M. to 8:00 P.M. Closed Christmas. Abridged hours on Thanksgiving and New Year's. Admission is $$ for adults, $ for children ages 5 to 11. Children under 5 enter Free.

After $300,000 in renovations, the former Wax Museum of Lancaster County has emerged with a new name and many new exhibits. The original thirty-two wax tableaux are still here, newly restored and expanded. Now, when you see the animated exhibit in which Daniel Boone grows up before your eyes, you can also put on a Daniel Boone hat and, using one-way mirror imaging, observe yourself transforming into Daniel Boone, too. New interactive exhibits include touch-screen computers. You can learn to count tree rings and twist pretzels. Employees are now dressed in period costume, and more educational items are offered in the gift shop.

AMISH FARM AND HOUSE (ages 6 and up)

2395 Route 30 East, ½ mile east of Dutch Wonderland; (717) 394–6185; www.amishfarmandhouse.com. Open daily at 8:30 A.M., the site closes at 4:00 P.M. in winter, 5:00 P.M. in spring and fall, and 6:00 P.M. in summer. On selected dates in September and October, hours are extended for kerosene-lamp tours. Admission is $$ for adults and $ for children 5 to 11.

This is the only operating Amish farm open to the public. The farm itself dates from the 1700s, the house from 1805. Guided tours show the house and describe the history, culture, and clothing of Old Order Amish. You can take a self-guided tour of the farm, with its barns, carriage sheds, springhouse, and animals. A food pavilion is open seasonally, and there are changing tables in both men's and women's rooms. Sheep shearing days are in April, and there are kerosene lamp tours in the fall.

HANDS-ON HOUSE, CHILDREN'S MUSEUM OF LANCASTER (ages 2 through 10)

721 Landis Valley Road; (717) 569–KIDS; www.handsonhouse.org. Admission is $. Open Tuesday through Thursday 11:00 A.M. to 4:00 P.M., Friday 11:00 A.M. to 8:00 P.M., Saturday 10:00 A.M. to 5:00 P.M., and Sunday noon to 5:00 P.M.

The museum has eight interactive areas for children ages two through ten, including the exhibit "E-I-E-I-KNOW," which teaches kids about farming in Lancaster County through computer touch-screens, interactive games, and hands-on exhibits. The Hands-On House is now in its new quarters on the grounds of the Landis Valley Museum. The new building is twice the size of the old one, all on one level, completely wheelchair and stroller accessible.

LANDIS VALLEY MUSEUM (elementary-school age)

2451 Kissel Hill Road; (717) 569–0401; www.landisvalleymuseum.org. Open year-round, Monday through Saturday 9:00 A.M. to 5:00 P.M., Sunday noon to 5:00 P.M. Closed some holidays. Admission is $$ for adults and children 6 to 12. Children under 6 enter **Free.**

The Landis Valley Museum is a Pennsylvania German living-history museum with fifteen historic buildings, including a farmhouse, tavern, country store, and inn.

Downtown Lancaster

Downtown Lancaster is worth a visit, offering the Central Market, Lancaster Newspapers' "Newseum," Steinman Park, and more. A walking tour is available. For information contact the Pennsylvania Dutch Convention and Visitors Bureau at (717) 299–8901 or (800) PA-DUTCH, ext. 4255.

HERITAGE CENTER MUSEUM OF LANCASTER COUNTY (all ages)

Penn Square; (717) 299–6440; www.lancasterheritage.com. The museum and hands-on room are open Free *April to December, Tuesday through Saturday 10:00 A.M. to 5:00 P.M. Open daily from the day after Thanksgiving through December. Donations accepted.*

The Heritage Center Museum collects, preserves, and interprets the decorative arts of Lancaster County. In the midst of all the furniture, silver, paintings, needlework, folk art, and rifles, kids will be attracted to the Museum Classroom, where ten different stations will have them doing puzzles, playing games, cutting paper, naming quilt patterns, and more. A new children's guide to the museum poses a series of questions to get kids started on their hunt for answers.

CENTRAL MARKET (all ages)

West King Street; (717) 291–4739. Open Tuesday and Friday 6:00 A.M. to 4:30 P.M. and Saturday 6:00 A.M. to 2:00 P.M.

Next to the Heritage Center, breathe in the delicious smells of Amish baked goods coming from the Central Market, which has been operating as a farmers' market since the 1730s.

JAMES BUCHANAN'S WHEATLAND (ages 10 and up)

1120 Marietta Avenue; (717) 392–8721; www.wheatland.org. Open daily April through November 10:00 A.M. to 4:00 P.M. Admission is $$ for adults and $ for seniors, students (up through college with ID), and children 6 to 11.

In spite of the pivotal role that Pennsylvania played in our history, the Keystone State produced only one U.S. president, James Buchanan. Located on the outskirts of downtown Lancaster, James Buchanan's Wheatland, Buchanan's home, is an excellent example of a Victorian home.

Hands-on tours and educational programs are offered for school groups and Scout troops. Special events include "Mystery in the Mansion" in October and "Christmas Candlelight Tours" during the first two weekends in December.

Landisville

1852 HERR FAMILY HOMESTEAD (ages 6 and up)

1756 Nissley Road; (717) 898–8822. Hours vary seasonally.

Although open only seasonally, the folks at the 1852 Herr Family Homestead do a nice job for children. There is a pleasant park nearby if you'd like to pack a picnic lunch.

Columbia

NATIONAL ASSOCIATION OF WATCH AND CLOCK COLLECTORS MUSEUM (ages 8 and up)

514 Poplar Street, just off Route 30; (717) 684–8261; www.nawcc.org. Open Tuesday through Saturday 10:00 A.M. to 5:00 P.M. and Sunday noon to 4:00 P.M. from May to September. Closed Monday and holidays. Admission is $.

Water clocks, candle clocks, sundials, musical clocks, grandfather clocks, wristwatches, pocket watches. . . . You've never seen so many kinds of timepieces as you'll find at the National Association of Watch and Clock Collectors Museum. Parents of school-morning slugabeds will get inspiration from the alarm-clock collection. For example, there's one alarm clock that gives the sleepyhead's big toe a yank. One tall musical clock runs seven days and plays seven different tunes.

WRIGHT'S FERRY MANSION (ages 10 and up)

Second and Cherry Streets; (717) 684–4325; www.ohwy.com/pa/w/wryfryman. htm. Open May through October, Tuesday, Wednesday, Friday, and Saturday 10:00 A.M. to 3:00 P.M. Last tour begins at 3:00 P.M. Admission is $$ for adults, $ for children ages 6 to 18.

Susanna Wright was known as the "bluestocking of the Susquehanna," but she was really more of a "Renaissance woman." (*Bluestocking* was a derogatory term for an intelligent unmarried woman.) At Wright's Ferry Mansion, you can get acquainted with this colorful but little-known character in American history. Wright operated a ferry here, drew up legal documents, raised silkworms, practiced medicine, and corresponded with people like Benjamin Franklin.

York

HARLEY-DAVIDSON, INC. ANTIQUE MOTORCYCLE MUSEUM (all ages)

1425 Eden Road, just off Route 30; (717) 848–1177; www.pwl.netcom/~pow/ harleyfactorytour.html. Museum tours are offered at specified times Monday through Friday. Plant tours are offered Monday through Friday 10:00 A.M. to 2:00 P.M. and are open to people over 12. No cameras, no sandals allowed on factory tours. Call ahead to check for times of museum-only tours or to make reservations for factory tours. **Free**.

Our seven-year-old was disappointed to learn that kids under twelve are not allowed on the factory tours at Harley-Davidson, Inc. All ages are welcome, however, at the adjacent Harley-Davidson Museum, where antique motorcycles on display include police bikes, army bikes, and bikes owned by celebrities. Handicapped accessible.

Hershey

If ever there were a town made for family enjoyment, it's Hershey, Pennsylvania. What child could resist the city that chocolate built, with Hersheypark as its main attraction. Even the streetlights are shaped like Hershey kisses! If you park your car at the Hersheypark entrance, you can get around town on foot. After you've enjoyed Hersheypark, ZooAmerica, and the other big attractions, if you're in the mood for something more low-key, there's a great playground on Cocoa Avenue near Chocolate Avenue.

CHOCOLATE WORLD VISITORS CENTER (all ages)

Hersheypark Drive; (717) 534–4900. Open year-round, **Free***, from 9:00 A.M. to 4:45 P.M.; in summer it stays open until 6:45 P.M. Admission to the chocolate tour is* **Free**.

Enjoy a free ride on the chocolate-making tour. Even when the line here is long, it keeps moving. The ride gives an introduction to today's candy-making processes, and you'll get a **Free** sample at the end. Of course, there's also a gift shop where you can buy Hershey products and merchandise.

HERSHEYPARK (all ages)

100 West Hersheypark Drive; (800) HERSHEY or (717) 534–3090; www. hersheypa.com. Hersheypark's season runs from mid-May through mid-September. The gates open at 10:00 A.M., and the rides open at 10:30 A.M. Closing times vary from 6:00 to 11:00 P.M. Admission plans range from regular (ages 9 to 54) at $$$$ to junior and senior, both at $$$. Children 2 and under are Free, *and the sunset savings plan (after 5:00 P.M.) is $$$. Admission includes all rides, all live performances, and a same-day visit to ZooAmerica (see page 103). There is a separate charge for paddleboats and miniature golf.*

In 2001 Hersheypark introduced NightLights, a musical laser show presented every night on a 40-foot by 40-foot screen in Midway America. Hersheypark boasts eight big-time roller coasters, including the Wild Mouse, Lightning River, and Sidewinder. There's also Great Bear, a steel, inverted looping coaster that is the first of its kind in Pennsylvania. For persons who understand roller-coaster jargon, the Great Bear has multiple high-speed turns, a spiral, a loop, an immelmann (which is like a loop except that you change direction and then complete a barrel roll as you head out of the immelmann), a zero-G roll, a flat spin, and a corkscrew.

As you enter Hersheypark, have your kids stand next to the "measure-up" signs. Kids of a certain height are "Hershey Kisses" and can ride Hershey Kiss rides. Taller kids are "Reese's Peanut Butter Cups," "Hershey Milk Chocolate Bars," "Twizzlers," or "Nutrageous." If your kids would like to get a bracelet that shows what candy-height they are, you can stop by the rides office in the operations building, located inside the park beside Swing Thing. (If you don't choose to get a bracelet, there are signs next to every ride.)

This manageable theme park is divided into small sections, which are centered around a different theme—and there's something for everyone. This way, your family can stay together and everyone can stay happy. For example, little ones can ride the Swing Thing, which is a kid-size version of Wave Swinger. The antique carousel will delight many visitors, whereas others flock to the Comet with its 95-foot drop. And don't stand anywhere near Tidal Force unless you don't mind getting wet! If you get hot and tired, a visit to the air-conditioned Music Box Theater may be just the ticket. If you do decide to split up, the Kissing Tower makes a good meeting spot.

hat We Remember about Hersheypark

—by Judah (12½) and Seth (10)

Seth: At Hersheypark there was this booth with water guns and we had to shoot at a blue button. If you shot the blue button enough, a bell would go off and you could win a stuffed animal. Judah and I didn't win anything, but Judah's friend Gabbi won three times and she gave us each one of her prizes.

Judah: We went on a Ferris wheel. The cars on the Ferris wheel went around. When we got to the top, I said "AHHHH!" We all laughed.

You may choose to ride the water rides in your clothes or bathing suits, but shoes are required, so we recommend wearing something waterproof like flip-flops or water shoes.

Traveling with an infant, we were delighted to find that Hersheypark offers facilities for nursing mothers and baby food at the first aid station. Even some of the men's rooms have changing tables.

Besides its regular season, Hersheypark opens for two special family events: Creatures of the Night at Halloween, and Hersheypark Christmas Candylane. At each of these events the park is specially lighted and decorated, and most of the family-oriented rides are open.

ZOOAMERICA NORTH AMERICAN WILDLIFE PARK (all ages)

Hersheypark Drive; (717) 534–3860. Open year-round. Hours vary seasonally; the zoo is open 10:00 A.M. to 8:00 P.M. whenever Hersheypark is open and 10:00 A.M. to 5:00 P.M. the rest of the year. Admission is $$. Children under 2 enter **free**.

You can enter ZooAmerica North American Wildlife Park directly through Hersheypark, and admission to the zoo is included in your Hersheypark ticket. The zoo is open year-round, not just seasonally, and a separate admission is also available. ZooAmerica focuses on plants and animals from different regions in North America.

Many of Hershey's attractions grew out of Milton Hershey's special interests. The rose garden at the Hotel Hershey developed from his own passion for the flowers, ZooAmerica started out with the animals Hershey collected, and the Hershey Museum sprang from Hershey's original collection of artifacts.

THE HERSHEY MUSEUM (all ages)

170 Hersheypark Drive; (717) 534–3439. Open year-round. Admission to the museum is $$ for adults and $ for youth.

Administered by the Hershey Foundation, The Hershey Museum is located at the west end of Hersheypark Arena. Its permanent exhibits celebrate the history of Hershey—the town, its founder, and its industries. Younger children will enjoy the Discovery Room, which has hands-on activities on these themes.

ALSO IN THE AREA

You may want to check the schedule of events at **Hersheypark Stadium and Arena** (717–534–3911). Hershey also offers several golf courses, Milton Hershey School, and the Derry One-Room School.

Hummelstown

INDIAN ECHO CAVERNS (ages 8 and up)

368 Middletown Road; (717) 566–8131; www.indianechocaverns.com. Open daily except Thanksgiving, Christmas, and New Year's Day. Call for current admission prices.

Your young geologists can take a forty-five-minute tour of Indian Echo Caverns and hear the story of William Wilson, a hermit who lived in the caverns for nineteen years. You can also pan for gemstones at Gem Mill Junction (mid-May to mid-October). The cavern is open year-round, but the food cart is open only during the summer season.

Middletown

MIDDLETOWN AND HUMMELSTOWN RAILROAD (all ages)

136 Brown Street; (717) 944–4435. Operates seasonally. Call for fares and schedule.

All ages seem to get a kick out of this folksy ride in a 1920 vintage railroad coach. You take a guided scenic ride 11 miles to Indian Echo Caverns. Your train will cross Swatara Creek on a 35-foot-high bridge. You can get off at the caverns, if you like, and take a forty-five-minute tour. On your return trip an accordionist leads a sing-along.

Harrisburg

WHITAKER CENTER FOR SCIENCE AND THE ARTS
(ages 6 and up)

The Kunkel Building, 301 Market Street; (717) 221–8201; www.whitaker center.org. Open Monday through Saturday 9:30 A.M. to 5:00 P.M., Sunday 11:30 A.M. to 5:00 P.M. IMAX theater shows begin at 5:30 P.M. A combination ticket to both the science center and the theater costs $$. Tickets to the theater only and to the science center only are $$. For all tickets, children under 3 enter Free.

The Whitaker Center describes its theme as "science through the arts," making science fun through dance, film, music, and more. The center includes a state-of-the-art IMAX 3-D movie theater and a Broadway-size theater, which hosts many concerts and performances. If you park at Strawberry Square, you can enter the Whitaker Center by way of an enclosed walkway.

Walking Tour of Downtown Harrisburg It's convenient to park your car at the Walnut Street parking garage, located right at Strawberry Square (North Third and Market Streets), an urban shopping mall with a food court and many shops. The Whitaker Center is across the street in the Kunkel Building.

Look up and you'll see the dome of the State Capitol Building. The circular building to the right as you leave the capitol is the State Museum of Pennsylvania.

If your feet aren't sore yet, you can walk over to the riverfront and cross Walnut Street Bridge, now exclusively for pedestrians. The bridge spans the Susquehanna River from Riverfront Park to City Island. (At night this bridge is illuminated, adding to the nighttime view of the city.)

STATE CAPITOL BUILDING (ages 10 and up)

Third and State Streets; (717) 787–6810; www.pasen.gov. Open to the public daily. Tours are given Monday through Friday, every half-hour 8:30 A.M. to 4:00 P.M. and on Saturday and Sunday hourly 9:00 A.M. to 4:00 P.M. with no tour between noon and 1:00 P.M. Free.

The dome of the State Capitol Building is said to be the most impressive one of any state capitol in the country. Inside, huge murals depict scenes such as Penn's treaty with the Native Americans, the signing of the Declaration of Independence, and Washington's troops at Valley Forge. The floors are made of tiles from the Moravian Pottery and Tile Works in Doylestown (see Philadelphia Countryside, page 62). The main floor of the rotunda displays more than 350 flags formerly carried by regiments from Pennsylvania.

In the East Wing visit the eighteen interactive exhibits of the Welcome Center, including a kinetic sculpture that depicts how a bill becomes law.

STATE MUSEUM OF PENNSYLVANIA (all ages)

Third and North Streets; (717) 787–4978; www.statemuseumpa.org. Open Tuesday through Saturday 9:00 A.M. to 5:00 P.M. and Sunday noon to 5:00 P.M. Closed holidays except for Memorial Day and Labor Day. Admission is Free, but there is a small charge for Curiosity Corner and the planetarium show. Handicapped accessible.

This museum strives to describe the entire history and prehistory of the state. You'll work your way down, starting at the third floor. There you'll begin with geology and the earth and go on through paleontology, archaeology, and the beginning of civilization. In Dino-Lab you can observe a real paleontologist at work, freeing a dinosaur skeleton from the rock. Using an intercom, you can ask questions about this painstaking process.

Going down to the second floor, you can see a series of life-size dioramas that depict the life cycle of a Native American in this area. There are also displays about the Revolution and the Civil War, including a huge mural of the Battle of Gettysburg. One gallery re-creates a typical early American Main Street. In Curiosity Corner younger children can try on period clothing, handle birds' nests, and use interactive computers.

On the first floor the museum displays a facsimile of its treasure, the original charter from the British crown that gave Pennsylvania to William Penn in 1681. This charter granted William Penn "rights, privileges and obligations" to Pennsylvania, as a payment of debts owed to Penn's father by King Charles II.

CITY ISLAND ATTRACTIONS (all ages)

City Island sits in the middle of the Susquehanna, a spot of greenery amid the water. Its sixty-three acres of parkland now include Riverside

Stadium, where Class AA minor league baseball is played. You'll also find a steam-driven train for children, a paddle-wheel riverboat, an arcade, miniature golf, jogging and skateboarding facilities, Harbour-Town, and more.

Amazing Hershey-Pennsylvania Dutch Facts

William Penn The State Museum of Pennsylvania in Harrisburg displays the original charter that gave Pennsylvania to William Penn. It's amusing to note that Penn was to pay the king two beaver furs and all the gold and silver found in the colony. Of course, there was no gold or silver found in Pennsylvania.

PRIDE OF THE SUSQUEHANNA RIVERBOAT (all ages)

City Island; (717) 234–6500; www.harrisburgriverboat.com. Boat sails from May through October. Hours vary seasonally, with tours hourly in the summer. Fares are $. Children under 12 ride **Free**.

From City Island take a ride on the *Pride of the Susquehanna* (operated by Harrisburg Area Riverboat Society, P.O. Box 910, Harrisburg 17108).

The riverboat tour gives an excellent view of this riverside city. Kids love looking up at the underside of the six bridges under which you'll pass, including the Walnut Street Bridge. Take your choice: You may sit indoors in air-conditioned comfort, where there is a small snack bar, or on the lower or upper decks, where the wind blows through your hair.

From the riverboat you can see the wrought-iron railing around the grave of the city's founder, John Harris. You can visit his home, the John Harris/Simon Cameron Mansion, at 219 South Front Street. This historic home was built in 1766 and now houses the collection of the Historical Society of Dauphin County.

FORT HUNTER MANSION (ages 8 and up)

5300 North Front Street; (717) 599–5751. Open May through November, Tuesday through Saturday 10:00 A.M. to 4:30 P.M., Sunday noon to 4:30 P.M. Admission is $.

Just outside Center City, on a bluff overlooking the Susquehanna River, stands Fort Hunter Mansion, surrounded by its outbuildings and park. The Federal-style mansion, built in 1814 by Archibald McAllister, is in remarkably good condition. While touring the house, open the closet doors to discover surprises such as sets of china or collections of fashionable clothing left behind by Helen Reily, last owner of the house. In the guest-room closet, you can peek at Mrs. Reily's bonnets (she had some one hundred), fans, hat pins, and other accessories. She also left a collection of dolls, toy soldiers, and even paper dolls. The dollhouse features a tiny hobby horse, a little dog curled up in a minute dog bed, and postcards glued to the walls for paintings. And don't miss the garden with its spicebush, smokebush, and boxwood.

In December, when the mansion is decorated for Christmas, it is open Tuesday through Sunday from noon to 7:00 P.M. In September Fort Hunter Day brings the whole park alive with bagpipe music (in honor of the McAllisters), arts and crafts, children's activities, food, and more. Programs for children and families are offered periodically.

 ## Farm Bed-and-Breakfasts in Pennsylvania

- **Cedar Hill Farm,** *Mt. Joy; (717) 653–4655.*
- **Elver Valley Farm,** *Cochranville; (717) 529–2803.*
- **Meadow Spring Farm,** *Kennett Square; (610) 444–3903.*
- **Olde Fogie Farm,** *Marietta; (717) 426–3992.* Families with children welcome April through October.
- **Spruce Edge Guest House,** *Christiana; (717) 529–3979.*
- **Sweetwater Farm,** *Glen Mills; (610) 459–4711; www.sweetwaterfarmbb.com.*

Carlisle

The town of Carlisle is known for country inns and antiques shops—not exactly what most kids want to see. Perhaps more kid-friendly are attractions such as the Carlisle fairgrounds (depending on what's going on), and, for older children interested in history, the Carlisle Barracks.

 ### CARLISLE BARRACKS (ages 10 and up)

Enter from Claremont Road. The post is open to the public daily. The Military History Institute and Bradley Museum are open weekdays only, 8:00 A.M. to 4:30

P.M. *Closed weekends and federal holidays. Hessian Powder Magazine, starting point for self-guided tour, is* **Free** *and open daily 10:00 A.M. to 4:00 P.M. For information call the public affairs office at (717) 245–4101.*

Carlisle Barracks originated as a British post during the French and Indian War. Later, it served as the arsenal for General Washington's troops in the Revolutionary War. At the turn of the nineteenth century, the Carlisle Indian Industrial School educated thousands and produced famous athletes such as Jim Thorpe. Today, the U.S. Army War College educates the nation's senior military leaders.

Walking tours of the barracks begin in the 1777 Hessian Powder Magazine. History buffs will enjoy a visit to the General Omar N. Bradley Museum, located in Upton Hall, along with the U.S. Army Military History Institute, where research on many aspects of army history are conducted.

 ## CARLISLE FAIRGROUNDS (ages 8 and up)

1000 Bryn Mawr Road. For a schedule of events, contact Carlisle Productions at (717) 243–7855.

Maybe somebody in your family is nuts about cars or antiques. The eighty-two-acre Carlisle Fairgrounds hosts major collector events on many weekends throughout the year. The antiques show takes advantage of the abundance of antiques dealers based in this area, plus many from outside the county. The automobile shows offer car flea markets and car corral, as well as "new old stock," parts, memorabilia, and displays of rare and pristine collector cars. Special events include Kids at Carlisle, in which children three to eight can show off their own miniature pedal-, battery-, or gas-powered cars.

ALSO IN THE AREA

For hiking, cross-country skiing, hunting, and other outdoor activities, contact **King's Gap Environmental Center** on Route 174 West (500 Kings Gap Road) at (717) 486–5031.

Boiling Springs

This lovely lakeside town is the home of the Allenberry Resort Inn and Playhouse. The Allenberry stretch of the Yellow Breeches River attracts many families to try their hands at fly-fishing. Here, the rules are "catch and release" and "artificial lures only." It's a little different on the Letort Spring Run (pronounced *lee-tort*), which is considered more challenging, and attracts devotees of *A River Runs Through It*.

ALLENBERRY RESORT INN

Route 174; (717) 258–3211; www.allenberry.com.

An eighteenth-century estate where you can enjoy professional theater, fishing, and special events. Call for a list of upcoming dinner theater productions.

Gettysburg

Every schoolchild in America should get the chance to experience Gettysburg. Before your visit, older kids and parents can prepare by watching either Ken Burns's PBS *Civil War* series or the 1993 movie *Gettysburg*. The better prepared they are, the more they'll get out of it.

Another great way to prepare for your trip is the *Gettysburg Expedition Guide*, offered by TravelBrains or at the visitors center. It includes a CD-ROM, driving tour tape or CD, and a fifty-six-page guidebook. Check out the Web site, www.TravelBrains.com.

You may also plan ahead by choosing a tour ahead of time. A tour will help you get a handle on this remarkable shrine. To find the one that best suits your needs and to receive a sixty-four-page booklet about Gettysburg, contact the Gettysburg Travel Council, Department R-67, Gettysburg 17325; (717) 334-6274.

You may choose a personal tour, bus tour, bicycle tour, a tour on tape or CD, or a tour on horseback. Tapes and CDs are available for purchase or rent at Farnsworth House bookstore, Dobbin House, the Lincoln Room, or the National Civil War Wax Museum.

- Bus tours on a double-decker bus or an air-conditioned enclosed bus are available through Gettysburg Battlefield Bus Tours, 778 Baltimore Street, across from the National Cemetery (717-334-6296; www. gettysburgbattlefieldtours.com).

- Tours on a Yellowstone Park bus are available through Historic Tours (717-334-8000).

- Tours on tape or CD are available from Gettysburg Battlefield Tape Tours (717-338-0631), CC Inc. Auto Tape Tours (717-334-6245), or Battlefield Driving Tours (717-337-1217).

- Tours on horseback, called "Ride Into History," are available through National Riding Stables (717-334-1288). Two-hour tours include a history of the battle; one-hour tours leave the history lesson out. Reservations six to eight weeks in advance are highly recommended. Tours are $$$$. Ninety percent of tour riders have never been on a horse before, so have no fear.

- For your own personal tour, contact the Association of Licensed Battlefield Guides at (717) 334-1124.

- If you are interested in an 8-mile educational tour on a mountain bike, call Battlefield Bicycle Tours. Information is available at (800) 830-5775 or (717) 691-0236 or teribiker@aol.com. Bicycle tours are also offered by Blazing Saddles, (717) 337-0700 or www.blazingsaddles.com.

Our Class Trip to Gettysburg
—by Judah Paulsen-Sacks, age 12½

When I was in the fifth grade, my classmates and I went to Gettysburg. Our social studies teacher was telling us about the Civil War. Each of us brought some lunch and money. I also brought my camera.

First we went to a museum of the Civil War. We came to see a special room. The walls were electronic. They showed in pictures the story of the Battle of Gettysburg.

We ate lunch in the van. (We were careful not to get the car messy.) Then we went to a horse stable. My horse was named Cowgirl. Anthony's horse was Bubblegum, and Mike's was Abbey. I've forgotten the other horses' names. Abbey was always leaving the trail. Bubblegum kept eating off the trees. The owner of the stable had warned us not to let our horses eat leaves or grass because once they'd started, they'd never stop. Even though the horses didn't always behave right, it was fun. I mean, who doesn't like horseback riding? It was that trip that inspired me to someday get a horse.

My favorite part of the trip was Devil's Den. That's a place where many people claimed to have seen ghosts and demons and things like that. Me and Anthony went exploring there. We found a little cave-type place that I was just thin enough to squeeze through. We all went inside. I was the leader. In the dark, we thought we saw two green eyes!

None of us are quite sure whether what we saw was a demon or not. It could have been a ghost. Or maybe a hoax.

The trip to Gettysburg was one of the funnest, most memorable trips I've ever taken and it really made me think, "Ain't this a great planet?"

The Gettysburg Travel Council recommends a minimum visit of three days to see all that Gettysburg has to offer. Several package plans are available from Gettysburg Battlefield Bus Tours. For example, Package Plan A includes a bus tour plus four other Gettysburg attractions for $$$$. For details about this and other package plans, call (717) 334–6296 or check the Web site at www.gettysburgbattlefieldtours.com. To prevent an overdose of history, plan for breaks and vary your activities. Here are some highlights.

GETTYSBURG NATIONAL MILITARY PARK (ages 8 and up)

Steinwehr Avenue (Business Route 15 South); (717) 334–1124; www.nps.gov/gett. The visitors center is open daily 8:00 A.M. to 5:00 P.M. Although admission to the park and visitor center are Free*, there is a small charge for the* Cyclorama *and Electric Map attractions. Twenty-minute* Cyclorama *showings are offered every half hour from 9:00 A.M. to 4:30 P.M. The thirty-minute Electric Map showings are given every forty-five minutes from 8:15 A.M. to 4:15 P.M. For either show the fees are the same: $. Children under 6 are* Free.

A walk or horseback ride across this ghostly battlefield can be a truly moving experience.

Gettysburg National Military Park brings to life the story of three days in July 1863. About 400 artillery guns stand along the Union and Confederate battle lines, and more than 1,000 monuments help visitors picture what happened here.

Plan to stop at the visitors center first thing. Don't miss the *Cyclorama,* a 356-by-26-foot circular painting by Paul Phillippoteaux. You'll feel as if you're standing on the battlefield just before Pickett's charge. (Just think what an effect this painting must have had when it was completed in the 1880s!) A sound-and-light program brings the painting to life and adds to the experience. The visitors center also has an Electric Map of the battlefield and the Museum of the Civil War, the largest collection of Civil War artifacts anywhere.

There is a self-guided driving tour that takes about two or three hours. The park roads are open 6:00 A.M. to 10:00 P.M. Hikers, bikers, and horses are welcome. Licensed battlefield guides are also available from the National Park Visitor Center. Tours begin at 8:00 A.M. and depart hourly. The fee is $$$$ per car for each two-hour tour.

Gettysburg National Military Park has just introduced its Junior Ranger program. Go to the information desk to pick up a free Junior Ranger booklet. Complete the instructions while touring the park, and you'll receive a Junior Ranger badge at the end of your visit.

From mid-June to mid-August, the park offers a new, free kids' program called "Join the Army." This hour-long program takes place daily at 11:00 A.M. (Just sign up at the Cyclorama Center.) You'll learn how to march and drill, get to try out the job of captain or drummer, and even get to charge.

We found that when children have prepared by studying the battle before their trip, many are able to imagine themselves as soldiers on the field. When "reenacting" Picketts' Charge with our kids, we heard them say, "That was really hard! Imagine how hard it would be if we were carrying rifles and surrounded by cannon smoke!"

Walking Tour of Downtown Gettysburg

After you've toured Gettysburg National Military Park and, optionally, Eisenhower National Historic Park, you may think you've "done" Gettysburg. Well, think again, because you've only just begun! Downtown Gettysburg offers an array of museums, shops, and attractions.

Start at the town's official information center, located at 35 Carlisle Street, across Lincoln Square from the center of town.

Cross Lincoln Square from the information center to visit the Lincoln Room Museum.

After the Lincoln Room Museum, you may choose to turn left down Baltimore Street, where most of the museums and sights are, or turn right for a ride on the Gettysburg Steam Railway.

Going down Baltimore Street away from Lincoln Square, you can stop at points of interest such as Schriver House Tour, Farnsworth House, and Greyston's Story Theater.

Baltimore Street then forks. The left fork is the continuation of Baltimore Street, where you'll find such sites as the Confederate States Armory Museum, Jennie Wade House and Olde Town, Soldiers National Museum, and Hall of Presidents and First Ladies.

The right fork is Steinwehr Avenue, where you'll find Magic Town, the National Civil War Wax Museum, and the Lincoln Train Museum.

🏛 EISENHOWER NATIONAL HISTORIC PARK (ages 10 and up)

Located on Business Route 15 South, adjacent to the battlefield; (717) 344–1124; www.nps.gov/eise. The farm is open daily from April through October. It is closed Monday and Tuesday from November through March. Admission: Adults $$, children ages 6 to 16 $, under 6 **Free**.

Adjacent to the battlefield is the Eisenhower National Historic Site, the 189-acre retirement home and farm of President and Mrs. Dwight Eisenhower. If you wish to tour the home, pick up tickets at the Gettysburg National Park Visitor Center, and then take a shuttle bus to the Eisenhower farm.

To liven up the visit for children ages five to thirteen, there's a new Junior Secret Service Agent program. Pick up a free booklet at the information desk. Kids get a chance to use a park radio, look through binoculars, learn how the President is protected, and earn a Junior Secret Service Agent badge at the end.

Pace yourself, because you've only just begun. You may wish to take a walking tour of downtown Gettysburg to get yourself oriented before visiting some of the many sites in town. The town's official information center is located at 35 Carlisle Street, across from Lincoln Square in the center of town.

Cross Lincoln Square from the information center to visit the Lincoln Room Museum.

 ## LINCOLN ROOM MUSEUM (ages 7 and up)

12 Lincoln Square; (717) 334–8188. Open in summer Monday through Thursday 9:00 A.M. to 7:00 P.M., Friday and Saturday 9:00 A.M. to 8:00 P.M. In the off-season, open Monday through Friday 10:00 A.M. to 3:00 P.M. Admission is $.

This is the room where Abraham Lincoln spent the night before he delivered the Gettysburg Address. The room is still furnished as it was that night. You can follow in Lincoln's footsteps with a ten-minute sound-and-light program, and you can view original drafts of the famous speech.

 ## JENNIE WADE HOUSE (ages 8 and up)

758 Baltimore Street; (717) 334–4100. Admission is $$ for adults, $ for children. The Jennie Wade House and Olde Town are open daily. In summer hours are 9:00 A.M. to 9:00 P.M. and in the off-season 9:00 A.M. to 5:00 P.M.

In addition to the thousands of men who died at Gettysburg, there was one woman. Twenty-year-old Jennie Wade was baking bread for the Union soldiers when she was hit by a stray bullet. You can see the bullet hole. A clever holographic display tells Jennie's story. Jennie Wade's house is adjacent to Olde Town, where the streets of Gettysburg of 1863 are re-created.

HALL OF PRESIDENTS AND FIRST LADIES (ages 8 and up)

789 Baltimore Street; (717) 334–5717. Open daily 9:00 A.M. to 5:00 P.M. Admission $$ adults, $ students.

You can hear U.S. presidents "speak" at the Hall of Presidents and First Ladies. A series of life-size mannequins and taped messages can help kids learn the difference between Andrew Jackson and Andrew Johnson. The first ladies appear in reproductions of their inaugural gowns.

THE NATIONAL CIVIL WAR WAX MUSEUM (ages 8 and up)

297 Steinwehr Avenue; (717) 334–6245; www.e-gettysburg.cc. Hours vary seasonally, but usually 9:00 A.M. to 5:00 P.M. daily. Admission: $; children 5 and under, Free.

The National Civil War Wax Museum has organized its more than 200 life-size figures into an audiovisual presentation including thirty different scenes. You can see animated figures reenact the Battle of Gettysburg and an animated Lincoln deliver the Gettysburg Address. On weekends from May until Labor Day, special events include living reenactments.

LINCOLN TRAIN MUSEUM (ages 8 and up)

Steinwehr Avenue; (717) 334–5678. Open in summer 9:00 A.M. to 9:00 P.M. and in spring and fall 9:00 A.M. to 5:00 P.M. Closed during the winter months. Admission is $$ for adults, $ for children.

You can join Lincoln for the train ride to Gettysburg on a twelve-minute simulated trip at the Lincoln Train Museum. The museum also exhibits a toy train collection including a model-railroad layout that represents the Civil War.

GETTYSBURG SCENIC RAILWAY (all ages)

106 North Washington Street; for schedules and fares, plus information about theme trains, call (717) 334–6932; www.gettysburgrail.com. Open seasonally. Tickets cost $$ for adults, $ for children.

Board the Gettysburg Railroad Train about 2 blocks from Lincoln Square and choose between the 16-mile and 50-mile trips on trains that pass by the Gettysburg Battlefield.

Lighter Attractions in Gettysburg

Okay, so your younger ones have had enough history. Now's the perfect time for some lighter fare. For something spookily different, hear stories by candlelight at **Farnsworth House Ghost Stories** at 401 Baltimore Street. In season, stories are given Tuesday through Friday at 9:30 P.M. and Saturday at 8:00 and 9:30 P.M. Hours vary seasonally. Call (717) 334–8838 for details and the current schedule. Tickets are $$ for adults; children under six are **Free**. Not recommended for children who are afraid of the dark or for very young children.

Younger kids will enjoy a break from history at **Magic Town,** 49 Steinwehr Avenue. You'll want to look very closely at the minute details and "magic" illusions that make this tiny town seem so real. Open evenings. Call (800) 878–4276 or (717) 337–0492.

In season you can enjoy these lighter attractions: **The Gettysburg Family Fun Center,** 1 mile from Town Square on Route 30 East (717–334–GOLF), has miniature golf, batting cages, an arcade, and a snack bar. **Mulligan McDuffer Adventure Golf,** adjacent to the battlefield, offers miniature golf and ice cream. Call (717) 337–1518.

Land of Little Horses is outside Gettysburg at 125 Glenwood Drive. The smallest Falabella horses may weigh seventy pounds and stand less than 20 inches high. Kids less than eighty pounds can climb up on their backs (for an additional fee). The horses perform tricks three times a day from Memorial Day through Labor Day. There's also a carousel, train tram, nature area, gift shop, and snack bar. The Land of Little Horses is open 10:00 A.M. to 5:00 P.M., daily, April through October. Call (717) 334–7259; www.landoflittlehorses.com. Admission is $$ for adults, $ for children two to twelve. "Herd" rates are available. Handicapped accessible.

SOLDIERS NATIONAL MUSEUM (ages 10 and up)

777 Baltimore Street; (717) 334–4890. Hours vary seasonally. Admission $$ adults, $ children.

Ten Civil War dioramas are housed in the building that was General Howard's headquarters during the battle and later the Soldiers' National Orphanage. The museum features artifacts and memorabilia from the Civil War as well as other major American conflicts.

GENERAL LEE'S HEADQUARTERS (ages 10 and up)

Route 30 West, 8 blocks west of Lincoln Square; (717) 334–3141; www. civilwarheadquarters.com. Open daily 9:00 A.M. to 5:00 P.M. mid-March through November. Admission is $.

In this house General Lee and his staff made plans for the battle. Now the building houses a collection of Civil War relics.

Where to Eat

IN READING/BERKS COUNTY

These non-fast food restaurants offer kid-friendly dining:

Antique Airplane Restaurant, *Best Western Dutch Colony Inn, 4635 Perkiomen Avenue, Route 422, East Reading; (610) 779–2345.* An authentic 1927 airplane hangs from the ceiling, and aviation memorabilia hang from the walls.

Arner's Family Restaurants, *four convenient locations throughout Berks County: 2101 Howard Boulevard, Reading; (610) 779–6555; Ninth and Exeter Street, Reading; (610) 929–9795; 1714 State Hill Road, Wyomissing Hills; (610) 372–6101; and 4643 Pottsville Pike, Route 61, Reading; (610) 926–9002.* Casual atmosphere.

Peanut Bar and Restaurant, *332 Penn Street, Reading; (610) 376–8500; www.peanutbar.com.* Lunch through late night, it's one of the few places where parents can enjoy gourmet selections while youngsters eat more kid-friendly choices. Besides, where else can you tell the kids, "go ahead, throw the peanut shells on the floor"?

IN GETTYSBURG

These non-fast food restaurants in Gettysburg offer children's menus:

Dobbin House Tavern, *89 Steinwehr Avenue; (717) 334–2100.* A historic building with country store, bakery, and underground slave hideout.

Farnsworth House Inn, *401 Baltimore Street, (717) 334–8838.* A historic building with one hundred bullet holes. Gettysburg's only Civil War dining.

General Lee's Family Restaurant, *US 30, (717) 334–2200.* Casual, country dining rooms.

Where to Stay

IN LANCASTER AND PENNSYLVANIA DUTCH COUNTRY

Bird-in-Hand Family Inn, *2740 Old Philadelphia Pike, Bird-in-Hand; (800) 537–2535.* Indoor/outdoor pools, **Free** bus tour, restaurant, bakery.

Fairfield by Marriott—Lancaster, *150 Granite Run Drive, Lancaster; (717) 581–8122 or (800) 228–2800.* Indoor pool.

Historic Strasburg Inn, *1 Historic Drive off Route 896, Strasburg; (800) 872–0201.*

Quality Inn & Suites, *2363 Oregon Pike, Lancaster; (717) 569–0477.* Restaurant, outdoor pool.

Outdoor World: Pennsylvania Dutch Country, *185 Lehman Road, Manheim; (717) 665–2500 or (800) 588–2222 (for reservations).* One of the Outdoor World camping resorts.

Red Caboose Motel, *P.O. Box 303, Strasburg; (717) 687–5000.* Sleep in authentic cabooses and dine in authentic dining car. Seasonal buggy rides, petting zoo, flea market, country music.

IN HERSHEY

Chocolatetown Motel, *1806 East Chocolate Avenue, Hershey; (717) 533–2330.* Good location.

Cocoa Nights Motel, *1518 East Chocolate Avenue, Hershey; (717) 533–2384.*

The Hershey Lodge, *West Chocolate Avenue and University Drive, Hershey; (717) 533–3311 or (800) 533–3131.* Casual resort with indoor/outdoor pool, a playground, children's pool, and **Free** shuttle buses to Hersheypark.

The Hotel Hershey, *Hotel Road, Hershey; (717) 533–2171 or (800) 533–3131.* Luxurious resort hotel with indoor/outdoor pool, children's pool, and **Free** shuttle buses to Hersheypark. Has two restaurants to suit different tastes. Choose the Fountain Cafe if you're traveling with young children.

Spinners Inn, *845 East Chocolate Avenue, Hershey; (717) 533–9157; www.spinnersinn.com.*

IN HARRISBURG

Best Western Hotel Crown Park, *765 Eisenhower Boulevard, Harrisburg; (717) 558–9500.* Convenient to Hersheypark, Amish country. State capitol minutes away.

Double Tree Club Hotel Harrisburg, *815 Eisenhower Boulevard (exit 19 off the Pennsylvania Turnpike and Highway 283), Middletown; (717) 939–1600 or (800) 222–TREE.* Indoor pool, restaurant. Convenient to Hersheypark and Amish country.

Ramada Inn on Market Square, *23 South Second Street, Harrisburg; (800) 2–RAMADA or (717) 234–5021.* Restaurant, indoor pool. Minutes from Hershey, Lancaster, Gettysburg.

For More Information

While surfing the Web, you may wish to check out the Web site of the Harrisburg-Hershey-Carlisle Tourist and Convention Bureau at www.visithhc.com or any of the Web sites given in this chapter.

Laurel Highlands Region

The beauty of the Laurel Highlands area of Pennsylvania will take your breath away. One hundred miles of countryside, mountains, and valleys; two mountain ridges; and thirteen state parks and forests provide the setting for golfing, skiing, fishing, and hiking. The Youghiogheny River (the "Yock") means white-water rafting, and Raystown Lake offers calmer boating, swimming, and more.

In this area the Rails-to-Trails Conservancy is converting old railroad paths to hiking and biking trails. (For information contact Rails-to-Trails of Blair County at 814–832–2400 or Rails-to-Trails of Pennsylvania at 717–238–1717.)

Here you'll find a master-

Faith & Emily's
Favorite Laurel Highlands Attractions

1. Idlewild Park, Ligonier

2. Family float trip on Youghiogheny River, Ohiopyle

3. Laurel Caverns, Uniontown

4. Lincoln Caverns, Huntington

5. Raystown Lake, Hesston

6. Old Bedford Village, Bedford

7. Bat hike in Canoe Creek State Park, Hollidaysburg

8. Rockhill Trolley Museum, Rockhill

9. Horseshoe Curve Railroad, Altoona

10. Johnstown Incline, Johnstown

piece of modern architecture, Frank Lloyd Wright's Fallingwater. Old Bedford Village re-creates our history, and Idlewild Park takes us to the Land of Make-Believe.

LAUREL HIGHLANDS REGION

The Laurel Highlands is rich in history, especially sites associated with the French and Indian War, such as Fort Necessity and the authentically restored Fort Ligonier. In 1806 the National Road was built to link the East with what was then the Western frontier. This road is now Route 40, where every May wagoners with teams of horses commemorate the opening of the nation's first turnpike (the National Pike Festival). Two old tollhouses still exist along Route 40, which is also a great foliage route in October.

This area saw remarkable industrial development: coal mining, the steel industry, the growth of railroading, and the building of canals. Many families enjoy driving the 500-mile Path of Progress Heritage Route, which takes them past many of the sites described in this chapter. (For further information about the Path of Progress, call 800-898-3636 or check the Web site at www.allegheny.com.)

If you're looking for something completely different, a visit to Gravity Hill should give you something to talk about. In Bedford County, near the town of Schellsburg, is an area where gravity goes backwards. It may be an optical illusion, but in this area, cars seem to roll uphill and water flows the wrong way. For very clear directions go to www.bedfordcounty.net and select Gravity Hill.

Faith & Emily's
Favorite Events in Laurel Highlands

- **Hidden Valley Resort Winter Carnival** (late January); (814) 443-2600 or (800) 443-SKII.
- **Seven Springs Resort Spring Festival** (March); (800) 452-2223.
- **Ligonier Scottish Highland Games,** Idlewild Park (September); (412) 238-3666.
- **Pioneer Days,** Old Bedford Village (September); (814) 623-1156.
- **Fort Ligonier Days** (October); (412) 238-4200.
- **National Pike Festival** (October); (412) 329-1560.
- **Overly Country Christmas** (November through December); (412) 423-1400.

Point Marion

FRIENDSHIP HILL NATIONAL HISTORIC SITE (ages 10 and up)
Off Route 119; (724) 725–9190; www.nps.gov/frhi. Open daily year-round 8:30 A.M. to 5:00 P.M. Closed major holidays. **Free**.

Friendship Hill is the home of Swiss-born patriot Albert Gallatin, who was elected to the U.S. Senate and the House of Representatives, played an important role in the Whiskey Rebellion, was Secretary of the Treasury, a member of the team that negotiated the end of the War of 1812, and minister to France.

There are 8 miles of trails and a picnic area. You can take a pleasant walk to the grave of Gallatin's first wife, Sophia Allegre. The site overlooks the Monongahela River, but watch out for the steep banks. Also, be aware that there may be potential dangers in old buildings and mine works that have not yet been restored. Since the house is sometimes closed for restoration work, it's wise to call ahead: (412) 725-9190.

Uniontown

In the Uniontown area, you can visit Searight Toll House, Fort Necessity National Battlefield, and Laurel Caverns.

SEARIGHT TOLL HOUSE (ages 8 and up)

Route 40 West; (724) 439–4422. Open Tuesday through Saturday 10:00 A.M. to 4:00 P.M. and, from mid-May to mid-October, Sunday 2:00 to 6:00 P.M. Admission is $ for adults; children enter Free. *Group tours arranged by appointment.*

The U.S. government authorized construction of the National Road in 1806 to connect the East and the West. One of the National Road's tollhouses, Searight Toll House is open to the public and is administered by Fayette County Historical Society. Built in 1835 and recently restored, the octagonally shaped tollhouse includes the toll keeper's office, kitchen, living room, and living quarters.

FORT NECESSITY NATIONAL BATTLEFIELD (ages 9 and up)

On Route 40 (the National Road), 11 miles east of Uniontown; (724) 329–5512. The fort building is open daily from dawn to dusk. The visitors center is open 9:00 A.M. to 5:00 P.M. Closed all federal holidays except Memorial Day, July 4th, Labor Day, and Columbus Day.

At Jumonville Glen, 5 miles from here, the young George Washington met with his first experience of battle, during the French and Indian War. Washington's forces won the first encounter. The fort was built afterward in expectation that the French would return, which they did, but this time Washington was forced into the only surrender of his career. Here you can also visit the grave of General Braddock.

Fort Necessity was reconstructed in 1952. At the visitors center here, you can view an audiovisual presentation about the fort, the battle, and the research behind the reconstruction effort. You'll probably be surprised when you see the size of the reconstructed fort. The circular stockade is 53 feet in diameter. The gate is only 3½ feet wide.

While you're in the neighborhood, you may wish to visit the Mount Washington Tavern, built in the 1820s on land once owned by George Washington himself. The tavern has been restored to look as it might have in the period when it was constructed to serve travelers along the new National Road, which was built in 1818.

LAUREL CAVERNS (all ages)

Located 5 miles east of Route 40, at the crest of Summit Mountain; (800) 515–4150; www.laurelcaverns.com. Open daily from May to October, 9:00 A.M. to 5:00 P.M., and weekends only in March, April, and November. Family guided tours leave every twenty minutes. Tours: $$; preschoolers are Free. *Group rates are available with advance notice. Indoor miniature golf course: $$ per person, $ group rate.*

Located on a mountainside, Pennsylvania's largest cave offers not only the underground caves but a breathtaking view. Although the adventurous may choose the challenging Caving Adventure, the guided family tour is recommended for families with children under twelve and the physically challenged. Watch your step in the narrow passageways.

At the end of the tour, don't miss the sound-and-light show, sort of an underground *Fantasia*. There's even "Cavern Putt," a handicapped-accessible miniature golf course housed in a huge man-made cave.

Bring a jacket and a flashlight. Rappelling and climbing sessions are available to groups inside the caverns, as are fossil-hunting excursions. Bathrooms in the visitors center are handicapped accessible and include changing tables. There is a picnic shelter, or you can pick up Zeb's Pizza nearby.

Brownsville

 ### NEMACOLIN CASTLE (ages 8 and up)

Front Street in Brownsville; (724) 785–6882; www.nemacolincastle.org. Open 11:00 A.M. to 5:00 P.M. Easter weekend through mid-October. In June, July, and August, it's also open Tuesday through Friday 11:00 A.M. to 4:30 P.M. Admission: adults $$, children 12 and under $.

Despite its name, Nemacolin Castle is not a castle but the home of Jacob Bowman, who opened a trading post in Brownsville in 1786. It does look a little like a castle, though, with its turreted tower and battlements. You can take a guided tour of more than twenty furnished rooms. Around the holidays, Christmas candlelight tours are offered.

Connellsville

CRAWFORD CABIN (ages 6 and up)

North Seventh Street at the Youghiogheny River; (724) 628–5640; www.fay-west.com. Open by appointment only. **Free**.

The Connellsville Area Historical Society (275 South Pittsburgh Street; 724-628-5640) administers Crawford Cabin. George Washington visited his lifelong friend Col. William Crawford in this humble log cabin, 14 by 16 feet, built in 1765. Colonel Crawford and his men served Washington at the crossing of the Delaware and the battles of Trenton, Princeton, Brandywine, and Germantown.

Ohiopyle

Ohiopyle State Park's Youghiogheny River (affectionately nicknamed the Yough, pronounced "Yock") offers a wide range of river adventures. From March into October thousands of vacationers challenge the Yough. Find the guided or unguided trip that suits your family's taste and ages.

RAFTING ON THE YOUGHIOGHENY (ages 4 and up for the Middle Yough only)

For novices or families with younger children, the **Middle Yough** is the best choice, with its gentler class I and II rapids and relaxing scenery. Laurel Highlands River Tours offers a guided trip on the Middle Yough, which they call their Family Float Trip, for families with children ages four and up. (Many seniors also enjoy this trip.) Both Wilderness Voyageurs and White Water Adventures offer similar relaxing float trips. For kids under twelve, Mountain Streams offers free rafting on Tuesday. Wilderness Voyageurs rents easily maneuverable rafts for unguided rafting. (See below for information on these establishments.)

The **Lower Yough's** class III and IV rapids are a little wilder. The minimum age for this 7½-mile stretch of the river is twelve. Mountain Streams offers a minitrip on the Lower Yough that lasts about two hours. Many of these organizations also provide bike rentals, kayaks, or "duckies." A duckie is sort of an inflatable kayak, used with a double-ended paddle, available with one or two seats. Most outfitters recommend duckies rather than canoes. A Thrillseeker, also used with a double-ended paddle, is made of a harder plastic.

Teenagers with a taste for adventure can take on the **Upper Yough.** This 11-mile stretch of the river includes class IV and V rapids and is recommended for experienced paddlers only. The minimum age is sixteen.

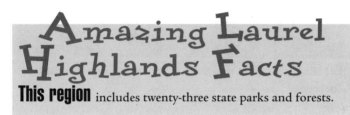

Amazing **L**aurel **H**ighlands **F**acts

This region includes twenty-three state parks and forests.

OHIOPYLE STATE PARK (all ages)

Park office, located on Dinnerbell Road; (729) 329–8591. Open dawn to dusk.
Ohiopyle is also the starting point for the **Laurel Highlands Hiking Trail.** You can hike 70 miles here from Ohiopyle to an area near Johnstown. Eight overnight sites have been set up along the trail, which is designed for serious hikers.

There are flush toilets and shower facilities in Ohiopyle State Park, and **Fox's Pizza** is not far away. Nearby, the community center offers a licensed day-care center for children under the minimum rafting age of four.

Any of the following outfitters can help you select your trip:

- **Laurel Highlands River Tours,** P.O. Box 107, Ohiopyle 15470, (800) 4-RAFTIN or (724) 329-8531; www.laurelhighlands.com

- **Mountain Streams and Trails Outfitters,** P.O. Box 106, Route 381, Ohiopyle 15470, (800) RAFT NOW (723-8669); www.mtstreams.com

- **White Water Adventurers, Inc.,** P.O. Box 31, Ohiopyle 15470, (800) WWA-RAFT; www.wwaraft.com

- **Wilderness Voyageurs, Inc.,** P.O. Box 97 Department PA, Ohiopyle 15470, (800) 272-4141 or (724) 329-5517; www.wilderness voyageurs.com

KENTUCK KNOB (ages 9 and up)

Kentuck Road, Chalk Hill; (724) 329–1901; www.kentuckknob.com. Open Tuesday through Sunday and Monday holidays. Regular tours depart from 10:00 A.M. to 4:00 P.M. Reservations are recommended. Tours are $$$. Longer, in-depth tours are $$$$ and depart at 8:30 A.M. or by reservation.

This home, designed by Frank Lloyd Wright, is a great side trip if you enjoyed Fallingwater. Children nine and up are welcome to join the regular tour. There are no day-care facilities for younger ones.

Mill Run

 ### FALLINGWATER (ages 9 and up except for children's tours for ages 5 to 9)

Route 381; (724) 329–8501; www.paconserve.org. Open for guided tours April to mid-November, Tuesday through Sunday and Monday holidays 10:00 A.M. to 4:00 P.M. In December tours are offered weekends only 11:00 A.M. to 3:00 P.M. Closed January and February. On weekends, tours are $$$; on weekdays, tours are $$. Children under 9 are not permitted on the regular tour. Special tours for children ages 5 to 9; call for schedules and admission prices.

The story goes that Frank Lloyd Wright told Edgar Kaufmann, "I want you to live with the waterfall, not just look at it." Because of the technology of cantilevers, Wright was able to do just that.

In a beautiful wooded setting, Wright placed Fallingwater, one of his most significant architectural achievements. It seems as if it has always been here, with the waterfall cascading from it. Inside the house, walls of windows look out into the woods. The American Institute of Architects has called Fallingwater "the best all-time work of American architecture."

The regular tour takes about forty-five minutes to an hour, but if you like, you may make a reservation for a longer tour, which is very detailed and can take up to two hours. (These in-depth tours are available at 8:30 A.M. and carry a fee of at least $$$$ per person.) Tours do require a fair amount of walking. Only the first floor is handicapped accessible.

Please note that children under nine are not permitted to take the regular tour of the house. If you wish to see it yourself, however, you may take advantage of child care provided here ($ per child per hour). If you have children five to nine who might like to see the house, call to find out when special children's tours are scheduled. Reservations are strongly recommended for both children's and adult tours. Lunch is available in Fallingwater's restaurant.

If you would like to see more of Wright's work, try Kentuck Knob in Ohiopyle.

ALSO IN THE AREA

Fallingwater is operated by the Western Pennsylvania Conservancy, which also runs **Bear Run Nature Preserve,** ½ mile away. It is very convenient to Ohiopyle.

The family can camp at **Yogi Bear's Jellystone Park,** but even if you're not camping here, you can take advantage of the water slides, playground, and other recreational activities. For information and pricing schedule, call (800) HEY-YOGI.

Mill Run Water Slides (724-455-2929) offers two 400-foot slides to cool you off.

Champion

SEVEN SPRINGS MOUNTAIN RESORT (all ages)

Located between exits 9 and 10 on the PA Turnpike; (800) 452–2223; www. 7springs.com.

Ski magazine has rated Seven Springs Mountain Resort among the top fifty ski resorts in North America. New features include two new chairlifts and a "magic carpet" conveyor lift. This large facility offers lodging for more than 5,000 people in hotel rooms, condos, and chalets. Besides ski and snowboard rentals and ski lessons, the resort offers snowtubing (eight chutes), swimming, bowling, indoor miniature golf, and game rooms.

Donegal

CADDIE SHAK FAMILY FUN PARK (all ages)

Located 1½ miles east on Route 31 off exit 9 of the PA Turnpike; (724) 593–7400; www.caddieshak.com. Open daily March through October. Admission and parking are **Free.**

You can't drive past Caddie Shak Family Fun Park without a reaction from your kids. ("Their tongues hang out," says one parent.) Convenient to the turnpike, Caddie Shak has three go-cart tracks, miniature golf, batting cages, games, and food. Recently added attractions include bumper cars with water cannons, a petting zoo, paint ball, and horseback riding. A nice way to break up the trip. The rides and attractions are moderately priced, and family discounts are available. Handicapped accessible.

LIVING TREASURES ANIMAL PARK (all ages)

Route 711, south of Route 31; (724) 593–8300; www.ltanimalpark.com. Open Memorial Day through Labor Day 10:00 A.M. to 8:00 P.M. In April, May, September, and October, open daily 10:00 A.M. to 6:00 P.M. Admission is $$ for adults and $ for children 3 to 11; children 2 and under are **Free***. Please note that there are two "Living Treasures" locations. The other, also listed in this guide, is in Moraine.*

Get up close to more than one hundred species of friendly animals from all over the world at Living Treasures Animal Park.

Hidden Valley

HIDDEN VALLEY SKI (all ages)

4 Craighead Drive; (814) 443–2600 or (800) 443–SKII; www.hiddenvalley resort.com.

The instructors at Hidden Valley Ski want you to learn to ski with them. One of the mid-Atlantic's most popular family ski resorts, Hidden Valley has twenty-five ski slopes and trails, more than 30 miles of cross-country ski trails, and a half-pipe for snowboarders. There's also a kids' camp, indoor and outdoor pools, boating, fishing, tennis, ecotouring, and more.

In spring and summer, there's still a lot to do, such as golfing, mountain biking, and swimming. The many restaurants cater to a variety of tastes, and all are kid-friendly with the possible exception of the Snow Shoe Lounge (kids may be served with parents, but it is a lounge). Mountain Munchkins Child Care offers baby-sitting for children eighteen months to eight years. There are changing tables in both men's and women's rest rooms.

Greensburg

HANNA'S TOWN (ages 8 and up)

951 Old Salem Road; (724) 836–1800; www.wchspa.com. Open Memorial Day through Labor Day, Tuesday through Sunday 1:00 to 5:00 P.M. Open weekends only in May, September, and October.

Archaeological research in Greensburg has revived Hanna's Town. A stockade fort, the home of Robert Hanna, the town jail, and a wagon shed are reconstructed. Klingensmith House has been moved here. You can visit the field museum and see archaeological artifacts unearthed here.

ALSO IN THE AREA

You may want to check out the **Westmoreland Museum of American Art** (221 North Main Street, 412-837-1500) or the **Westmoreland Symphony Orchestra** (412-837-1850).

Jeannette

Depending on how you look at it, Bushy Run Battlefield is in either Jeannette or Harrison City. Either way, it's about 11 miles northwest of Greensburg, and it's an interesting place to visit.

BUSHY RUN BATTLEFIELD (ages 8 and up)

Route 993; (724) 527–5584; www.bushyrunbattlefield.com. Visitors center: April through October, Wednesday to Saturday 9:00 A.M. to 5:00 P.M. and Sunday noon to 5:00 P.M. Battlefield: Wednesday to Sunday 9:00 A.M. to 5:00 P.M. year-round. From November to March the museum is closed. Admission is $.

Here's an opportunity to acquaint your family with a lesser-known conflict: Pontiac's War. In 1763 Native American forces, under the command of war chief Pontiac, struggled against the British, eventually laying seige to Fort Pitt. At the Bushy Run Battlefield, the British turned the tide against this rebellion and saved Fort Pitt.

At the visitors center a fiber-optic map helps you get your bearings. Take some time to observe the new interactive exhibits, maps, flags, and weapons and learn about this episode in our history. In the Kids' Corner you can try on a reproduction uniform. Then you can take a guided tour of the battlefield. There are 3 miles of historic hiking trails, education programs, and special events. On the Edge Hill Trail, each stop represents one aspect of the Battle of Bushy Run, including the Flour Bag Entrenchment in which flour bags were used to protect the British wounded. There is also a gift shop. Handicapped accessible.

Another trail, the Flour Sak Discovery Trail, focuses on how humans have used things from the forest. For example, the black walnut tree provided food, dye, insect repellent, gunstocks, and furniture.

The Iroquois Nature Trail was designed by the Boy Scouts to demonstrate the changes in the environment between the nineteenth and twenty-first centuries. There are thirteen stations, such as Beauty in Nature Through Adaptation, where you can see how nature has healed itself in what was once a stone quarry.

Ligonier

 IDLEWILD PARK (all ages)

Route 30 West; (724) 238–3666; www.idlewild.com. Open Tuesday through Sunday, June through August, on weekends only mid-May to June and on holiday Mondays. The gates open at 10:00 A.M., and closing times vary. Fun Day passes, which include all rides and attractions, are $$$; children 2 and under enter Free.

"America's Most Beautiful Theme Park," Idlewild Park is the home of Mister Rogers' Neighborhood of Make-Believe, complete with the Neighborhood Trolley your preschoolers have always wanted to see. Fred Rogers himself served as creative consultant for this charming replica with the castle, King Friday, Queen Sarah Saturday, and all the details you'll recognize right away. In July, characters such as Mr. McFeeley may appear in person.

This relaxing and manageable park, nestled in the woods, is perfect for children twelve and under, but it also has rides for older kids such as the new Wild Mouse and the Rollo Coaster, built in 1938. Located about 50 miles east of Pittsburgh and also a sister park to Kennywood and Sandcastle, it began as a picnic area in 1878. At present the three-row carousel, built by Philadelphia Toboggan Company in the 1930s, still entrances children of all ages.

You'll literally step through the pages of a storybook to visit the homes of "Peter, Peter, pumpkin eater," "The Three Little Pigs," and the "Little Crooked Man," among others. The beloved Story Book Forest was added in 1956, with its more than forty scenes and characters from fairy tales and nursery rhymes. It takes about an hour to explore the Story Book Forest.

Jumpin' Jungle gets families climbing and crawling and, well, jumping. Climb up the netting; jump in the ball room. Soak Zone is a giant water attraction for all ages. It has Hydro Racers, Pipeline Plunge, Tipping Bucket, and a huge swimming pool, plus Little Squirts, wet fun for younger ones. Bring your bathing suit if you plan to go on any of the water slides or swim in the pool.

FORT LIGONIER (ages 8 and up)

Intersection of Routes 30 and 711; (724) 238–9701. The fort is open daily April to October, Monday through Saturday 10:00 A.M. to 4:30 P.M., and Sunday noon to 4:30 P.M. Admission is $$ for adults, $ for children 6 to 14 years old.

Fort Ligonier was built by the British during the French and Indian War. The entire fort, except for its foundation, was destroyed by 1800, but it has been carefully reconstructed. It has gun batteries and a retrenchment. The visitors center offers exhibits and a film. You can visit several restored buildings such as a quartermaster's storehouse, magazine, hospital, and commissary.

Every October, on the anniversary of its most famous battle, the fort celebrates Fort Ligonier Days.

Amazing Laurel Highlands Facts

Mt. Davis in Somerset County is the highest peak in Pennsylvania.

Laughlintown

COMPASS INN MUSEUM (ages 8 and up)

Three miles east of Ligonier, on Route 30 East; (724) 238–4983; www.compass inn.com. Open May through October, Tuesday through Saturday 11:00 A.M. to 4:00 P.M. and Sunday noon to 4:00 P.M. Admission is $$ for adults, $ for students, **Free** *for children under 5.*

If you want to get a picture of what it was like in a typical roadside inn of the eighteenth and nineteenth centuries, visit the Compass Inn Museum. The log part was built in 1799, and the stone addition in 1820. The Ligonier Valley Historical Society has restored the building, and the kitchen, blacksmith's shop, and barn have been reconstructed on their original sites.

You can find out where terms like "upper crust" and "toasting" came from. You can see how travelers spent the night crammed into beds with other guests. You can visit the family's quarters, as well as the barn, where old horse- and ox-drawn vehicles still remain, and sometimes a blacksmith is on duty, demonstrating the craft. You can also see tools of the period.

During summer, living-history days are held on the third weekend of each month. In November and December candlelight tours are offered on weekends only.

Johnstown

The town of Johnstown will always be remembered as the site of the tragic flood that occurred on May 31, 1889. The stress of a storm proved too much for the town's neglected dam, which broke, sending a wall of water down the mountain and through the town, killing more than 2,000 people.

But Johnstown is not just a place of tragedy; it is a town full of life. In late June, Johnstown hosts "Thunder in the Valley," an unusually family-oriented motorcycle rally. In August, the Cambria County Ag-Tour offers a day in the country with **Free** refreshments at several area farms. The Log House Arts Festival, during Labor Day weekend, has many activities for children. Also, the Pasquerilla Performing Arts Center has "Sydney's Series" of plays for children. Besides these annual events, Johnstown has the BOTTLEWORKS Ethnic Arts Center.

 JOHNSTOWN FLOOD NATIONAL MEMORIAL (ages 8 and up)
Located in St. Michael, 10 miles northeast of Johnstown; (814) 495–4643; www.nps.gov/jofl. Open Memorial Day to Labor Day 9:00 A.M. to 6:00 P.M. Open the rest of the year 9:00 A.M. to 5:00 P.M. Closed on Veterans Day, Martin Luther King Jr. Day, Presidents' Day, Thanksgiving, Christmas, and New Year's Day. Admission $; children 16 and under enter **Free**. *Call for details. Take US 219 to the St. Michael/Sidman exit. Head east on PA 869, and turn left onto Lake Road at the sign.*

The Johnstown Flood began on the site in Saint Michael where you can see the Johnstown Flood National Memorial, administered by the National Park Service. In fact, you can see what little is left of the South Fork Dam from here. A weakness in this dam is suspected of having made the flood so disastrous.

An award-winning documentary, *Black Friday*, brings the events to life. The thirty-five-minute film puts you inside the terror of the flood. In fact, it is so effective parents are warned that it may be too frightening for young children.

In summer you can see reenactments of some of the events surrounding the flood. You can also take a tour around the dam. The flood happened on Memorial Day, so every year during that holiday weekend, the abutments of the dam glow with the light of thousands of luminaries. Special presentations are offered, including *Tales of the Great Flood,* a theater event in which costumed interpreters read from eyewitness accounts of the flood.

JOHNSTOWN INCLINE (all ages)

711 Edgehill Drive; easily accessible to Routes 56 and 403, and Route 271; (814) 536–1816; www.asme.org/history. Weekdays the ride runs from 6:30 A.M. to 10:00 P.M. On Saturday hours are 7:30 A.M. to 10:00 P.M., and on Sunday, 9:00 A.M. to 10:00 P.M. Call for fares and schedules. **Free** *parking is available at both the top and the bottom.*

After visiting the memorial, you'll want to complete the story with a tour of the Johnstown Flood Museum. But first you might want to break up the seriousness with an exhilarating ride on the Johnstown Inclined Plane. You'll travel up on an amazing 71.9 percent grade, the steepest vehicular inclined plane in the world. Your car can ride the incline with you, if you desire, so that you can drive around the town of Westmont.

After the Johnstown Flood, the frightened residents of the area wanted to live at the top of the hill, but they needed a way to commute to and from the city, so this incline was built. An "incline" is an unusual kind of cable railway found in Johnstown and Pittsburgh. During Johnstown's two subsequent floods (1962 and 1977), the incline became the people's escape route. At night, when both the tracks and the cars are lit up, the incline is a spectacular sight.

At the top of the incline, 634 feet above the city, there is an observation deck, visitors center, and the Incline Station Restaurant and Pub. The view of the Conemaugh Valley is spectacular, as seen from the glass-walled Plane Visitor Center. From this vantage point you can see one of the largest American flags anywhere.

 ## THE JOHNSTOWN FLOOD MUSEUM (ages 6 and up)

304 Washington Street (P.O. Box 1889); (814) 539–1889; www.jaha.org. Open May though October, Sunday to Thursday 10:00 A.M. to 5:00 P.M.; Friday and Saturday 10:00 A.M. to 7:00 P.M. From November through April open daily 10:00 A.M. to 5:00 P.M. Call for information and admission charges.

The museum, located in a former Carnegie Library, tells the story of the Johnstown flood disaster. Photos show how the town looked before the waters came, and after. An animated map with light and sound effects shows how the water swept through Johnstown, destroying thousands of homes and businesses.

First, see the documentary film *The Johnstown Flood,* which won the Academy Award for Best Documentary Short Subject in 1989. This twenty-five-minute movie is shown hourly and was made using black-and-white still photos taken after the flood. A longer version of this movie has been shown on PBS's *The American Experience.*

Then visit the two floors of permanent exhibits, artifacts, and a 3-D multimedia presentation. The museum store offers a large selection of books and gifts.

BOTTLEWORKS ETHNIC ARTS CENTER (ages 6 and up)

411 Third Avenue; (814) 536–5399. Open Tuesday through Friday 10:00 A.M. to 4:00 P.M. and Saturday 11:00 A.M. to 3:00 P.M. Admission is **Free.** *Some special events have additional fees.*

In 1994 the old Tulip Bottling Company building was converted into the BOTTLEWORKS, whose mission is "to educate, preserve, and celebrate the ethnic heritage of the people of the Johnstown region." The Tulip Bottling Company was founded by a family of Russian and Hungarian Jews. In just a few years, the BOTTLEWORKS has become well known in the area for its Celebrations of Heritages through visual, performing, and folk arts. Summertime offers ethnic camps for children and ethnic arts and crafts at the FolkFest.

ALSO IN THE AREA

Every September, the Johnstown Area Heritage Association hosts **Johnstown FolkFest,** three days of music and culture reflecting the historical and ethnic heritage of the area. For information call (888) 222–1889, or check the Web sites www.visitjohnstownpa.com and www.jaha.org/folkfest.

The Johnstown Area Heritage Association also administers the **Heritage Discovery Center** at Broad Street and Seventh Avenue, which tells the story of immigrant families, and the **Wagner-Ritter House,** which will open its doors in 2002 to re-create life in the late 1800s to early 1900s. For information check the Web site www.jaha.org.

Stackhouse Park offers many special programs for children in its 277 acres of wooded land.

The **Windber Coal Heritage Center,** in the nearby mining town of Windber, offers an interesting interactive view of the everyday life of a coal mining family. Open 10:00 A.M. to 5:00 P.M. daily May 1 to October 31. Adjacent to outdoor Miner's Park and within walking distance of the shops and restaurants of Windber. Call (814) 467–6680 for admission fees and information, or check the Web site www.allegheny.org/windber.

Claysburg

 BLUE KNOB RECREATION (all ages)
Route 20 North (from PA Turnpike, exit 11). For details call in-state (814) 239–5111; out-of-state, call (800) 458–3403; www.blueknob.com.

One of the top ski resorts in the area, Blue Knob offers a KinderSki program, a ski school, an outdoor ice rink, swimming pools, and both junior and senior rates.

Amazing Laurel Highlands Facts

The Laurel Highlands get more than 100 inches of real snow per year, plus another 60 to 80 inches from man-made snow machines.

Cresson

ALLEGHENY PORTAGE RAILROAD NATIONAL HISTORIC SITE (ages 8 and up)

Twelve miles west of Altoona and 10 miles east of Ebensburg on Route 22, off the Gallitzin exit; (814) 886–6150; www.nps.gov/alpo. Open daily 9:00 A.M. to 5:00 P.M. Closed all federal holidays except Memorial Day, July 4th, Labor Day, and Columbus Day. Admission is $; children under 17 enter **Free**.

In the middle of the nineteenth century, when Philadelphia was being linked to Pittsburgh by rail and canal, this portion of the Allegheny Mountains between Hollidaysburg and Johnstown seemed impassable. So someone came up with a "portage railroad." A series of inclines carried the freight and passengers up the hills.

The Engine House Interpretive Building features full-scale models, a movie, and hands-on exhibits. The railroad no longer exists, but you can walk along a portion of its route and see one section of restored track. As you enjoy the view from the overlook, be sure to note Skew Arch

Bridge, which is actually twisted so that a wagon road could pass over the track. Costumed presentations and ranger-led hikes are available during the summer months.

Hollidaysburg

TROUGH CREEK STATE PARK (all ages)

Route 994. Twenty-four-hour access. **Free**. *For information and pricing schedule, call (814) 658–3847; www.dcnr.state.pa.us.*

If you want to stay in comfort in a beautiful forested setting, Trough Creek Cottage, at Trough Creek State Park, is available for rental year-round. It is a two-story home built in the 1800s as an ironmaster's house and is now completely renovated, including a modern eat-in kitchen, four bedrooms, a bathroom, and central heat.

CANOE CREEK STATE PARK (all ages)

On Route 22, about 13 miles east of Altoona, and about 7 miles east of Hollidaysburg or 11 miles west of Water Street; (814) 695–6807; www.dcnr.state. pa.us. The "day use" side is open 8:00 A.M. to sunset. The cabin area and east side have twenty-four-hour access. Admission is **Free**.

You can reserve either a rustic or modern cabin and enjoy a wide variety of nature education programs at Canoe Creek State Park, one of a few parks that offer bat hikes, a favorite with our boys. At Canoe Creek you can join in on a bat hike to look in on Pennsylvania's largest bat nursery colony (females and young) in the attic of an old church. As night falls, they emerge from their home—about 10,000 of them! Children under twelve must be accompanied by an adult. Bring a flashlight. Other programs teach about bluebirds, birds' nests, frogs and toads, and wildflowers. Persons with disabilities may call (814) 695-6807 if assistance will be needed to participate in the program.

Patton

SELDOM SEEN TOURIST COAL MINE (ages 8 and up)

Located on Route 36, 4 miles north of Patton, 7 miles from Prince Gallitzin State Park; (800) 237–8590 or mine phone in season only (814) 247–6305; www. seldomseenmine.com. Open Memorial Day, July 4th, and Labor Day, plus weekends throughout June and September, as well as Thursday and Friday in July and

G̲oing Batty
For Judah's tenth birthday, we took about twelve of his friends on a bat hike. We also brought Seth, who was seven and a half, and Gideon, a newborn in a baby sling. Judah was very interested in bats.

The guide told us that July was a good time for a bat hike because the bats would recently have had young, and the colony would be at its largest.

As the sun set we waited outside the dilapidated barn that was the bats' home. The kids were all impatient to see the bats fly out to feed on the millions of insects that congregated over the nearby field.

Our guide had brought a device that amplified the bats' sonar sounds. He explained how to distinguish the sounds the bats made as they located and devoured their prey.

As darkness fell, first one bat emerged from a crack in the roof of the barn. Then another. Then another, then more and more until we counted more than 200, then lost count. The sky over the field was dark with bats.

August. Hour-long tours are conducted daily from noon to 6:00 P.M. Admission: adults, $$; children under 12, $. Group rates available.

Many of the coal mines in southwestern Pennsylvania were small, family-run mines like this one. This nonprofit educational attraction is one of the region's most popular sites. Many of the tour guides are former miners and descendants of immigrant miners. Somehow once your kids have imagined themselves hand digging and hand loading coal for 25 cents a ton, taking out the garbage doesn't seem so bad.

Altoona

Altoona has a lot to offer, including its new minor-league baseball team, the Altoona Curve.

ALTOONA RAILROADERS MEMORIAL MUSEUM (all ages)
1300 Ninth Avenue; (888) 4–ALTOONA; www.railroadcity.com. From November through March open Tuesday through Sunday 10:00 A.M. to 5:00 P.M. From April through October open daily 9:00 A.M. to 5:00 P.M. Admission is $$; children under 5 are Free.

There are many museums devoted to the technology of railroading, but the Altoona Railroaders Memorial Museum tells the story of the men and women of the Pennsylvania Railroad. Here, you'll experience Altoona at the height of industrial America. Located in the former Pennsylvania Railroad Master Mechanics building, this high-tech interpretive facility guides visitors through a firsthand experience of life in a booming railroad town. A film about the men and women of the PRR is also featured and included in the admission price.

The museum is across from the Amtrak station, so real fanatics can come by train, see the trains, and go home by train. There are changing tables in the bathrooms only in the new building. If you get hungry, the shopping center next door has fast food, pizza, and Chinese food.

 ## HORSESHOE CURVE NATIONAL HISTORIC LANDMARK (all ages)

Located 6 miles west of Altoona; (814) 946–0834 or (888) 4–ALTOONA; www.railroadcity.com. Open daily April through October 10:00 A.M. to 7:00 P.M. and November through December, Tuesday through Sunday 10:00 A.M. to 4:00 P.M. Closed on Monday and January through March. Admission is $; a yearly pass is $$. Children under 5 are Free.

At the Altoona Railroaders Museum, you can see a film that describes how the **Horseshoe Curve Railroad** was built. Then you can drive about 5 miles to watch the trains at Horseshoe Curve National Historic Landmark. Administered by the Altoona Railroaders Museum, this incredible engineering feat revolutionized rail travel, cleared the way for the westward expansion of the railroad, and made the Allegheny Portage Railroad obsolete (see page 135).

The story of Horseshoe Curve is told at a modern interpretive center. Visitors can ride to track elevation onboard the single-track funicular or walk the 194 evenly spaced stairs. At track elevation, more than fifty trains can be viewed every day along the Norfolk Southern mainline. One round-trip funicular ride is included in the admission.

There is a food concession open seasonally, and all bathrooms have changing tables.

 ## QUAINT CORNER CHILDREN'S MUSEUM (ages 3 to 10)

On Route 36, at 2000 Union Avenue, only a few blocks from the railroad museum; (814) 944–6830. Open Thursday, Friday, and Saturday from 1:00 to 5:00 P.M. Admission is $.

Kids love exploring closets and attics, and they're welcome to snoop around in the Quaint Corner Children's Museum. Peek in the International Closet or the Amish Closet, and climb up the ladder to Grandma's Attic.

The Quaint Corner Children's Museum was designed as a place for families to explore together, promoting creative hands-on learning and an appreciation for art, history, and science. The house itself is charming with its stained-glass windows and fine woodwork. Children love the craft room, dress-up clothes, and the sandbox in the basement. There's even a player piano in the gift shop. The gift shop has a nice selection of 25-cent items. The bathroom, like the house, is old, with no changing or handicapped facilities. The annual Quaint Corner Children's Fair comes in mid-August with puppet shows, games, and food.

BENZEL'S PRETZEL BAKERY (all ages)

5200 Sixth Avenue (Route 76); (814) 942–5062; www.benzels.com. Open Monday through Friday 9:00 A.M. to 5:00 P.M. and Saturday 9:00 A.M. to 1:00 P.M. Tours are Free.

You can walk to Benzel's from the Quaint Corner Children's Museum. Operated by a third generation of the Benzel family, Benzel's Pretzel Bakery makes about five million pretzels every day. At one time the pretzels were shaped by hand, but at present the dough goes through an extruder. To order pretzels by mail, call (800) 344–GIFT. There is a changing table in the handicapped-accessible rest room.

LAKEMONT PARK (all ages)

700 Park Avenue; (814) 949–PARK; www.lakemontparkfun.com. Open early May through mid-September, plus selected weekends in October, November, and December. Several different passes are available, with the most expensive All Day Ride & Slide Pass costing $$ per person.

In 2000, Lakemont Park reopened its treasured historic Leap the Dips roller coaster, the world's oldest roller coaster and the last remaining example of the side friction figure-eight design. In 2001 the Tin Lizzy Antique Auto ride opened. In all, there are more than thirty rides and attractions, including the Island Waterpark, two roller coasters, two go-cart tracks, an arcade, food, and more.

Sinking Valley

FORT ROBERDEAU (ages 8 and up)

Off PA 433 north or the Bellwood exit of I–99. Open May 15 through September 30, Tuesday to Saturday 11:00 A.M. to 5:00 P.M. and Sunday 1:00 to 5:00 P.M. Closed on Monday. (814) 946–0048; www.fortroberdeau.org.

Sinking Valley, which is between Altoona and Tyrone, is the site of Fort Roberdeau. This 1778 stockade has been reconstructed, and it now offers living-history reenactments, nature trails, tours, and a picnic area.

Tipton

DEL GROSSO'S PARK (all ages)

Twelve miles north of Altoona on old US 220, off I–99 exit 41 or 46 ; (814) 684–3538; www.delgrossos.com. Open seasonally. All-day Waterworks and rides: $$. All-day Waterworks, rapids, and rides: $$$.

Del Grosso's (formerly Bland's Park) features more than thirty rides, five water slides, an interactive children's park, an eighteen-hole mini-golf course with five waterfalls and two lakes, go carts, and miniature train rides.

Tyrone

GARDNERS CANDIES (all ages)

30 West Tenth Street; (814) 684–0857; www.gardnerscandies.com. Open Monday through Saturday 9:30 A.M. to 9:00 P.M. and Sunday 1:00 to 9:00 P.M. Admission is **Free***.*

A sweet taste of nostalgia for children of all ages, Gardners Candies has been making candies for more than a century. Inside its newly renovated History of Candyland Museum, you can see antique candy-making equipment, a 10-cent Coke machine, and other nostalgic artifacts.

Spruce Creek

INDIAN CAVERNS (all ages)

Eleven miles east of Tyrone on Route 45, between Water Street and State College in Huntington County; (814) 632–7578; www.indiancaverns.com. During June,

July, and August, hours are 9:00 A.M. to 6:00 P.M. daily. In April, May, September, and October, hours are 9:00 A.M. to 4:00 P.M. daily. Closed November through April. Call for admission prices.

There are real cave paintings on the walls of Indian Caverns: a turtle, a tepee, and a Mohawk chief.

More than 400 years ago, Native Americans used these caverns as a winter shelter, council chamber, and burial ground. Adjacent to Indian Caverns is a second cavern, Giant's Hall, where you can view the Grotto of the Wah Wah Taysee, a cave that glows, and the Frozen Niagara, which is more than two stories tall. Kids enjoy the sounds made by a musical rock.

The wide concrete walkways and Native American artifacts make this an excellent cavern if your family includes a wide range of ages, attention spans, and energy levels.

Huntingdon

GREENWOOD FURNACE STATE PARK (all ages)

On PA Route 305; 5 miles west of Belleville; park office (814) 667–1800; visitors center: (814) 667–1805; www.dcnr.state.pa.us. The visitors center is open 9:00 A.M. to 5:00 P.M. Wednesday through Sunday during the summer and 9:00 A.M. to 5:00 P.M. on weekends only in spring and fall.

Less than thirty minutes from Huntingdon, Lewistown, or State College is a green park area on the site of the Greenwood iron furnaces and the "village built around an inferno." You can take a one-hour, self-guided walking tour of a portion of the historic district and see parts of the town such as the tramway, historic roads, charcoal hearths, a stone mansion, stone church, and stables. History and nature programs are presented every weekend during the summer. The park's most popular event is Old Home Days, during the first full weekend of August, when living-history interpreters offer historical demonstrations such as soap making, brew making, and bonnet making. Campsites are available.

LINCOLN CAVERNS AND WHISPER ROCKS (all ages)

On Route 22, 3 miles west of Huntingdon; (814) 643–0268; www.lincoln caverns.com. Tour hours vary seasonally. Admission is $$ and Free for children 3 and under. A single admission fee gets you into Lincoln Caverns and Whisper Rocks.

These two caverns are a bit more challenging than some other nearby caverns. The walkways are often damp, but the minerals in the water droplets keep this a living cave. The rock formations are spectacular: flowstones, stalactites, calcite, and crystals.

Ann Dunlavy Molosky, third-generation manager of the cave, emphasizes education as well as fun. Many educational programs are available, including geology and speleology workshops, as well as programs focused on debunking common misconceptions about bats. Bring a sweater. Special offerings include a kids cave camp in June and Ghosts and Goblins tours in October.

 ## THE SWIGART MUSEUM (all ages)

Route 22 East, 4 miles east of Huntingdon; (814) 643–0885; www.swigart museum.com. Open daily Memorial Day through October, 9:00 A.M. to 5:00 P.M. Admission is $;children under 6 enter Free.

This museum is the oldest automobile museum in America, established by the late W. Emmert Swigart in 1920. The present owner, William E. Swigart Jr., continued the collection upon his father's death in 1949. The Swigart collection emphasizes the era when America was first becoming a mobile society. Featured cars include a 1900 Winton, 1904 Rambler, and the only remaining Carroll. Other highlights include two Tuckers and Herbie, the "Love Bug." About thirty-five cars from the collection of 200 are on display at any given time. Supporting these is an outstanding collection of license plates and name plates. Children will enjoy seeing the exhibits of antique toys, trains, and bicycles.

Hesston

Area residents believe that **Raystown Lake** doesn't get the attention it deserves. This huge man-made lake is located in Huntington County, surrounded by two state forests, trout-stocked streams, museums, historic sites, campgrounds, and lots of family recreation. Call (814) 658-0060 or (800) RAYSTOWN.

 ## SEVEN POINTS MARINA (all ages)

Raystown Lake, off Route 26; (814) 658–3074 for departure times and details; www.7pointsmarina.com. The boats operate for both private charter and for the public, April through October. Public cruises depart up to three times a day at the height of the summer season and cost $$ for adults, and $ for children under 12.

Seven Points Marina, Pennsylvania's largest marina, offers a variety of ways to enjoy the lake and its countryside, including houseboat rentals and daily boat rentals. The 75-foot lake cruiser *Princess* is available for public cruises, dinner cruises, and private charters. Seven Points Restaurant, with both indoor and outdoor tables, overlooks the inner harbor. Kids enjoy feeding the hundreds of carp at the Fish Feeding Station.

Entriken

 LAKE RAYSTOWN RESORT AND LODGE

100 Chipmunk Crossing, Raystown Lake; (814) 658–3500; www.raystown resort.com.

Raystown Resort is a great spot for recreation. The resort includes 122 campsites, several different kinds of cabins (some with hot tubs), luxury houseboats for rent, and a lodge. The list of activities for families goes on and on: the WildRiver Water Park (with a heated pool), Caddy's Revenge miniature golf, bank-shot basketball court, and a full-service marina featuring boat rentals, Jet Skis, etc. From Memorial Day to Labor Day, there are daily organized activities for children.

Rockhill

East Broad Top Railroad and the Rockhill Trolley Museum jointly host a Fall Spectacular during Columbus Day weekend. On the first Saturday in December, Santa's Trolley runs with decorations, an outdoor train display, and hot cocoa.

EAST BROAD TOP RAILROAD (all ages)

Route 994, 1 mile west of Orbisonia in Rockhill; (814) 447–3011; www.spikesys. com/EBT. Open from June through October, Saturday and Sunday, with three train trips daily. Trains depart at 11:00 A.M., 1:00 P.M., and 3:00 P.M. Fares are $$; children under 2 ride Free. *Group rates available for groups of twenty or more.*

Now a National Historic Landmark, East Broad Top Railroad once carried coal and other raw materials. At present it is the most complete and authentic rail site in North America.

Board the train for a ride on the only narrow-gauge railroad in the East still running at its original site. The narrated train ride takes about fifty minutes and carries you past countryside that is virtually unchanged since the days when East Broad Top Railroad transported coal along these tracks. If you like, bring along a picnic lunch. You can get off at Colgate Grove, picnic, and go back on a later train.

Every year during Columbus Day weekend, railroad buffs come from all over the United States to East Broad Top's Fall Spectacular. For this event all four locomotives operate at once, and scheduled shop tours are available.

ROCKHILL TROLLEY MUSEUM (all ages)

Meadow Street (Route 994); on weekends call (814) 447–9576; other days call (610) 965–9028; www.rockhilltrolley.org. Open weekends only Memorial Day to mid-October, 10:30 A.M. to 4:30 P.M., plus some holidays. Trolleys operate 11:00 A.M. to 4:30 P.M. Fares are $; children under 2 ride **free**. *For more information write to Railways to Yesterday, Inc., P.O. Box 1601, Allentown 18105.*

Adjacent to East Broad Top Railroad, the Rockhill Trolley Museum has twenty-six trolleys and streetcars, including cars from Philadelphia, Johnstown, Harrisburg, Scranton, and York. Nine trolleys are currently operational, including open cars, closed cars, an interurban car, a snowplow, a sweeper, and a Philadelphia PCC. You can take a more-than-3-mile ride on a restored trolley, passing the Rockhill Iron Furnace.

Like the National Trolley Museum near Pittsburgh, the Rockhill Trolley Museum is staffed by volunteers who love what they're doing. Volunteers here are members of Railways to Yesterday, Inc. Your trolley ticket is good for unlimited rides on the date purchased. Most days, you can try out two or three different cars. If you time it right, you can meet the returning East Broad Top Railroad train, passing just a few feet away.

Amazing Laurel Highlands Facts

This region includes more than twenty golf courses (including the Latrobe Country Club owned by Arnold Palmer); 700,000 acres of game land; 120 lakes and streams, plus white-water rafting on the Youghiogheny River; and Raystown Lake, Pennsylvania's largest man-made lake.

Robertsdale

BROAD TOP AREA COAL MINERS MUSEUM AND ENTERTAINMENT CENTER (ages 8 and up)

Reality Theater, Main Street; (814) 635–3807, (814) 635–3220, or (814) 635–2013. Open Friday and Saturday 10:00 A.M. to 5:00 P.M. and Sunday *noon to 5:00 P.M. Admission is $. On show nights, tickets are $$ for adults, $ for children.*

This museum offers exhibits about coal mining and railroading in the area.

Bedford

If you like the tradition of stealing a kiss on a kissing bridge, you'll love Bedford County. It has fourteen covered bridges, and you can cuddle your toddlers and embarrass your older kids on every one of them.

OLD BEDFORD VILLAGE (all ages)

Business Route 220, 1/2 mile south of PA Turnpike exit 11, also reachable from Route 30; (814) 623–1156; www.oldbedfordvillage.org. Spring and summer hours: Memorial Day weekend through Labor Day weekend, open 9:00 A.M. to 5:00 P.M. daily except Wednesday. Fall hours: Thursday through Saturday 9:00 A.M. to 5:00 P.M., Sunday 10:00 A.M. to 4:00 P.M. Admission is $$ for adults and $ for students and children 6 and over.

Drive over the Claycomb Covered Bridge to Old Bedford Village. This restored village of more than forty log structures is beautifully laid out to re-create a typical village of about 1750 to 1900, with homes, schools, a church, and shops. Interpreters in period costumes bake cookies and make brooms, and much more. About fourteen indigenous crafts are represented. The kids will love stopping for ice cream or doughnuts as you tour the town.

Meals are available at Pendergrass Tavern in the village. Dress comfortably and wear walking shoes. Wheelchair accessible. The Village Craft and Gift Shop offers many unusual crafts made in the village, as well as souvenirs.

Annual special events include a crafts festival in June, gospel music and a storyteling festival in August, Civil War reenactments in September, pumpkin festivals in October, and a holiday celebration in December.

You can take a pleasant walking tour of Historic Downtown Bedford, including several historic houses and the Fort Bedford Museum.

FORT BEDFORD MUSEUM (ages 8 and up)

Fort Bedford Drive; (814) 623–8891 or (800) 259–4284; www.bedford county.net. Open daily May through October, except Tuesday in May, September, and October, 10:00 A.M. to 5:00 P.M. Admission is $; children under 6 are **Free**. *Family rate $$.*

Old Fort Bedford was a British stockade built in 1758 during the French and Indian War. Later it was used as a British outpost on the frontier until the early 1770s. Fort Bedford is gone, but you can learn about its past by touring the Fort Bedford Museum. The museum includes a large scale model of the fort, Native American artifacts, weapons, uniforms, a Conestoga wagon, and children's toys of the period. Handicapped accessible.

Where to Eat

IN JOHNSTOWN AREA

Applebee's Neighborhood Grill & Bar, *425 Galleria Drive, Johnstown; (814) 269–4500.* This popular chain is consistent and family-friendly. Children's menu.

Coney Island Lunch, *127 Clinton Street, Johnstown; (814) 535–2885.* This casual place serves hot dogs, hamburgers, etc. Children always welcome.

Fazoli's Italian Restaurant, *2550 Old Route 220, Altoona; (814) 949–8229.* Casual Italian-style food such as pizza, spaghetti, lasagna, and ravioli are offered on the children's menu.

Grubb's Diner, *Route 22 at Fourth and Moore, Huntingdon; (814) 643–3934.* Casual dinners. Children welcome.

Johnnie's Restaurant and Lounge, *415 Main Street, Johnstown; (814) 536–9309.* Greek-style food including Greek salads and gyros, but also spaghetti and rigatoni. Children always welcome.

The Train Station, *Philadelphia Street, Indiana; (724) 349–9005.* Subs, steaks, seafood. Children's menu.

Where to Stay

IN OHIOPYLE

Ohiopyle State Park Kentuck Campground, *(729) 329–8591.*

Scarlett Knob Campground, Inc., *Route 381 North; (412) 329–5200.* Adjoining Ohiopyle State Park. Both campsites and cabins available.

Yough Plaza Motel, *(800) 992–7238.* Within walking distance of the river.

IN JOHNSTOWN

Comfort Inn Ebensburg, *Route 22 West, Ebensburg; (814) 472–6100 or (800) 221–2222.* Suites available, indoor pool, **Free** continental breakfast.

Comfort Inn Johnstown, *455 Theatre Drive, Johnstown; (814) 266–3678 or (800) 228–5150.* Centrally located near all major attractions.

Days Inn Johnstown, *1540 Scalp Avenue; (814) 269–3366.*

Holiday Inn, *downtown, 250 Market Street, Johnstown; (814) 535–7777.* Indoor pool, Harrigan's restaurant, sidewalk cafe.

Sleep Inn Johnstown, *453 Theatre Drive, Johnstown; (800) 753–3746.*

IN RAYSTOWN LAKE AREA

Lake Raystown Resort & Lodge, *100 Chipmunk Crossing, Route 994, Entriken; (814) 658–3500.* Wild River Waterpark, miniature golf, hiking, fishing, picnic areas, camping, and restaurants all nearby.

Seven Points Marina/Houseboat Rental, *Seven Points Marina, off Route 26; (814) 658–3074.* Fully equipped houseboats for rent. Cruises aboard the *Raystown Bell* and *Queen.*

For More Information

Allegheny Mountains Convention and Visitors Bureau, *Logan Valley Mall, Route 220 and Goods Lane, Altoona 16602; (800) 84–ALTOONA or (814) 943–4183; www.alleghenymountains.org.*

Bedford County Visitors Bureau, *141 South Juliana Street, Bedford 15522; (800) 765–3331 or (814) 623–1771; www.bedfordcounty.net.*

Fulton County Tourist Promotion Agency, *112 North Third Street, P.O. Box 141, McConnellsburg 17233; (717) 485–4064; www.fultoncountypa.com.*

Greater Johnstown/Cambria County Convention and Visitors Bureau, *111 Market Street, Johnstown 15901–1608; (800) 237–8590 or (814) 536–7993; www.visitjohnstownpa.com.*

Greene County Tourist Promotion Agency, *17 South Washington Street, Waynesburg 15370; (412) 627–TOUR; www.co.greenepa.net.*

Huntington Country Visitors Bureau, *RD 1, Box 222A, Seven Points Road, Hesston 16647; (888) RAYSTOWN; www.raystown.org.*

Indiana County Tourist Bureau, *Indiana Mall/2090 Route 286 South, Indiana 15701; (724) 463–7505; www.indiana-copa-tourism.org.*

Laurel Highlands Visitors Bureau, *120 East Main Street, Ligonier 15658; (800) 925–7669 or (724) 238–5661; www.laurelhighlands.org.*

Pittsburgh and Environs

From the dizzying height of one of its two inclines, with the city spread below you, to the *Gateway Clipper* riverboat, from which you see the city at the confluence of the Monongahela, Allegheny, and Ohio Rivers, Pittsburgh comes as a pleasant surprise. As the boat passes the tip of Point State Park, you'll see a striking fountain that shoots a blast of water straight up into the sky.

Entering Pittsburgh through the Fort Pitt Tunnel, you'll see why the *New York Times* has called this "the only city in America with an entrance." Pittsburgh has the Golden Triangle (downtown area) with the cleanest **Free** subway system in the United States, and the Wayfinder system of 1,500 brightly colored signs to help you navigate.

For one hundred years the names Pittsburgh and Carnegie have been inextricably linked. Andrew Carnegie believed that wealth should

Faith & Emily's
Favorite Pittsburgh Attractions

1. Kennywood, West Mifflin

2. Sandcastle Action Park, West Homestead

3. Carnegie Science Center, Pittsburgh

4. The Pittsburgh Children's Museum, Pittsburgh

5. Carnegie Museums of Art and Natural History, East Pittsburgh

6. Duquesne or Monongahela Incline, Pittsburgh

7. Pittsburgh Zoo and Aquarium, East Pittsburgh

8. The Gateway Clipper Fleet, Pittsburgh

9. The Pennsylvania Trolley Museum, Washington

10. Children's Studio at Society for Contemporary Craft, Pittsburgh

PITTSBURGH AND ENVIRONS

be used to benefit the public. Thanks to Andrew Carnegie, and the museums he helped to create, your trip to Pittsburgh can include dinosaur bones, paintings, sculpture, a submarine, and more. Celebrating its centennial in 1996, the Carnegie museums include the Carnegie Science Center, Museum of Art, Museum of Natural History, Library of Pittsburgh, Music Hall and Performing Arts Center, and The Andy Warhol Museum.

You'll also benefit from the legacies of some of Pittsburgh's other leading families: the Mellons, Fricks, Phippses, and now, the Heinzes.

You won't want to miss the Senator John Heinz Regional History Center. Its Children's Discovery Place uses hands-on activities to teach about the everyday life of children from the region's history.

And then, within minutes, you can be squealing with excitement at America's favorite traditional amusement park or at an outstanding water park. If you're looking for a decidedly different way to tour Pittsburgh, check out Just Ducky Tours, Inc, which offers tours aboard a World War II military amphibious vehicle. Call (412) 928-2489 for information.

When planning your visit, you may want to check out the Greater Pittsburgh Convention and Visitors Bureau Web site, www.pittsburgh.net, or any of the Web sites of the museums and attractions listed in this chapter.

Faith & Emily's
Favorite Pittsburgh Area Events

- **Pittsburgh Children's Festival,** Pittsburgh's North Side (mid-May); (412) 321-5520.

- **Three Rivers Arts Festival** (first two weeks of June); (412) 281-8723.

- **"Fireworks Capital of the World" July Fourth Celebration** in New Castle; (412) 654-5593.

- **Greater Pittsburgh Renaissance Festival** (last three weeks of August through September on Saturday, Sunday, and Labor Day); (724) 872-1670; www.pgh-renfest.com.

- **"Pumpkin Patch Trolley"** (October); (412) 228-9256.

- **Holidays at the Carnegie** (November through December); (412) 622-3131.

Pittsburgh's North Side

Start your adventure in downtown Pittsburgh's North Side with a stop at the visitors center on Liberty Avenue near Stanwix Street, a handy place to pick up maps, brochures, and advice. Also in this area is The Pittsburgh Children's Museum (PCM).

THE PITTSBURGH CHILDREN'S MUSEUM
(ages 12 and under)

10 Children's Way, Allegheny Square–North Side; (412) 322–5059; www. pittsburghkids.org. Open Tuesday through Thursday and Saturday 10:00 A.M. to 5:00 P.M., Friday 10:00 A.M. to 8:00 P.M., Sunday noon to 5:00 P.M. Open Mondays from mid-June through August. Admission: adults $$, children 2 to 18 and seniors $; children under 2 are Free.

The Pittsburgh Children's Museum is reaching "great heights" with exciting exhibits and programs for the young and young-at-heart. Visitors can scale the two-story Kids' Climber, build and launch airplanes from Flying Machines, and raise themselves up in human-powered elevators. Get creative in the multimedia studio: create silkscreen prints, play with clay, paint a masterpiece, and design on a computer. Learn about health and anatomy with 7-foot-tall blue-haired mascot Stuffee and Riddle, the 25-foot poodle sphinx, and explore the basics of car, bicycle, bus, and pedestrian safety on Safety Street. Put on a puppet show at one of four stages and enjoy the original puppets from *Mister Rogers' Neighborhood*. There are even areas for the youngest visitors to explore and learn.

This hands-on museum, located in the historic Old Post Office building, is a top attraction for family fun in Pittsburgh. There are also fun, unique educational programs; outreach performances; and classes.

POINT STATE PARK (all ages)

Point State Park is at the tip of Pittsburgh's "Golden Triangle." The thirty-six-acre park is accessible from the east and west by I–376 and I–279, from the north by PA Route 8, and from the south by PA Route 51. Web site: www.dchr.state.pa.us.

You can stroll the park's paved promenade along the riverfront, enjoying the view. At the tip of the park, you can see the fountain also known as "The Point." The sites of both Fort Duquesne and Fort Pitt are located in Point State Park.

Fort Duquesne was built by the French and destroyed by the British in 1758. Today only a bronze marker shows where that fort once stood.

FORT PITT MUSEUM (ages 8 and up)

Point State Park; (412) 281–9284. Open in winter Wednesday to Saturday 10:00 A.M. to 4:30 P.M. and Sunday noon to 4:30 P.M. In summer open Tuesday as well. Admission is $. If you bring in a losing Pennsylvania lottery ticket, you can save $1.00. Maximum family rate is $$.

The British occupied Fort Pitt until 1772, when the Americans took over. You can see the Fort Pitt Blockhouse and the Fort Pitt Museum. Here you can view exhibits that describe Pittsburgh's early years.

CARNEGIE SCIENCE CENTER (all ages)

One Allegheny Avenue; (412) 237–3400; www.carnegiesciencecenter.org. The Carnegie Science Center is open Sunday through Friday 10:00 A.M. to 5:00 P.M. and Saturday 10:00 A.M. to 9:00 P.M. Extended hours are offered from mid-June to early September. The UPMC SportsWorks exhibit is open Sunday through Thursday noon to 5:00 P.M. and Friday and Saturday noon to 10:00 P.M. Extended hours are offered from mid-June through August. General admission, $$$, includes permanent and traveling exhibits, planetarium show, theater demonstrations, submarine tour, and UPMC SportsWorks. General admission for seniors is reduced to $$ on Tuesday. Omnimax-only and other combination tickets also available. The science center is fully accessible to persons with disabilities; the submarine requires full mobility. Assistive listening systems are available for the Omnimax.

In August 2001, the Carnegie Science Center opened UPMC Sports-Works, a brand-new exhibit in a building adjacent to the science center and across from the new Heinz Field. UPMC SportsWorks explores the science in sports in a setting that evokes the excitement of a sporting event, with banners, concession stand, scoreboards, and sound effects. UPMC SportsWorks contains more than forty exhibits in six major theme areas: Safe Adventure, Try It Yourself, Sports & Science, Virtual Sports, MiniGolf Math, and UPMC SportsWorks Jr. Kids can scramble up a 25-foot rock wall or bounce on a trampoline wearing a bungee harness. They can challenge a virtual Jackie Joyner-Kersee to an "Olympic Sprint," ski down a virtual slope, or jump over a virtual sand dune. In UPMC SportsWorks Jr. children ages three to seven get their own play zone to crawl through arches, climb across a rock wall, or skip river stones. It's fun with a purpose: to teach the underlying science of sports. After all, Pittsburgh is a great sports town.

But with all the new exhibits in SportsWorks, don't miss the science center, with its Omnimax Theater, planetarium, submarine, and more than 250 hands-on exhibits.

Carnegie Science Center's permanent exhibits include: SeaScape, SciQuest, The Miniature Railroad & Village, and the USS *Requin*. Enjoy the ultimate audiovisual experience at the four-story-tall Omnimax Theater.

Now open throughout the year, you can visit Pittsburgh's famous Miniature Railroad & Village. This replica of western Pennsylvania of the 1920s includes a minute Ferris wheel, a circus parade, and real smoke puffing out of the steel mill.

NATIONAL AVIARY (all ages)

Allegheny Commons West; (412) 323–7235; www.aviary.org. Open daily 9:00 A.M. to 5:00 P.M. Closed Christmas. Admission: $$ for adults, $ for seniors and for children 2 to 12. Children under 2 enter Free.

There are nearly 500 live birds of more than 220 species, many of them endangered, at the National Aviary. You'll see birds of all sizes and colors, from a tiny hummingbird to an Andean condor with a 10-foot wingspan, and more, including highly endangered red-crowned cranes. The aviary itself presents a lush green indoor oasis, with few obstructions between you and the birds' habitats.

Open exhibits, free-flight atriums, and hands-on demonstrations bring excitement and fun to the experience. The Animal Encounters program introduces visitors to the birds up close in informal presentations. Guided tours by reservation. Educational programs are available for children and adults, and new interactive graphics will invigorate your imagination. The entire facility and spacious parking lot are handicapped accessible.

THE ANDY WARHOL MUSEUM (all ages)

117 Sandusky Street, on Pittsburgh's North Side near the cultural district, and across the Seventh Street Bridge from downtown; (412) 237–8300; www.warhol. org. Open Tuesday, Wednesday, Thursday, Saturday, and Sunday 10:00 A.M. to 5:00 P.M. and Friday 10:00 A.M. to 10:00 P.M. Closed Monday and legal holidays. Admission is $$ for adults, $ for children (3 and over) and students.

Artist and pop icon Andy Warhol was born in Pittsburgh. Opened in 1994, The Andy Warhol Museum is the largest single-artist museum in the United States. Housed in a funky historic industrial warehouse are

3,000 original works of art, including paintings, drawings, prints, films, and a lot more. Public parking lots with attendants are located under the North Shore Expressway, 1 block north of the museum off Sandusky Street. There is additional parking across the street from the museum.

At the Warhol museum children are especially drawn to the Silver Clouds gallery on the fifth floor, where silver, pillow-shaped balloons float around you. Hands-on activities are offered in the Weekend Factory on Saturday and Sunday noon to 4:00 P.M.

MATTRESS FACTORY (all ages)

500 Sampsonia Way; (412) 231–3169; www.mattress.org. Open Tuesday to Saturday 10:00 A.M. to 5:00 P.M., Sunday 1:00 to 5:00 P.M. Admission: Adults $$, students and seniors $. Children under 12 enter Free. Free *parking is available at 505 Jacksonia Street. Handicapped accessible.*

The Mattress Factory is a museum of contemporary installation art that presents "art you can get into" created by in-residence artists. Located on Pittsburgh's North Side since 1977, the Mattress Factory is one of few museums of its kind anywhere. Visitors of all ages examine the unique nature of site-specific art and explore a range of nontraditional media and environments—from recorded sound and running water to mirrored rooms and projected light. The museum's multisensory permanent collection includes works by Yayoi Kusama, Rolf Julius, Winifred Lutz, and more.

From June 2002 through April 2003, the Mattress Factory features "Into the Light: James Turrell." Artist/scientist/pilot James Turrell uses light to explore the relationship between art, light, the solar system, and volcanic craters.

The Mattress Factory offers a variety of Family Fun Activities. In the Art Lab, families can participate in thematic art-making projects that illuminate the creative process. Art lab activities are offered on the first and third Saturdays of every month, 11:00 A.M. to 4:00 P.M., Free with suggested admission. Children must be accompanied by an adult.

Amazing Pittsburgh Facts

With seven floors and more than 3,000 original works of art, The Andy Warhol Museum is the largest single-artist museum in the United States.

The "Strip District"

Pittsburgh's "Strip District" has nothing to do with exotic dancing. This is the nickname given to Pittsburgh's open-air marketplace. It's fun to take in the atmosphere on this ½-mile strip along Penn Avenue and Smallman Street, starting at Eleventh Street. Enjoy the colorful produce, the smells of ethnic food, bakeries, restaurants, and other shops.

Near the Strip District give your children a really extraordinary experience by participating in a children's workshop at the Society for Contemporary Craft.

 SOCIETY FOR CONTEMPORARY CRAFT (ages 4 to 12)

2100 Smallman Street; (412) 261–7003; www.contemporarycraft.org. Open Tuesday through Friday 10:00 A.M. to 5:00 P.M. and Saturday 9:00 A.M. to 5:00 P.M. The Exhibition Gallery and Drop-In Studio are **Free** *and open during public hours. Guided group tours of exhibitions are $ per person. Tour with artist-led craft activity is $$ per person. Please schedule group tours in advance.*

The Society for Contemporary Craft (SCC) provides an unusual chance to make art a part of your life. In 2001 SCC completed a major expansion and now offers a larger exhibition gallery, an education center, The Studio, and The Store, featuring one-of-a-kind handmade works for all ages.

The gallery stages four craft exhibitions per year. Each exhibition is accompanied by a related artist-designed project that invites families to create art together in the Drop-In Studio. Past visitors have made object jewelry and cereal-box-cardboard quilts. Come as you are and stay until your masterpiece is complete.

More in-depth art experiences are available through studio classes in book arts, fiber, metal, and wood for adults, children, and families. SCC also hosts special family events throughout the year. Both the building and the rest rooms are accessible to all visitors.

 THE SENATOR JOHN HEINZ PITTSBURGH REGIONAL HISTORY CENTER (all ages)

1212 Smallman Street; (412) 454–6000; www.pghhistory.org. Open daily 10:00 A.M. to 5:00 P.M. Admission: $$ for adults, $ for children ages 6 to 18, seniors (ages 65 and older), and students with ID.

This museum features permanent exhibits spotlighting life in western Pennsylvania from 1750 to the present. In the Great Hall children immediately notice a 1949 restored trolley, a Conestoga wagon, and the Pittsburgh city fire bell, cast after the great fire of 1845.

The Children's Discovery Place tells the story of eight real children from the region (two are still living today) whose lives exemplify different aspects of history. For example, kids can learn about the everyday life of a child who worked in a steel mill, one who was an indentured servant, and one who lived a privileged life. Hands-on activities get the kids involved in these lives. For example, kids learn to pack pickles in the Heinz factory as one of these children did, beginning at age fourteen.

The building is handicapped accessible, and there are baby-care facilities on the first and third floors. There is also a cafe and a museum shop.

South Side

On the South Side of Pittsburgh, you'll have an excellent opportunity to see the city from the water or from one of two inclines.

Board the *Gateway Clipper* at Station Square, a five-minute stroll across the Smithfield Street Bridge from downtown Pittsburgh. Two contiguous railroad buildings have been beautifully restored to create Station Square, a collection of sixty-five shops, eleven restaurants, and a hotel.

JUST DUCKY TOURS, INC. (all ages)

Station Square Dock; call (412) 928–2489 for information and reservations.

There's a unique way to tour the city of Pittsburgh—by DUCK! Not the kind of duck with feathers, but a World War II military amphibious vehicle, a bright green bus-boat that carries passengers on a tour of Pittsburgh, on land and water. The only requirement for passengers is that they quack. Hour-long tours depart from Station Square on Pittsburgh's South Side.

THE GATEWAY CLIPPER FLEET (all ages)

9 Station Square Dock; call (412) 355–7980 for information and a schedule of cruises. Web site: www.gatewayclipper.com.

The Gateway Clipper Fleet has a schedule of day and night cruises year-round, ranging from narrated sight-seeing trips to elegant dinner cruises with entertainment. Family Fun cruises are aimed at children twelve and under, such as the Goodship Lollipop Ride and seasonal cruises like Santa Family Fun, Halloween Monster Fun, and Bunny Fun. All the riverboats are climate controlled. The different vessels vary in facilities, but all have plenty of rest rooms, some with changing tables, others with wide counters. Some also have snack bars, and certain cruises include boxed lunches or pizza. Goodship Lollipop cruises feature Lolli the clown.

MONONGAHELA INCLINE (all ages)

Across the street from Station Square; (412) 442–2000. It runs Monday through Saturday 5:30 A.M. to 12:45 A.M. On Sunday and holidays it is open 8:45 A.M. to midnight. The fare is $ each way.

The "Mon," the first passenger incline in the United States, is 635 feet long and rises to an elevation of about 368 feet at a thirty-five-degree angle.

DUQUESNE INCLINE (all ages)

Located on Carson Street, directly across the river from Three Rivers Stadium. Call (412) 381–1665 for information. The Duquesne operates Monday through Saturday 5:30 A.M. to 12:45 A.M., Sunday 7:00 A.M. to 12:45 A.M. The fare is $ each way. **Free** *parking is available at the lower station.*

The Duquesne Incline has been in operation since 1877. The interiors are made of hand-carved cherry panels, with oak and bird's-eye maple trim and amber glass transoms. You can rise up 400 feet at a thirty-degree angle to the New Observation Deck at the upper station and take in the spectacular vista.

Inclined Planes of Pittsburgh

Two of Pittsburgh's famous inclines are located near Station Square: the Monongahela Incline and the Duquesne Incline.

So what is an "incline" anyway? It's a cable railway designed to carry passengers or freight up Pittsburgh's steep hills. Inclines were invented before electric streetcars and before automobiles. At one time the city had seventeen of these steam-driven engineering marvels. At present two survive, although now they are driven by electricity. Thousands of commuters use the inclines every day. (Both stations and inclines are now wheelchair accessible.)

What's the difference between the two? Well, the Duquesne has red cars, and the tracks are lit with red lights. The Monongahela has green and yellow lights on the tracks, and the cars are ivory with black trim. Both have overlooks from Mount Washington, with a great view of the city. Both have historical information in their upper stations.

East Pittsburgh

Three miles east of downtown, you'll discover Pittsburgh's Oakland cultural district, where you can see the University of Pittsburgh, Carnegie-Mellon University, the Carnegie Museums of Art and Natural History, Schenley Park, and the Phipps Conservatory. Also in this area you can visit Kennywood, Sandcastle Waterpark, and the Pittsburgh Zoo and Aquarium. (Technically, Kennywood is in West Mifflin and Sandcastle is in West Homestead, both of which are east of the city, so it gets a little confusing. In this guide we have listed them under West Mifflin and West Homestead respectively.)

 CARNEGIE MUSEUMS OF ART AND NATURAL HISTORY (all ages)

Located side by side on Forbes Avenue; (412) 622–3131; www.carnegiemuseums. org. Both museums open at 10:00 A.M. Tuesday through Saturday and close at 5:00 P.M., except on Thursday, when they are open until 9:00 P.M. Open Sunday noon to 5:00 P.M.; closed on Monday, except in July and August. A combination admission to both museums is $$. Handicapped accessible.

The Carnegie Museum of Natural History has one of the world's finest dinosaur collections, a hall of gems and minerals, Egyptian artifacts (including mummies), and Polar World.

The dinosaur collection has full skeletons of fifteen different species of dinosaur, including the the first *T. rex* ever discovered. The Hillman Hall of Minerals and Gems includes some of the finest specimens of their kinds, plus a dazzling display of fluorescent minerals. Polar World explores the culture of the Inuit, including their keenly observed carvings.

Big Dinobones! I'll never forget the first time we took Judah to an exhibit of dinosaur bones. He was about three-and-a-half years old, and he looked up at the huge skeletons with his enormously wide eyes and shouted, "B-I-I-I-G dino-bones!"

There are also Egyptian artifacts; African and North American wildlife; colorful displays of insects, butterflies, birds; and so much more.

The Discovery Room, for all ages, is open selected hours. There are also special programs for children, including Camp Earth, a summer camp program.

Founded in 1896 by Andrew Carnegie, the Carnegie Museum of Art was planned as a collection of "the old masters of tomorrow." At that time, that meant artists like Winslow Homer, James McNeill Whistler, and Camille Pisarro. Today the museum is known for its collections of American, French Impressionist, and Post-Impressionist works. It also includes European and American decorative arts, Asian and African art, and a new architectural department.

Schoolchildren will get a kick out of the Hall of Sculpture, patterned after a real Greek temple. Family, youth, and children's programs are available.

Since the museum of natural history and the museum of art are attached, one admission gets you into both, and there are often joint programs such as tours of both facilities. Also adjacent you'll find the Carnegie Music Hall and the Carnegie Library of Pittsburgh.

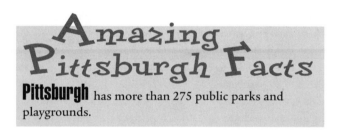

Amazing Pittsburgh Facts

Pittsburgh has more than 275 public parks and playgrounds.

 ### NATIONALITY ROOMS (ages 6 and up)

Fifth Avenue entrance, Cathedral of Learning; (412) 624–6000; www.pitt.edu. Reservations are recommended. Tour fees are $.

At the University of Pittsburgh's Cathedral of Learning you can compare New England Colonial architectural style with French Empire, Japanese, Indian, Austrian, Russian, Byzantine, Chinese Empire, first-century Israeli, or Irish Romanesque. Twenty-six different nations are represented in the Nationality Rooms Tours. Funded by gifts from Pittsburgh's ethnic communities, the Nationality Rooms are functioning classrooms in which your family can tour "around the world" with a university student guide who has been trained to adapt the tour to different ages and interests.

Younger children enjoy patting the laughing lion in the Chinese Room or identifying the fairy tales depicted in the German Room. The gift shop carries many unusual publications and an array of international gifts.

Also at the Cathedral of Learning:

HEINZ MEMORIAL CHAPEL (ages 8 and up)

Cathedral of Learning; (412) 624–4157; www.pitt.edu. Open 9:00 A.M. to 4:00 P.M. on weekdays. Mass is celebrated at noon every day. Services are also offered on Sunday, when the chapel is open 1:30 to 5:30 P.M.

Stained-glass windows set a tone of Gothic other-worldliness.

STEPHEN FOSTER MEMORIAL/CENTER FOR AMERICAN MUSIC (ages 8 and up)

Forbes Avenue at Cathedral of Learning; (412) 624–4100. Open weekdays 9:00 A.M. to 4:30 P.M. Guided tours by reservation only. Admission to museum is **Free**.

A collection of memorabilia reflecting the life of the popular composer, a Pittsburgh native.

PHIPPS CONSERVATORY (all ages)

Schenley Park; (412) 622–6914; www.phipps.conservatory.org. Open year-round Tuesday through Sunday 9:00 A.M. to 5:00 P.M. Admission: $$ for adults, $ for students and children 2 to 12. Outdoor gardens are open dawn to dusk, **Free**.

Inside the Victorian glass structure of the Phipps Conservatory, you can see hundreds of orchids, palms, ferns, and other plants. The Japanese Courtyard Garden has an excellent collection of bonsai. In winter the indoor gardens soothe your cabin fever, and in warm weather you can enjoy both indoor and outdoor gardens and fountains.

THE FRICK ART AND HISTORICAL CENTER (ages 8 and up)

7227 Reynolds Street; (412) 371–0600; www.frickart.org. Open year-round Tuesday through Saturday 10:00 A.M. to 5:00 P.M., Sunday noon to 6:00 P.M. Closed Monday. Admission to the museum is **Free***. Admission to Clayton is $$.* **Free***, secure parking at the Reynolds Street entrance.*

Another one of Pittsburgh's leading citizens was Henry Clay Frick, who lived at Clayton until 1905, when he moved to New York City (where his next house also became a favorite museum). The Frick Art and Historical Center is a six-acre site that includes Clayton, the Frick Art Museum, historic Car and Carriage Museum, visitors center, and cafe. The Victorian home has been meticulously restored, and about 95 percent of the furnishings are original. The Car and Carriage Museum displays old-fashioned automobiles, sleighs, and carriages. Little ones will be interested in the visitors center, which was once the playhouse of Helen, the Fricks' daughter. (Please note that neither backpacks nor strollers are permitted in Clayton.)

 PITTSBURGH ZOO AND AQUARIUM (all ages)

One Hill Road, in Highland Park (ten minutes from downtown Pittsburgh); (412) 665–3640; www.pittsburghzoo.com. Open daily except December 25. In winter the gates are open 9:00 A.M. to 4:00 P.M. If you're already inside the gate, you can stay until 5:00 P.M. In summer the gates open at 10:00 A.M. and close at 5:00 P.M., and you can stay inside until 6:00 P.M. Parking is $ per vehicle. Admission is $$.

In June 2000 the Pittsburgh Zoo became the Pittsburgh Zoo and Aquarium. It is the only public aquarium in Pennsylvania, a 45,000-square-foot, state-of-the-art facility featuring more than 4,000 aquatic animals: penguins, barracuda, piranha, stingrays, jellyfish, sharks, a rare Amazon River dolphin, and much more. Innovative tank designs include a crawl-through stingray tunnel, two-story shark tank, and the first revolving tanks ever publicly displayed.

Out of the Mouths of Babes

We were looking at the photos we'd taken at the zoo. Seth was three and fascinated with all the animals.

I told him, "A gorilla is very strong." He said, "So is a boy-rilla."

Kids Kingdom, the Children's Zoo at the Pittsburgh Zoo, has been ranked one of the top three children's zoos in the country. Kids Kingdom includes exciting interactive exhibits. Parents enjoy the fact that they can sit on the patio in Kids Kingdom while the kids learn to swing like spiders, slide like penguins, and enjoy the playground and live animals.

The animals here have natural enclosures. Highlights include the Siberian tigers in the Asian Forest; lions, leopards, rhinos, elephants, and gazelles of the African Savannah; and family groups of lowland gorillas, plus monkeys, gibbons, and orangutans of the Tropical Forest.

ALSO IN THE AREA

Pittsburgh is also a great sports town. The Pirates and Steelers both moved to brand-new stadiums in 2001, the Pirates to **PNC Stadium** and the Steelers to **Heinz Stadium**. For information and tickets for the Pirates, call (800) BUY–BUCS, or check the Web site at www.pittsburghpirates.com. For the Steelers, call (412) 432-7800 or visit www.pittsburghsteelers.com. The Pittsburgh Penguins (NHL hockey) still play in the same arena, but it's now called the **Mellon Arena** (formerly the Civic Arena). Call (800) 642-PENS, or visit www.theticket service.com.

While in Pittsburgh, you may wish to take in a performance at one of the many cultural venues: **Heinz Hall for the Performing Arts** (600 Penn Avenue, 412-392-4900); **Civic Light Opera** (Benedum Center, 719 Liberty Avenue, 412-281-2022); **The Playhouse** (222 Craft Avenue, 412-621-6695); **Pittsburgh Center for the Arts** (6300 Fifth Avenue, 412-361-0873); **Pittsburgh Opera** (711 Penn Avenue, 412-281-0912); or call TicketMaster at (412) 323-1919.

West Mifflin

Memories of a childhood in Pittsburgh usually include scrambling around a rocking Noah's Ark in Kennywood. Voted "Favorite Amusement Park" for eleven years in a row by the National Amusement Park Historical Association (NAPHA), Kennywood has also been called the "Roller Coaster Capital of the World." In 2001 the popular Steel Phantom was improved to include a faster speed (82 mph), a longer drop (228 feet), and new thrills. The reborn coaster was renamed Phantom's Revenge. And if all that isn't reason enough to visit the park, it has also been said that Kennywood's french fries are the best in the world.

Amazing Pittsburgh Facts

Kennywood, now more than one hundred years young, is one of only two amusement parks that are National Historic Landmarks.

KENNYWOOD (all ages)

4800 Kennywood Boulevard; (412) 461–0500; www.kennywood.com. Open daily mid-May through Labor Day 11:00 A.M. to 10:00 P.M. Prices vary seasonally, but, in general, you can get a Ride-All-Day ticket for $$$$. Senior general admission is $.

Now more than a century young, Kennywood is only minutes away from downtown Pittsburgh, off the Swissdale exit (exit 9) of I-376

(Penn-Lincoln Parkway). Although some rides will get you wet, none require bathing suits.

A Pittsburgh landmark since 1898, Kennywood is now also a National Historic Landmark. The carousel pavilion and a restaurant are the original structures. Others were added over the years. One roller coaster, for example, the Jack Rabbit, with its "camel back" (double dip), looks just the way it did in 1921. "Pittsburgh's Lost Kennywood" re-creates Luna parks of the past. But Kennywood has continued to evolve, with rides like Phantom's Revenge, and the Pitt Fall, the world's tallest and fastest free-fall ride. Kennywood's Exterminator combines a roller coaster with virtual reality to give you the ride of your life, in the dark, through underground tunnels and sewers where you'll encounter who knows what.

Kennywood makes your visit easy on your wallet in several ways. First, you're welcome to bring along a cooler and eat in the picnic grove. Another unique feature is the pricing schedule. Kennywood offers both a Ride-All-Day ticket that includes everything and a general admission for seniors. General admission can be a bargain for anyone who doesn't plan to go on many rides but still wishes to accompany the family. This ticket lets you into the park, but you have to pay for any rides separately. These two features allow families to save a little money and still have a great time together.

There are changing tables in all the bathrooms. In Kiddieland, there are kid-size bathrooms and an area for nursing mothers.

West Homestead

 ### SANDCASTLE ACTION PARK (all ages)

1000 Sandcastle Drive, on Route 837 between the Homestead High Level Bridge and Glenwood Bridge; (412) 462–6666; www.sandcastlewaterpark.com. Open daily in season, usually June through Labor Day weekend, 11:00 A.M. to 6:00 P.M. The park stays open until 7:00 P.M. in July and August. Admission: Whitewater Pass (includes all water activities—hot tubs, pools, Lazy River, and fifteen water slides) is $$$ for adults and children three and older.

Sandcastle Action Park, Kennywood's sister park in West Homestead, began life as an abandoned steel mill and was opened as a water park in July 1990. Sandcastle is a major riverside water park with a boardwalk, fifteen water slides, two pools, and a Lazy River. It also has two race-car tracks, video games, and miniature golf. Mon-Tsunami is a

20,000-square-foot wave pool with huge roller waves as well as diamond waves.

Only the bravest water-sliders should attempt the Lightning Express twin body slides, 60 feet high and 250 feet long, each with a double dip, followed by a monster free fall. (AAAH!)

Another slide, Cliffhangers, uses a new concept in water-slide design: sky ponds. Each pond is at a different level above the ground. You and your inner tube can float in one pond before sliding down to the next.

If that doesn't sound like your speed, relax on the Lazy River, with its whirlpools, fountains, and gentle current. Wet Willie's Waterworks is recommended for younger children, and The World's Largest Hot Tub is perfect for stressed-out parents.

Parking and boat docking are **Free**. Special events and festivals are held in Sandcastle's Riverplex entertainment complex.

Springdale

Rachel Carson said, "Those who contemplate the beauty of the earth find reserves of strength that will endure as long as life lasts." The famous author of *Silent Spring* was born in 1907 in the farmhouse now known as the Rachel Carson Homestead, in Springdale, within minutes of Pittsburgh. As your family travels this region that is so much a part of our industrial development, a visit to Carson's home is a healthy reminder of the downside of "progress."

 RACHEL CARSON HOMESTEAD (ages 8 and up)

613 Marion Avenue, approximately 30 minutes from downtown Pittsburgh; (724) 274–5459; www.rachelcarsonhomestead.org. Open Saturday and Sunday noon to 4:00 P.M. At other times you may call (724) 274–5459 for an appointment. Admission is $.

Tour this nineteenth-century house and find out about one woman who made a difference. This is the birthplace and childhood home of Rachel Carson, author of *Silent Spring*, published in 1962. Carson's books pointed out for the first time the dangers of DDT and other pesticides. Her special interest in exposing children to nature was illustrated by her 1956 article "Help Your Child to Wonder." You'll also enjoy the nature trail that Rachel Carson walked and the gardens, especially the Butterfly Garden.

Special children's programs are offered. In May Rachel Carson's birthday is celebrated.

Tarentum

In Tarentum, only a few miles northeast of the Rachel Carson Homestead, you can find out what life was like for miners in this area.

TOUR-ED MINE AND MUSEUM (ages 8 and up)

748 Bull Creek Road at exit 14 of Route 28 North, located on the Allegheny Valley Expressway, opposite Woodlawn Golf Course; (724) 224–4720; www. Tour-Edmine.com. Open Wednesday to Monday, Memorial Day to Labor Day, 1:00 to 4:00 P.M. Admission is $$ for adults, $ for children 12 and under. Group rates available.

You'll have to wear a miner's hard hat and mind your head as you board a mining car, modernized for comfort and electrically powered, to travel a ½-mile underground at Tour-Ed Mine and Museum into a genuine coal mine. Your tour guide, a real miner, will help you learn about the history of coal mining. It's chilly down here, so bring your sweater. This is not for the claustrophobic.

Kids will enjoy the newest addition: a tour in a locomotive on the surface to see a demonstration strip mine and auger mine. You can also see the company store, 1785 log home, and sawmill. You can even see a bedroom set up like the ones where the miners slept. There are covered picnic areas and snacks available.

Butler

The Butler County Historical Society administers several historic sites in the county, which are open seasonally. For information on any of these sites or to arrange a group or off-season tour, call the Historical Society at (724) 283–8116, or check the Web site www.butlercountyhistoricalsociety-pa.org.

BUTLER COUNTY HERITAGE CENTER (ages 8 and up)

119 West New Castle Street; (724) 283–2505; www.butlercountyhistorical society-pa.org. Hours vary seasonally.

This center presents temporary exhibits on the history of this area. On permanent display are artifacts from Butler County's many industries, including a tin shop, a Bantam jeep, Spang oil tools, Franklin glasswork, and farm tools.

COOPER CABIN (ages 8 and up)

Off Route 356 on Cooper Road; (724) 283–8116; www.butlercountyhistorical society-pa.org. Hours vary seasonally.

Built around 1810, Cooper Cabin was an original county homestead. On Halloween families gather around a bonfire at the cabin to hear ghost stories. On weekends from April to October the cabin offers demonstrations of horse shoeing, basket weaving, quilting, spinning, and weaving, as well as an herb garden and outbuildings such as a spinning house, spring house, and tool shed.

 ### LITTLE RED SCHOOL HOUSE MUSEUM (ages 6 and up)

200 East Jefferson Street; (724) 283–8116; www.butlercountyhistoricalsociety-pa.org. Hours vary seasonally.

At the Little Red School House, built in 1838, you sit down in a real old-fashioned desk as your tour guide transforms into a teacher.

Zelienople

Twenty-eight miles north of Pittsburgh on Route 19 is the historic town of Zelienople. The Zelienople Historical Society has restored the **Passavant House** and **Buhl House** (243 South Main Street and 221 South Main Street, respectively). Passavant House is primarily devoted to the furnishings and memorabilia of the Passavant family, who played an important role in the town's history. Buhl House displays a collection that tells the history of the entire community. Open May 1 to September 30, Wednesday and Saturday 1:00 to 4:00 P.M., otherwise by appointment. Call (412) 452–9457.

Harmony

The village of Harmony was founded in 1804 by members of a religious communal group, the Harmony Society. This group eventually built about 130 buildings including two outlying villages. At present, Harmony is known for its antiques shops, museums, restaurants, and parks.

 ### THE HARMONY MUSEUM (ages 8 and up)

Mercer Street; (724) 452–7341 or (888) 821–4822; www.harmonymuseum. org. Open year-round 1:00 to 4:00 P.M. daily except Monday. Appointments

strongly recommended for weekends. Closed holidays. Admission is $; children under 6 enter **Free***.*

The Harmony Museum displays Native American artifacts, as well as artifacts of the Harmonists and Mennonites. The museum also offers walking tours of the historic district of Harmony, as well as the Ziegler Log House and the Wagner House. Limited handicapped accessibility.

Amazing Pittsburgh Facts

The Pittsburgh Crawfords are considered the greatest Negro League baseball team of all time.

Portersville

MORAINE STATE PARK (all ages)

225 Pleasant Valley Road, off Route 422; (724) 368–8811; www.dcnr.state.pa. us. Open year-round 8:00 A.M. to sundown. **Free***, but there are rental fees for boats, cabins, etc. The beach is* **Free***.*

Moraine State Park offers 17,000 acres of family-oriented nature programs. There are nature walks and canoe trips. Having recently reintroduced ospreys to Lake Arthur, the park offers educational programs about these and other waterfowl. You can rent motorboats, pontoons, or sailboats. A 7-mile paved bike trail winds around the north shore of the lake.

McCONNELL'S MILL STATE PARK (all ages)

Five miles west of Moraine State Park, off Route 422; (724) 368–8091 or (724) 368–8811; www.dcnr.state.pa.us. The gristmill is open for **Free** *guided tours Memorial Day to Labor Day, 10:00 A.M. to 6:00 P.M. This scenic park features a covered bridge and a waterfall. For more information and park hours, call (724) 368–8091.*

Also administered by Moraine State Park is McConnell's Mill State Park. It's definitely worth the walk to see the 400-foot Slippery Rock Creek Gorge, formed by the glaciers thousands of years ago. The huge boulders literally "slipped" down the walls of the gorge, creating a strange and wonderful landscape. You can also explore the 2,500 acres of park land, have a picnic, hike one of the trails, or take a 𝐅𝐫𝐞𝐞 guided tour. If you have your own boat, you can go kayaking or rafting.

JENNINGS ENVIRONMENTAL CENTER (all ages)

2951 Prospect Road; (724) 794–6011; www.dcnr.state.pa.us. The education center is open Monday through Friday, 8:00 A.M. to 4:00 P.M. or whenever educational programs are offered. 𝐅𝐫𝐞𝐞 *admission. Some programs have fees. Call for information.*

Jennings Environmental Center is the only state park environmental education center in western Pennsylvania, and one of only four in the state. This site is a true relict prairie ecosystem.

A what? A relict prairie ecosystem is a prairie formed by prehistoric glacial activity. Here, the glacier left only 4 to 6 inches of topsoil, with clay underneath. As a result, trees don't grow here, but grasses and wildflowers do. If you visit in late July or August, you can see spectacular wildflowers in bloom, such as the spiky purple blazing star. The prairie also supports unusual wildlife, such as the eastern massasauga rattlesnake, one of Pennsylvania's three species of poisonous snakes and an endangered species in the state.

You can hike or picnic here from dawn to dusk, seven days a week. Public interpretive programs are offered on weekends. Please call for program schedules. In spring and summer special programs highlight the wildflowers in bloom. In March you can learn about maple sugaring, and in April Earth Day programs teach about biodiversity and related topics. Many other programs are also available.

Volant

Main Street in the quaint rural town of Volant offers more than fifty shops and restaurants featuring Victorian collectibles, arts and crafts, Christmas specialties, housewares, pottery, and special events such as a Quilt Show and Sale in July, an Autumn Pumpkin Festival, Old Fashioned Christmas, and more. Volant is located north of New Castle, on Route 208, ten minutes from routes I-79 and I-80. It is just minutes away from McConnell's Mill State Park and Living Treasures Animal Park. There's also a thriving Amish community in this area.

The shops are open daily except for New Year's Day, Easter, Thanksgiving, and Christmas. Hours are 10:00 A.M. to 5:00 P.M. Monday through Saturday and noon to 5:00 P.M. on Sunday. For more information contact the Volant

Merchants Association at (724) 533-2591.

New Castle

Bet you didn't know that New Castle, Pennsylvania, is the "Fireworks Capital of America." Two of the largest fireworks manufacturers, Pyrotecnico and Zambelli Internationale, are based in this city northwest of Pittsburgh.

So, if you happen to be in the area around the Fourth of July, check out the **"Fireworks Capital of America Fireworks Festival"** here. Fourth of July weekend in Lawrence County has recently been named one of the top one hundred events in North America by the American Bus Association. Besides the fireworks festival, there's also "Back to the Fifties Weekend" at Cascade Park and the Ellwood City Arts, Crafts, and Food Festival at Ewing Park. All of these events feature fireworks, all are within a week of July 4th, and all are within a few miles of each other.

For details contact the Lawrence County Tourist Promotion Agency, Shenango Street Station, 138 West Washington Street, New Castle 16101; call (888) 284-7599 or (724) 654-8408. Or, check the Web site www.lawrencecounty.com.

 HARLANSBURG STATION'S MUSEUM OF TRANSPORTATION (all ages)

Routes 19 and 108; (724) 652–9002. Open seasonally, so call for current hours. Generally, the museum is open weekends only in fall and winter, Saturday 10:00 A.M. to 5:00 P.M. and Sunday noon to 5:00 P.M. In summer and fall, it is open Tuesday through Saturday 10:00 A.M. to 5:00 P.M. and Sunday noon to 5:00 P.M. Closed Monday, and January through February. Admission is $. Group tours available by appointment.

Family-owned, family-operated, and family-friendly, Harlansburg Station's Museum of Transportation looks just like an old railroad station, with four Pennsylvania Railroad cars in front. Inside one of the cars, you can see displays of railroad memorabilia such as uniforms, silver, linens, and more. As you enter the museum, a model conductor greets you. Inside the museum you're surrounded by planes, trains, trolleys, cars, and trucks—all kinds of transportation. In 2002 the museum will open a new exhibit focusing on aviation in the 1920s. The highlight will be a 1928 Franklin aircraft.

Amazing Pittsburgh Facts

The City of Pittsburgh contains more than 70 miles of riverfront land, one of the highest totals in the United States.

HOYT INSTITUTE OF FINE ARTS (ages 8 and up)

124 East Leasure Avenue; (724) 652–2882. Open Tuesday and Thursday 10:00 A.M. to 8:00 P.M., Wednesday, Friday, and Saturday 10:00 A.M. to 5:00 P.M. Closed Sunday and Monday. General admission is **Free***. Period House Tours $ by appointment only.*

This regional arts center is housed in two neighboring 1917 mansions on five manicured acres of New Castle's historic North Hill. Collections include significant regional artwork, decorative arts, and Shenango china. Adult and youth art classes are offered year-round. Every year the Hoyt hosts a Summer Art Camp and a **Free** Children's Summer Arts Festival.

LIVING TREASURES ANIMAL PARK (all ages)

Route 422, 4 miles west of I–79 in Moraine; (412) 924–9571; www. ltanimalpark.com. Open weekends 10:00 A.M. to 6:00 P.M. in May, September, and October, and daily 10:00 A.M. to 8:00 P.M. Memorial Day through Labor Day. Admission is $$ for adults, $ for children 2 to 12, and children under 2 are **Free***. Please note that there are two "Living Treasures Animal Park" locations: this one, in Moraine; and the other in Donegal on Route 711 south of Route 31. For the Donegal location, please call (724) 593–8300.*

Get up close to more than one hundred species of friendly animals from all over the world at Living Treasures Animal Park.

New Brighton

MERRICK FREE ART GALLERY (ages 8 and up)

Fifth Avenue at Eleventh Street; (724) 846–1130; e-mail: merrick@ccia.com. Open Tuesday through Saturday 10:00 A.M. to 4:30 P.M. and Sunday 1:00 to 4:00 P.M. **Free** *admission.*

The Merrick Free Art Gallery houses the collection of French, German, English, and American paintings of the eighteenth and nineteenth centuries that belonged to Edward Dempster Merrick. It has a display of artifacts belonging to the New Brighton Historical Society as well. The gallery also mounts many special exhibits, such as its annual Victorian Christmas Toy Show.

Ambridge

OLD ECONOMY VILLAGE (ages 8 and up)

Fourteenth and Church Streets, 18 miles northwest of Pittsburgh on Route 65; (724) 266–4500; www.oldeconomyvillage.org. Open Tuesday through Saturday 9:00 A.M. to 5:00 P.M., Sunday noon to 5:00 P.M. Closed Monday and winter holidays and January through February 2002. Admission: ages 6 to 12 and 60 and over, $; ages 12 to 59, $$; family rate, $$$.

Old Economy Village was built by the same Christian communal society that built Harmony (see page 161). Here you can visit seventeen restored buildings and gardens and learn about how this unusual community lived. Your whole visit takes about an hour and a half, including the orientation film *Those Who Believed* and a tour of the exhibits, gardens, and buildings. The society had its own textile mill, as well as a tailor, printer, shoemaker, cabinetmaker, locksmith, and more, and the village store still posts the 1827 price list. Kids will enjoy using the hand pump to pour themselves a drink. The Harmony Society's Natural History Museum opened in fall 2001, and a new visitors center will open in 2003.

Many special events and tours are available, including events such as the Family Festival in June, Erntefest (food festival) in September, and Candlelight Christmas at the village in December. ADA rest rooms, diaper-changing areas.

RACCOON CREEK STATE PARK AND WILDERNESS RESERVE (all ages)

Located in southern Beaver County, 25 miles west of Pittsburgh (take Route 22 or Route 30; access to the park is via Route 18); (412) 899–3611; www.dcnr.state. pa.us. Trails are open year-round from 8:00 A.M. to sunset. **Free** *admission.*

One of the largest and most beautiful state parks in Pennsylvania, Raccoon Creek State Park has about 7,000 acres and Raccoon Creek Lake, which itself is more than one hundred acres.

Located within Raccoon Creek State Park, only steps east of the park entrance, is the 315-acre Wildflower Reserve, where you can choose between easy walking trails and trails with gentle grades. Your best bet to see the most blooms is April or May, but something is blooming from late March through summer. If you're lucky, you might see deer, raccoons, wild turkeys, mink, birds, and other wildlife. Comfortable shoes are a must. On Soldier Days you can view historic reenactments, military displays, and more.

Recreational facilities include boating, hiking, camping, swimming, and picnicking. Modern family cabins are available year-round, with electric heat, kitchens, and toilets.

While you're in Raccoon Creek State Park, you may wish to visit **Frankfort Mineral Springs,** about ½-mile south of the park entrance. From the 1790s to 1932, this was the site of a popular spa where many people were attracted to the purported medicinal properties of the spring water. Call (412) 899–2200.

Avella

 MEADOWCROFT MUSEUM OF RURAL LIFE (ages 6 and up)
401 Meadowcroft Road; (724) 587–3412; www.meadowcroftmuseum.org. Open weekends in June, July, and August; Saturday noon to 5:00 P.M., Sunday 1:00 to 5:00 P.M., otherwise open by appointment. Admission: $$ for adults, $ for children 6 to 16; children under 6 enter **Free**. *The last complete tour starts at 3:00 P.M. Call for information about group reservations and many special workshops and events.*

Sixteen thousand years of history and prehistory in western Pennsylvania are brought to life at the Meadowcroft Museum of Rural Life. The grounds here include the archaeological site that contains the earliest evidence of human life in eastern North America. (This part of the site is not open to the public at this time, but displays explain about the work in progress.)

Tours are designed to engage the entire family. Everyone can sit down in a one-room schoolhouse and take part in a real school lesson, reading from *McGuffey's Reader.* Then try some of the playground games children played 150 years ago. Explore log houses, a covered bridge, a blacksmith's shop, and other exhibits.

Located off Route 50, less than an hour from Pittsburgh, the museum offers many hands-on educational programs for groups. Wear good walking shoes, because the paths between the buildings are natural. There is a snack bar and gift shop.

Washington

THE PENNSYLVANIA TROLLEY MUSEUM (all ages)

One Museum Road; (724) 228–9256 or (877) PA–TROLLEY; www.pa-trolley. org. Open 11:00 A.M. to 5:00 P.M. daily from Memorial Day to Labor Day; weekends 11:00 A.M. to 5:00 P.M. April 1 through December 30. Admission is $$ for adults, and $ for children 2 to 15.

Faith's kids could never resist a trolley. And here in Washington, you'll find the only museum where you can see, learn about, and actually ride historic electric-rail vehicles from Pittsburgh, Philadelphia, Johns-town, and other cities. Take several generations along for an opportunity for reminiscing and intergenerational storytelling.

First, go to the Visitor Education Center to buy your tickets and view an exhibit. Stop and browse through the exhibits or take in a film. During the winter holidays you can even find yourself at the controls of a model-train layout.

Rides leave from the Richfor Shelter across the picnic area and next to the car barn. You just won't believe how beautifully these streetcars have been restored. Your motorman and most of the staff are volunteers. You'll clatter on a 3-mile journey past a scenic section that was once an old coal-mining railroad. After you climb off the trolley, you may view about twenty-five trolley cars from the museum's collection, including the real "Streetcar Named Desire" from New Orleans. You can even peek in on the car shop where volunteers restore the cars. Bring along a picnic lunch if you like.

Just 25 miles southwest of Pittsburgh, off I-79, exit 41 southbound or exit 40 northbound, the trolley museum is convenient to Meadowcroft Village in Avella. Special events include: the "Anything on Wheels" Fair in June, with a trolley parade, antique vehicle display, and motorcar and caboose rides; the "Pumpkin Patch Trolley" in October; and "Santa Trolley" in December.

WASHINGTON COUNTY HISTORICAL SOCIETY'S LEMOYNE HOUSE (ages 8 and up)

49 East Maiden Street; call (724) 225–6740 for admission prices; www.wchspa. org. Open February to mid-December, Tuesday to Friday 11:00 A.M. to 4:00 P.M., *and Saturday and Sunday noon to 4:00 P.M. Admission is $.*

Dr. Francis Julius LeMoyne, a successful nineteenth-century physician, took the courageous step of opening his home and properties as stops along the Underground Railroad. LeMoyne House is now the headquarters of the Washington County Historical Society, including its collection of Civil War weapons and a time capsule prepared by President Ulysses S. Grant. The beautiful stone home, which also served as Dr. LeMoyne's medical office, still contains some of his old medical instruments and books.

Where to Eat

IN PITTSBURGH

Bobby Rubina's Place for Ribs, *10 Commerce Court Station Square; (412) 642–7427.*

Crewser's Restaurant, *1501 Smallman Street, Strip District; (412) 281–1099.* Nautical theme, located on the boardwalk in the strip.

Houlihan's Restaurant, *#15 Freight House Shops, South Side; (412) 232–0302.*

Italian Spaghetti Warehouse, *2601 Smallman Street; (412) 261–6511.* Italian food, casual atmosphere, located on the strip.

Riverview Cafe, *Carnegie Science Center, One Allegheny Avenue, North Side; (412) 237–3417.* Casual atmosphere, city view on the Ohio River. Kid-friendly foods, booster seats.

Where to Stay

IN PITTSBURGH

Best Western University Center Hotel, *3401 Boulevard of the Allies; (412) 683–6100 or (800) 245–4444.* Nearby: Oakland, downtown, stadiums, museums, university, Station Square, zoo, Kennywood.

Club House Inn Pittsburgh, *5311 Campbells Run Road; (412) 788–8400.* Nine miles from downtown, Carnegie Cultural Center.

Doubletree Hotel Pittsburgh, *1000 Penn Avenue; (412) 281–3700 or (800) 222–TREE.* Full-service luxury hotel in heart of cultural district.

Green Tree Marriot, *101 Marriott Drive; (412) 922–8400 or (800) 525–5902.* Three miles from downtown.

Pittsburgh Hilton & Towers, *600 Commonwealth Place, Gateway Center; (412) 391–4600.* Adjacent to Point State Park. Walking distance to sports games and Carnegie Museum.

For More Information

Greater Pittsburgh Convention & Visitors Bureau, *(800) 359–0758; www.visitpittsburgh.com.*

VisitPittsburgh Help Center, *(888) 849–4753 twenty-four hours a day, seven days a week, e-mail: support@ visitpittsburgh.com.*

Northeastern Pennsylvania

With the Delaware and Susquehanna Rivers, the Pocono Mountains, wilderness areas, numerous lakes, and crystal clear rivers, northeastern Pennsylvania has attracted vacationers since the 1800s. But northeastern Pennsylvania is more than just a resort area. The discovery of one of the world's largest deposits of anthracite coal made the region a center for industry. Entrepreneurs, immigrant workers, and others came to the area to make money or find work. The country's first railroads were built to transport the coal to the cities. Other industries moved their operations here to take advantage of the cheap fuel.

Thanks to its history—both natural and industrial—northeastern Pennsylvania offers a special mix to family vacationers today. Those looking for hiking, skiing, boating, and relaxing resorts will not be disappointed. But the region's industrial

Faith & Emily's
Favorite Northeastern Pennsylvania Attractions

1. Float trip on the Delaware River
2. Mountain biking in the Lehigh Gorge
3. Skytop Lodge, Skytop
4. World's End State Park, Forksville
5. Pocono Environmental Education Center, Dingmans Ferry
6. Steamtown National Historic Site, Scranton
7. Lackawanna Trolley Museum, Scranton
8. Lackawanna Coal Mine tour, Scranton
9. Woodloch Pines Resort, Hawley
10. Inn at Starlight Lake, Starlight

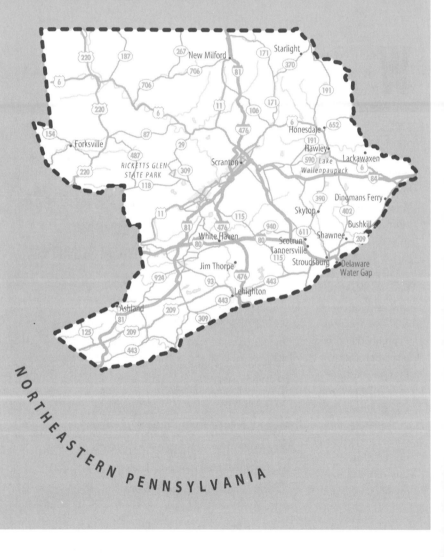

NORTHEASTERN PENNSYLVANIA

history adds some more unusual attractions, such as factories, railroad excursions, and coal-mine tours.

The Poconos may be the classic vacation destination—but there's good reason, especially where families are concerned. With so many resorts to choose from, every family can find one that fits its needs.

Despite overdevelopment in some areas, the unspoiled areas of the Poconos are absolutely beautiful—and very accessible. We're not talking huge snowcapped mountains; we're talking gentle hills, lovely trails, and babbling brooks that are easy for all members of the family to enjoy.

For example, the Poconos ski resorts are perfect for families. The vertical drops are steep enough to keep it interesting for Mom and Dad while gentle enough for kids to learn easily. Most of the resorts have great learn-to-ski programs for kids, starting as young as three years old.

One of the hottest things on the slopes in recent years is snowtubing. This is also very good news for families. Though parents may worry a bit the first time the kids take to the slopes on skis or snowboards, snowtubing—with its cushy, fit-the-whole-family inflatable rafts—is something everyone can do together.

Faith & Emily's
Favorite Events in Northeastern Pennsylvania

- **Delaware River Sojourn** at sites along the Delaware (mid-June).
- **Patch Town Day** at Eckley Miner's Village in Weatherly (mid-June); (570) 636–2070.
- **Central Pennsylvania Festival of the Arts** in State College (July); (814) 237–3682; www.arts-festival.com.
- **Wildflower Music Festival** in Hawley-Lake Wallenpaupack (July and August); (570) 253–5500.
- **Moscow Country Fair** (mid-August); (570) 842–9804.
- **Rail Expo** at Steamtown National Historic Site in Scranton (early September); (570) 340–5200 or (888) 693–9391.
- **Shawnee Mountain Lumberjack Festival** in Shawnee-on-Delaware (early October); (570) 421–7231; www.shawneemt.com.

Delaware Water Gap and the Stroudsburg Area

For vacationers arriving in Pennsylvania from New Jersey, the Delaware Water Gap serves as a gateway to the Poconos. This natural land formation along the Kittatinny Ridge is a dramatic backdrop for a host of outdoor activities. The town of Delaware Water Gap is a good place to start exploring.

Stroudsburg and East Stroudsburg are the commerce centers of this part of the Poconos. You'll find restaurants and some lodgings in these towns, but most of the tourist attractions and resorts are located in the surrounding smaller towns. For information on this area, check the Delaware Water Gap home page, www.microserve.net/~magicusa/delawarewatergap.html.

THE DELAWARE WATER GAP NATIONAL RECREATION AREA (all ages)

 Bushkill; (570) 588–2435; www.nps.gov/dewa/parkstatus.html. Open year-round. Visitors centers and hiking are Free*; day-use fee at beaches and some picnic areas.*

The 37-mile portion of the Delaware River extending from the Delaware Water Gap north to Milford was designated a National Recreation Area in the 1960s. The river offers great family canoeing, fishing, and rafting opportunities, and the hills on either side offer some fun trails and historic sites to explore on foot, skis, or snowmobile. There's excellent hiking in the area—the Appalachian Trail cuts through at the Water Gap—with some shorter trails that even little legs can handle without problems.

Other attractions that kids enjoy are visiting Millbrook Village (actually, it's about 16 miles from the Gap on the New Jersey side), gazing at dramatic waterfalls located around the area, and swimming in the cool, clear river at Milford and Smithfield beaches. Best of all, the park is less than two hours from New York or Philadelphia.

The best places to view the Gap itself are three overlooks along Route 611 just south of Route 80. Route 209 going north offers a nice family drive along the river valley, with the Pocono Plateau rising to the west. (The Poconos are not a typical mountain range but rather a plateau.)

There's a visitors center at Kittatinny Point, just off I-80 on the New Jersey side of the river. It's open daily May through October and on weekends year-round. Another visitors center, located at Dingmans Falls, about 30 miles north of I-80 on Route 209, is open during the summer. To find out what's happening in the park during your visit and to get a

Delaware River Canoe and Rafting Trips (ages 5 and up)

The Delaware is a wonderful, calm river for family rafting and canoeing. Although children eight to twelve get the most out of this kind of trip, most liveries will accommodate younger children—even toddlers. Rafting is recommended over canoeing for children under twelve, says David Jacobi of Adventure Sports in Marshalls Creek. His organization is one of several that offer Delaware River rafting and canoe trips. Typical excursions range from a couple of hours to all day. Be sure to specify your family members' ages and abilities when talking with the liveries; they'll help you decide which excursion is best for you.

- **Adventure Sports in Marshalls Creek,** Route 209, Marshalls Creek; (800) 487-2628 or (570) 223-0505; www.adventuresport.com. Trips run seven days a week in summer. Fees: $$$$ for adults, $$$ for children ages 13 through 17, and $$ for children ages 2 to 12.

- **Chamberlain's Canoes, Inc.,** River Road, Minisink Hills 18341; (800) 422-6631 or (570) 421-0180; www.chamberlaincanoes.com.

- **Kittatinny Canoes, Inc.,** 102 Kittatinny Court, Dingmans Ferry; (800) FLOATKC; www.kittatinny.com. Rafting, canoeing, kayaking, tubing, and paintball.

- **Shawnee River Adventures,** River Road, Shawnee-on-Delaware 18356; (800) SHAWNEE or (570) 424-4000, ext. 1120; www.shawneeinn.com. Midweek specials. Open daily April through October.

ranger's recommendation on what to do and see, stop by one of the visitors centers. While you're there, pick up a Junior Naturalist Discovery Pack, a self-guiding booklet that helps children six to twelve explore the park. Kids who complete the pack are eligible to become Junior Rangers.

WATER GAP TROLLEY (ages 2 and up)

Main Street, Delaware Water Gap; (570) 476-9766; www.delawarewatergap. net/watergaptrolley. Open April through October (weather permitting), 10:00 A.M. to 4:00 P.M. Admission: $$ for adults, $ for children ages 2 to 12, children under 2 **Free**.

The Water Gap Trolley takes vacationers from the depot on Route 611 near the town's center (actually, it's right across from the town's only stoplight) into the National Recreation Area. The one-hour narrated tour covers the geological and cultural history of the region.

SHAWNEE PLACE PLAY AND WATER PARK (ages 2 and up)

Hollow Road, Shawnee-on-Delaware; (570) 421–7231; www.shawneemt.com.
Open weekends from Memorial Day to June 15 and daily from June 16 to Labor
Day, 10:00 A.M. to 5:00 P.M. Admission is $$$ for adults and children, $$ spec-
tators; children under 40 inches **Free***.*

Kids will enjoy swimming and sliding at Shawnee Place Play and
Water Park, located just north of Route 80 (take exit 52 to Route 209
and follow signs). Especially geared for children under age twelve, the
park has two slides and two pools, both about 3 feet deep. There are
three magic shows daily as well as fifteen unique play elements.

SHAWNEE MOUNTAIN (ages 4 and up)

Hollow Road, Shawnee-on-Delaware; (570) 421–7231; www.shawneemt.com.
Open mid-December to mid-March, 9:00 A.M. to 10:00 P.M. weekdays, 8:00 A.M.
to 10:00 P.M. weekends. Varying prices for lift tickets, rentals, and learn-to-ski
programs.

Shawnee Mountain has twenty-three trails, a snowboarding area,
snowtubing, and a vertical drop of 700 feet. In winter it also has an
extensive ski program for kids. There's a Ski Wee program for six- to
twelve-year-olds. Little ones (four to five years) can join the Pre-Ski Wee
group. More adventurous kids ages ten to fifteen will want to hook up
with the Mountain Cruisers. Beginning to early intermediate snowboard-
ers can join the Young Riders for eight- to fifteen-year-olds. Programs
are $$$$. Three- and five-day packages are available (reservations
required). For nonskiing children eighteen months and up, the Little
Wigwam Children's Center is open daily for baby-sitting 9:00 A.M. to
5:00 P.M. on weekdays and 8:00 A.M. to 5:00 P.M. on weekends.

SHANNON INN AND PUB (all ages)

Exit 52 off I–80, East Stroudsburg; (800) 424–8052 or (570) 424–1951. A
wide variety of ski and golf packages are available, custom-tailored to your needs,
at reasonable prices.

Several of the attractions nearby recommend the Shannon Inn for
families. With an indoor pool, on-site informal restaurant, and a kids-
stay-free policy, this 120-room hotel has everything a family needs for a
quality, budget-priced vacation. Through cooperative agreements with
Shawnee and Camelback ski areas and other nearby sites, the Shannon
Inn offers two-day ski and golf packages.

QUIET VALLEY LIVING HISTORICAL FARM (ages 3 and up)

Route 209, 3½ miles south of Stroudsburg; (570) 992–6161; www.quiet valley.org. Open June 20 through Labor Day, Tuesday through Saturday 10:00 A.M. to 5:30 P.M.; Sunday 1:00 to 5:30 P.M. Admission: $$ for adults, $ for children ages 3 to 12.

Take a trip back in time at the Quiet Valley Living Historical Farm. Here your family will spend time with the Zeppers, a German immigrant family that settled this land back in 1765.

After a brief welcoming presentation, leave the present day and step back into the 1800s. In the 1763 cellar kitchen you will learn how food was prepared and how nothing was wasted on the farm. The farmhand will introduce you to the animals, demonstrate the farm equipment, and let your kids jump in the hayloft. Special demonstrations of various crafts and skills necessary to early life are held throughout the summer.

In addition to regular tours during the summer months, the museum also has special presentations, with a Farm Animal Frolic in May, a Harvest Festival in October, and an Old Time Christmas celebration in December. Call for more information and specific dates. The Farm Animal Frolic is especially recommended for small children, with baby bunnies, hatching chicks, piglets, lambs, and more for children to touch and learn about.

Mount Pocono and Eastern Poconos (Tannersville, Scotrun, Skytop)

Mount Pocono is in the heart of Pocono resort country. There are lots of resorts and attractions—everything from petting zoos to cheesecake factories—to choose from within a few miles of Mount Pocono, but here are some of our top picks.

CAMELBACK SKI AREA and CAMELBEACH WATERPARK (ages 4 and up)

Camelback Road, off Route 80 (exit 45), Tannersville; (570) 629–1661; www. skicamelback.com (winter), www.camelbeach.com (summer). Open for skiing late November through late March, weather permitting. Water park open late May through Labor Day. Call for specific dates. Lift tickets: $$$$. Children's ski instruction: $$$$ per lesson (includes lift ticket, lesson, and rental). Check the

Web site for "Value Days." $$$$ for adults (12 to 64), $$$ for children (3 to 11) and seniors. Children 2 and under enter **Free**.

The Camelback Ski Area is worth a stop in any season. In winter Camelback is one of the Pocono's largest ski resorts, with thirty-three trails, thirteen lifts, and a vertical drop of 800 feet. Since 1996, the organization has spent more than $7 million to improve the property. One of the newer additions is snowtubing, a great family activity. There's a full-scale ski program where children ages four to twelve can spend the day learning to ski or snowboard.

From May until the end of fall, Camelback transforms from a ski resort to Camelbeach Waterpark, with eight water slides, an action river, swimming pool, kids' play area, miniature golf, an alpine slide, and more. Ride the chairlift to the top of the mountain, enjoy the view of the Pocono Mountains, and take the alpine slide down. Buy a full ticket and enjoy the waterpark attractions all day. There's also a summer day-camp program at the facility, and kids ages five to twelve can sign up for a day, a week, or the whole summer.

CAESAR'S BROOKDALE RESORT (all ages)

Route 611, Scotrun; (800) 233–4141; www.caesarspoconoresorts.com. Open year-round. Call for package rates.

Okay, I have to admit it: There's something a little comical about visiting a renowned couples resort with your toddler, but Caesar's really has something here. Though families don't have full use of all the couples-oriented facilities here (we were disappointed to know we weren't eligible for breakfast in bed), it is a great way to combine some time for yourselves *and* still have a family vacation. (After the kids are asleep, you can sneak into the bath and enjoy the Jacuzzi for two.) Kids five and older can join the Brookdale Kids Kamp and participate in a wide range of special activities just for kids, from face painting to special meals and magic shows.

We visited with our two youngest children, two and one-half and one and one-half at the time. The staff couldn't have been more accommodating, spreading out a tablecloth under the high chair at each meal, filling our sippy cups and bottles each day, and making us bagels for the road. At each meal we sat with a different family, which was fun for adults and children alike. While we ate, a clown, magician, or other entertainer made the rounds of the tables, creating animals from balloons or cracking jokes with the kids.

Many rooms have recently been upgraded, some now sleeping up to eight people, and some with 36-inch TVs or Bose Wave radios. During the summer and winter seasons, there are lots of activities at the nearby ski resorts, National Recreation Area, petting zoos, and other Poconos attractions.

SKYTOP LODGE (all ages)

Route 390, Skytop; (800) 345–7759; www.skytop.com. Open year-round.

When we were children, our parents took us to several resorts within a couple hours of our home in New York. Although some resorts were by the ocean, others in the mountains, all had a few elements in common: a stately lodge, a rocking-chair porch, great trails for hiking and walking, and a casual but classy approach to everything.

Skytop Lodge was one of those places—and it has only gotten better in the intervening years. A spa has been added, guest rooms renovated, and twenty executive-style bedrooms added.

Rather than a resort that caters to kids, Skytop accommodates families the same way it accommodates all its guests: with individual attention and concern for detail. Families can check into Skytop for a weekend or a week and find plenty to do for everyone: hiking and cross-country ski trails from 1 mile to 10; guided nature walks and self-guided fitness trails; downhill skiing, mountain bikes, rowboats, canoes, and sporting clays available on site; a swimming lake and indoor and outdoor pools; a game room; and a gorgeous golf course.

Skytop offers Camp in the Clouds for children ages four to ten every day in summer and weekends year-round. The program, which runs from 9:00 A.M. to 4:30 P.M., includes arts and crafts, nature walks, swimming, and other supervised activities. The cost is $$$ per full or half day.

Winter Camp in the Clouds is offered every Saturday January through March, 6:00 to 9:00 P.M. **Free** of charge. Parents can dine alone while kids ice skate, watch movies, and more, after a kid's dinner.

Skytop is a splurge; however, if you can swing it, it's an excellent family vacation. Accommodations are on the American plan, which means all meals are included. The menu includes some excellent entrees for adults and some favorites for kids. There is a per-day charge ($$$$) for children under sixteen who stay in their parents' room.

ALSO IN THE AREA

Pocono Cheesecake Factory, Route 611, Swiftwater; (570) 839–6844. Open daily 10:00 A.M. to 6:00 P.M. See cheesecakes made fresh daily.

Callie's Candy Kitchen and Pretzel Factory, Route 390, Mountainhome; (570) 595–2280 or (570) 595–3257. The Pretzel Factory is open daily April through December, weekends only January, February, and March. The candy factory is open year-round except January.

Located about 5 miles apart on Route 390, Callie's factories let you watch while candy and pretzels are made. Of course, then you'll want to buy some in the gift shop.

Bushkill

Route 209 from Route 80 up to Milford is a lovely drive along the Pennsylvania side of the Delaware River. Here are some suggested stops on the way.

 ## MARY STOLZ DOLL MUSEUM (ages 3 and up)

Route 209 North and McCole Road; (570) 588–7566. Open daily 11:00 A.M. to 5:00 P.M. Admission is $.

The Mary Stolz Doll Museum is definitely a don't-touch place, but if you have a doll lover in the family, the collection of more than 125 dolls from around the world makes it well worth resisting the temptation. Kids especially like the impressive array of Barbie and Jem dolls. There's also a fine display of miniature rooms, bears, and old toys.

 ## POCONO INDIAN MUSEUM (ages 6 and up)

Route 209 North; (570) 588–9338; www.pocoindianmuseum.com. Open daily (call ahead for hours and admission prices).

The Pocono Indian Museum is the only museum dedicated to portraying the lives of the Leni Lenape Indians from prehistoric times (about 10,500 B.C.) to their first contacts with Europeans. Its six rooms display artifacts, weapons, and tools, most of which were unearthed within a 20-mile radius of the museum. There's a reconstructed bark house you can actually walk through. Your admission includes a thirty-minute taped, self-guided tour.

BUSHKILL FALLS (all ages)

Route 209; (570) 588–6682; www.visitbushkillfalls.com. Open April through October, 9:00 A.M. to dusk. Admission: $$ adults, $ for children ages 4 through 10; under 4 enter Free. Free *parking.*

The Peters family started charging admission to see these eight magnificent falls, sometimes called the "Niagara of Pennsylvania," on their 300 acres back in 1905. The tourists haven't stopped coming since. Take a short nature walk back to the falls. Small children can usually manage the easy forty-five-minute to one-hour stroll. For the more energetic, there's a 2-mile hike that affords an even better view. A gift shop, food facilities, picnic area, and bathroom facilities are available to visitors. There are also paddleboat rides, fishing, miniature golf, an ice-cream parlor, a Pennsylvania Wildlife exhibit, and a Native American exhibit.

FERNWOOD HOTEL AND RESORT (all ages)

Route 209, Box 447 Bushkill; (570) 588–9500 or (888) FERNWOOD; www.fernwoodhotel.com.

The newly renovated Fernwood Hotel and Resort offers year-round vacation possibilities, including an eighteen-hole golf course, snowtubing, ice skating, two lakes, themed restaurants, live entertainment, indoor and outdoor pools, and a planned schedule of daily activities for children and adults. There's also "The Zone," a 10,000-square-foot game center. Fernwood is convenient to many popular ski resorts.

Dingmans Ferry

POCONO ENVIRONMENTAL EDUCATION CENTER (ages 4 and up)

RD 2; (570) 828–2319; www.peec.org.

For families interested in learning about the environment in a national park, there's no better deal than a weekend at the Pocono Environmental Education Center. The center conducts weekend and weeklong family vacation camps that include cross-country skiing, canoeing, hiking, "orienteering," natural history investigations, crafts, and field trips such as "The Waterfall Hunt." The thirty-eight-acre campus is located within the borders of the Delaware Water Gap National Recreation Area and includes classrooms, an indoor pool, a craft center, a dark room, a library, and a bookstore.

Accommodations are in one-room cabins that sleep between two and fourteen people. Meals are served at the dining hall. Sample rates for family programs are $$$$ per person for a three-day weekend including meals, lodging, and program activities (everything from candle making to birds-of-prey presentations). Children under two are **Free**, four and under are half price, and ages five to eight are 25 percent off. PEEC provides linens and towels for an additional cost. For more information write to the center at Box 1010, Dingmans Ferry 18328-9614.

ALSO IN THE AREA

Grey Towers, *Milford; (570) 296–9630; www.pinchot.org/gt.* Grey Towers, a national historic landmark, is managed and maintained by the USDA Forest Service in cooperation with the Pinchot Institute for Conservation. In August 2001, Grey Towers celebrated its reopening after two years of restoration. Public tours of the house are conducted daily, on the hour, 10:00 a.m. to 4:00 p.m. Many conservation programs are also offered.

Promised Land State Park, *Route 390, 5 miles south of Route 84; (570) 676–3428; www.dcnr.state.pa.us.* Promised Land State Park is a 3,000-acre park surrounded by state forest land—creating a total of 11,000 acres of preserved wilderness. The area is home to a wide variety of wildlife, including one of eastern Pennsylvania's bigger populations of black bear. There are numerous housekeeping cabin resorts along Route 390, and camping is available in the park. There are environmental programs for children during summer. One primitive campground stays open year-round for cross-country skiers who can't bear to go home at the end of the day.

Hawley—Lake Wallenpaupack

Lake Wallenpaupack, the state's third largest man-made lake, is 15 miles long with 52 miles of shoreline. It was created in the 1920s by Pennsylvania Power & Light (PPL) as part of a major hydroelectric project. The PPL Visitor's Center was closed after Septmeber 11; however, a new center will open in spring 2003 and will have exhibits that outline the development of the project as well as available recreation on and around the lake. PPL also maintains Shuman Point, Ledgedale natural areas, and Beech House Creek Wildlife Refuge for public use. They are great places for short nature hikes and spotting wildlife such as beavers, herons, hawks, and more.

Just north of the lake is the town of Hawley, a great town for antiquing. Kids will be more interested in the following area attractions.

TANGLWOOD SKI AREA & WINTER PARK (ages 3 and up)

Route 507, Lake Wallenpaupack; (570) 226–SNOW; www.tanglwood.com. Open daily December through March.

If you're in the area during winter, check out nearby Tanglwood Ski Resort, which offers nine trails of downhill skiing, a snowboarding area, a snowtubing park, and several cross-country ski trails. There's also a Ski Wee children's program and a nursery available for small children. The ski shop is one of the only ones in the area to rent cross-country as well as downhill equipment.

 CLAWS 'N' PAWS WILD ANIMAL PARK (ages 2 and up)

Off Route 590, near Hamlin; (570) 698–6154; www.clawsnpaws.com. Open daily May 1 through late October 10:00 A.M. to 6:00 P.M. Admission: $$$ adults, $$ ages 2 through 11 and seniors; children under 2 are **Free***.*

Claws 'n' Paws Wild Animal Park is a unique private zoo with 120 species of animals. Kids may feed the giraffes and lory parrots at scheduled feeding times. There are two different live animal shows through Labor Day. During the reptile show kids can pet an alligator and a python. Other exhibits include bears, otters, primates of several types, many species of birds, a rare snow leopard, and a white tiger. The Dino Dig in the children's zoo lets kids dig for buried "bones." A new Wild West Territory features animals of the west and panning for "gold." The easy-to-follow trails through the woods and the size of the facility help younger children from getting overwhelmed and overtired by the experience.

 TRIPLE "W" RIDING STABLES (ages 6 and up)

Follow blue and white state signs. Beechnut Drive, off Owego Turnpike near Lake Wallenpaupack; (570) 226–2620; www.triplewstable.com or www.doublewranch bnb.com. Stable (800) 450–2620. Open year-round (except hunting season).

Take a step beyond "follow-the-leader" riding at this 200-acre horse ranch in a secluded area on the top of the mountain, featuring western riding experiences tailored to the individual. The staff at Triple W ensure a fun and rewarding ride for all members of the family by taking into consideration level of expertise and ambition. Overnight camping on horseback, hayrides, and pony rides for children under seven are also available.

Triple W offers Wild West shows, complete with a beautiful stagecoach, at many local events, fairs, and rodeos. There are also Murder Mystery weekends, day trips, school trips, reunions, weddings, and company outings.

In the winter, there's enough snow at the top of the mountain to get a lot of use out of the horse-drawn sleigh with jingle bells.

If you're looking for overnight accommodations, stay at the Double "W" Ranch Bed and Breakfast, located on the same property. The B&B boasts a large dining room, ski lounge with fireplace, a game room, and a three-level outdoor deck with a hot tub and a great view. The grounds include flower gardens, gazebos, and hiking paths. For the bed-and-breakfast, call (877) 540–RANCH.

WOODLOCH PINES RESORT (all ages)

Route 590, Hawley; (800) 572–6658 or (800) 272–9428; www.woodloch.com. Open year-round.

If you follow 590 east from Hawley, you'll arrive at an excellent family resort, Woodloch Pines Resort. Named three times by *Better Homes & Gardens* magazine as one of America's favorite family vacation resorts and winner of the Pennsylvania Travel Council's 1999 "Spirit of Hospitality" award, Woodloch Pines was established as a small inn back in 1958. Since then, it has grown into a complex with 160 hotel rooms, a nightclub, several restaurants, game rooms, recreation complex, and more family activities and children's programs than you can cram into a seven-day stay.

The resort is located right on Lake Teedyuskung, sixty-five acres of crystal-clear waters with a sandy swimming beach and rowboats, pad-

Lake Cruises

Along the lake there are numerous resorts and marinas geared to vacationers who want to spend time on the water.

- **Pine Crest Yacht Club, Inc.,** *Route 507; (570) 857–1136. Open May through October.* Boat rentals available.

- **Pocono Action Sports,** *Route 507; (570) 857–1976.* Sailboats, rowboats, fishing, and waterskiing boats available.

- *Spirit of Paupack. Route 6 and Route 507; (570) 226–6266.* Open daily Memorial Day through October. Dinner, 7:30 to 9:00 P.M. Scenic tours, 9:00 A.M. to 5:00 P.M. daily; $$ for adults, $ for children under twelve. Dinner tours, 7:30 to 9:00 P.M., $$$$ for adults, $$ for children. One-hour scenic cruises: Adults $$, children $. Two-hour sunset cruises: Adults $$$, children $$. Two-and-a-half-hour dinner cruises: Adults $$$$, children $$$. For a sunset dinner cruise or a one-hour sight-seeing tour on the lake, the 48-foot double-decker *Spirit of Paupack* is a great way to see the lake.

dleboats, canoes, kayaks, and sailboats for exploring on your own. Woodloch Pines has the space and the layout that allow some families to be quiet and relax with one another while other groups applaud and cheer one another in games and contests. Other seasonal activities include hiking, biking, golf, snowtubing, snowmobiling, ice skating, bumper cars, go carts, rifle range, batting cages, and more.

Woodloch Pines rates include three meals a day, activities, and entertainment. For families who prefer a more independent vacation, homes are available for rent at Woodloch Springs, a planned village centered around an award-winning golf course. Rates vary according to package length and accommodation type. Please call for current rates and availability.

ALSO IN THE AREA

Lacawac Wildlife Sanctuary (ages 6 and up), *Lacawax Road, Ledgedale; (570) 689–9494.* Open year-round. One-mile self-guided nature trail overlooking Lake Wallenpaupack (pick up a trail guide at the parking lot), plus a host of special programs May through October.

Dorflinger-Suvdam Wildlife Preserve, *White Mills; (570) 253–1185.* Located off Route 6 between Hawley and Honesdale, this private preserve features hiking and cross-country ski trails and a great series of outdoor concerts in the summer months. The glass museum on the same property is interesting to adults and older children but not a great choice for toddlers and active kids.

Lackawaxen

Route 590 continues east from Woodloch Pines to the state line at Lackawaxen and the Delaware River. This tiny Pennsylvania town was the home of Zane Grey, author of such famous Western novels as *The Riders of the Purple Sage* and more than fifty others. Today the property is owned by the National Park Service as part of the Upper Delaware Scenic and Recreational River, which encompasses a 74-mile stretch of river from Sparrowbush, New York, to Hancock.

 ## ZANE GREY MUSEUM (ages 8 and up)

River Road; (570) 685–4871; www.nps.gov/upde.zgmuseum.htm. Open seasonally. No park entrance fee. A program fee is charged for the museum. Admission is $; children under 10 are **Free***. Call ahead for museum hours.*

This museum, operated by the National Park Service as part of the Upper Delaware Scenic and Recreational River, houses an impressive collection of memorabilia of Grey's life and his passion for the West. Little ones will be frustrated by the "don't touch" policy of the museum, but school-age and older kids interested in stories of the Wild West will enjoy the twenty-minute guided tour. The paintings on the walls of Grey's study depict scenes from the Southwest. If you luck out and get an individual tour, the guide may be able to gear his or her presentation to your family's interests.

Also at the museum is a gift shop (many of Grey's novels are on sale for some light vacation reading). The ranger on duty will be able to point out some of the highlights of the park, including Roebling's Delaware Aqueduct and the locks of the D&H Canal. Be sure to ask for the *Junior Ranger Program Activity Book*. Children who successfully complete six of the twelve activities in the pamphlet are awarded a certificate of achievement and a Junior Ranger patch.

ROEBLING'S DELAWARE AQUEDUCT (ages 6 and up)

Route 590; (570) 685–4871; www.nps.gov/upde. The bridge operates year-round.

Down the road about ½-mile from the Zane Grey Museum is the Delaware Aqueduct, also known as the Roebling Bridge. Believed to be the oldest existing wire suspension bridge in the Western Hemisphere, it was designed and built in 1848 by John Augustus Roebling, the man who later designed the famous Brooklyn Bridge in New York City. Recently, the National Park Service restored the bridge to its original appearance. The Tollhouse contains historic photos from the canal era (1825 to 1898). It is open daily for a self-guided tour, weather permitting, Memorial Day to Labor Day, Wednesday through Sunday 10:00 A.M. to 5:00 P.M. and weekends in September and October. The bridge is open twenty-four hours a day for vehicular traffic.

Fly-fishing Both the Delaware and the Lackawaxen Rivers are known by anglers as prime fly-fishing areas. Licensed guides will take you and your older kids out on the river for lessons. Check the list published by the park service.

Upper Delaware River Trips (ages 5 and up) The

Upper Delaware River is one of the last and longest free-flowing rivers in the northeastern United States. There are some rapids here, but most of the river is class I, which means it is safe for beginning boaters and older children. (Always wear life jackets and exercise caution when on or near the water.)

There are several river accesses along the Upper Delaware, including one in Lackawaxen. If you don't have your own boat to launch here, contact one of the liveries that rent canoes, rafts, and tubes and conduct guided trips down the Delaware. The Park Service publishes a list of liveries and licensed guides. Most outfitters provide boats, life jackets, and drop-off and pick-up service at various river access points. They also have campsites available, although most are located on the New York side of the river. Remember, although the river is open to the public, the land on either side is privately owned. Please respect the rights and privacy of landowners.

Some of the bigger operations on the northern portion of the river include the following:

- **Kittatinny Canoes, Inc.,** *102 Kittatinny Court, Dingmans Ferry; (800) FLOATKC; www.kittatinny.com.* Rafting, canoeing, kayaking, tubing, and paintball.

- **Lander's River Trips & Campgrounds,** *Route 97 P.O. Box 376, Narrowsburg; (800) 252-3925; www.landersrivertrips.com.* Children must be fifty pounds. With landings in Hancock, Hankins, Callicoon, Skinners Falls, Narrowsburg, Ten Mile River, Minisink, Pond Eddy, Knights Eddy, and Matamoras, Lander's has the Upper Delaware covered. In addition to conducting rafting and canoe trips, the company rents equipment for self-guided expeditions. Facilities include campgrounds, motel (Ten Mile River Lodge in Ten Mile River, New York), and large grassy areas for playing near the river.

- **Wild and Scenic River Tours,** *166 Route 97, Barryville, New York; (800) 836-0366.*

Honesdale

Honesdale, located at the intersection of Routes 6 and 191, is in many ways the quintessential American small town. Its Main Street is lined with shops and stores that have been operated by the same families for years. Through a special Main Street program, many of the stores have been renovated to reflect the town's historic architecture. And the Victorian homes and big porches of north Main Street are classic examples of American design.

WAYNE COUNTY HISTORIC SOCIETY MUSEUM (ages 2 and up)

810 Main Street; (570) 253–3240; www.waynehistorypa.org. Open year-round; call for current hours. Admission is $; children under 12 are **free**.

Here you can see a replica of the original Stourbridge Lion, the first commercial steam locomotive to run on an American rail in 1829. (The original is in the Smithsonian Institution in Washington, D.C.) Another exhibit traces the history of the D&H Canal, which connected Honesdale to the Hudson River, 108 miles away. There's also an impressive collection of Native American artifacts found in the Upper Delaware River Valley by a local archaeologist.

STOURBRIDGE LINE RAIL EXCURSIONS (all ages)

303 Commercial Street; (570) 253–1960; www.waynecountycc.com. Call for current schedule. Rates vary according to season and itinerary.

The Stourbridge Line Rail Excursions run on weekends in summer and for special occasions at other times. The excursions follow the Lackawaxen River to Hawley and Lackawaxen. Different themes include fall foliage tours, dinner-theater tours, the Great Train Robbery Run, the Halloween Fun Run, and the Santa Express.

The Wayne County Visitors Center, at the same address, will soon house a number of railroad exhibits, and there's a gift shop featuring railroad souvenirs.

ALSO IN THE AREA

Carousel Water and Fun Park, *Route 652, Beach Lake; (570) 729–7532; www.carousel-park.com. Open May through October.* Go carts, water slides, bumper boats, mini-golf, and batting cages are among the attractions here. Pay one price or pay by the ride.

Fun and Games, *Route 6 Plaza, Route 6; (570) 253–9111.* A pay-and-play center that can be just the ticket on rainy days.

Wayne County Fair, *Route 191.* The first week in August, the Wayne County Fairgrounds hosts a fairly traditional county fair. There are rides and food, but the best part is watching local 4-H kids with the animals they've raised and trained themselves.

Starlight and New Milford

Head north from Honesdale on Route 191 and you'll find yourself in northern Wayne County. The thick forests of this corner of the state add to the feeling of an escape from civilization.

INN AT STARLIGHT LAKE (all ages)

Lake Road, Starlight; (800) 248–2519; www.innatstarlightlake.com. Open year-round.

One of the best places to enjoy northern Wayne County is the Inn at Starlight Lake, which has been attracting vacationers since 1909. Guests can stay in the inn itself, but families will generally prefer the cottages. Each cottage is a little different: Some have fireplaces, others have sleeping lofts for kids. All have private bathrooms.

The inn, as the name suggests, is located right on Starlight Lake, a pretty little body of water that's great for swimming and exploring by rowboat or small sailboat (no powerboats allowed). There is a tennis court, shuffleboard, and a library and game room for evenings and rainy days. In winter visit nearby Mount Tone and Elk Mountain for downhill and cross-country skiing.

The inn is also the first stop on a four-day self-guided inn-to-inn bike tour of Wayne and Susquehanna Counties. For families with older children, this is a great combination of an active vacation and lovely accommodations.

OLD MILL VILLAGE MUSEUM (ages 5 and up)

Located 1 mile south of New Milford on Route 848 (exit 223 of I–81) and accessible from US Route 11; (570) 465–3448. Hours vary seasonally. Admission is $ for adults, ℱℛℯℯ for children under 2 with an adult.

Follow the signs from the interstate to this group of historic buildings and artifacts depicting life in the area in the 1800s. During summer artisans demonstrate different crafts, from blacksmithing to quilting. There are also special events and festivals throughout the season, including an Annual Arts and Crafts Day, an antique doll show, Old Time Country Music Contest, and more.

Scranton

Until the opening of the Steamtown National Historic Site in downtown Scranton in 1995 and the Lackawanna Trolley Museum in 1999, this industrial city was hardly thought of as a vacation destination. Visitors, however, are often pleasantly surprised that Scranton has a lot to offer—especially to family travelers.

STEAMTOWN NATIONAL HISTORIC SITE (all ages)
Entrance off Lackawanna Avenue, just west of Steamtown Mall; (570) 340–5200 or (888) 693–9391; www.nps.gov/stea. Open daily 9:00 A.M. to 5:00 P.M. (closed major holidays). Museum admission: $$ adults, $ children 6 to 12; children 5 and under, **Free**.

Railroad buffs of all ages won't want to miss Steamtown. Occupying fifty-two acres of a working railroad yard in downtown Scranton, Steamtown traces the history of railroading in the region and throughout the country. The structure, opened in 1995, includes a visitors center, a theater, technology and history museums, a renovated roundhouse, and a museum store.

Watch the eighteen-minute film *Steel and Steam* to learn about the history of American steam railroading. At the history museum meet the people (actually lifelike statues) who worked, used, and depended on the railroad. Visit the roundhouse to see several examples from the Steamtown collection of locomotives and railroad cars. Learn about locomotive design and railroad communications at the technology museum.

From Steamtown you can arrange to take a two-hour train excursion to the nearby town of Moscow ($$$ for adults, $$ for seniors and children) or to the historic Radisson Lackawanna Hotel (included in general admission). According to one park ranger, children are "glued to the window or fast asleep during these trips. Either way, it's great for parents!" Call the park for current information and train schedules.

The visitors center and most of the railroad yard and outdoor exhibits are **Free**. Admission is required for entry to the museums and the theater. If you plan to take a train ride to Moscow, you'll save money with a combination ticket.

The Steamtown site is handicapped accessible, and there are bathrooms with changing tables. The Moscow excursion is accessible, but prior reservations are required. There are chemical toilets on the train, and snacks are available during a brief stop at Moscow.

After touring Steamtown, walk up the long ramp to the Steamtown Mall. (On rainy days, or when little ones are tired, it may be better to drive to the mall and park in the lot there.) There's a food court with fast food for every taste. The mall now operates a seasonal shuttle along the boardwalk between Steamtown and the food court. If you prefer a more leisurely dining experience, head downstairs, where there are two restaurants to choose from.

LACKAWANNA TROLLEY MUSEUM (all ages)

300 Cliff Street on property of Steamtown; (570) 963–6590. Open Tuesday through Sunday. Ride and museum combo tickets are $$; children under 3 are Free.

The Lackawanna Trolley Museum shares a parking lot with Steamtown, making one-stop shopping for kids who love the rails. This museum tells the story of electric traction and trolley systems in northeastern Pennsylvania. Trolley excursions depart regularly from the same platform as the Steamtown trains, and go through the Crown Avenue tunnel. The Children's Gallery teaches "painless geography" through models set on maps of the area. Kids can generate their own electricity, run a trolley system, and build their own model anthracite communities.

Paulsen Family Adventure On a rainy weekend in November, Faith and I took Eli (one and a half years old) and Gideon (two and a half) to Steamtown National Historic Site in Scranton. It is tailor-made for train-loving toddlers who need a chance to run around. The boys loved the roundhouse and climbing up on the trains, as well as the train sounds and the photographs of trains in the museum.

On our way out to the car, the excursion train was pulling into the station. The boys were excited to see the big engine coming closer and closer. We picked them up so they could see better. They waved at the passengers and at the engineer. In reply, the engineer blew the loud train whistle. Both boys immediately burst into tears. It was probably not the reaction the engineer expected!

RADISSON LACKAWANNA STATION HOTEL (all ages)

700 Lackawanna Avenue; (570) 342–8300; www.radisson.com/scranton.pa.
Sticking with the railroad motif, why not stay in a glorious old railway station? The Lackawanna Station Hotel, a building on the National Register of Historic Places now operated by the Radisson chain of hotels, is just a few blocks from Steamtown. You can actually take the Steamtown Excursion train to Steamtown. The station's waiting area has been transformed into a palatial lobby with two restaurants and complete hotel facilities—including a game room that's a hit with kids.

 HOUDINI MUSEUM (ages 3 and up)

1433 North Main Avenue; (570) 342–5555; www.houdini.org. Open daily Memorial Day through September 15; other times by appointment. Admission is $$.
The Houdini Museum is a must-see for budding magicians. The museum takes visitors back to the days of vaudeville, when traveling performers like Houdini frequently visited the Scranton area. There are continuous guided tours, a film, and nonstop magic shows, along with Houdini memorabilia and exhibits about Scranton's vaudeville past. A wonderful magic show is performed by nationally known magicians Dorothy Pietrich and Bravo the Great. Lots of laughs, live animals, and audience participation.

The Halloween "Spook-tacular" Theater of Illusion takes place from Columbus Day through Halloween. Appropriate for all ages, this magic show features classic illusions with nothing too scary for little ones.

 LACKAWANNA COAL MINE (ages 3 and up)

McDade Park; (800) 238–7245 or (570) 963–MINE; www.visitnepa.org. Open daily April through November. Admission: $$, adults, $ children ages 3 to 12; children under 3 are **Free***.*
Coal is a major part of this region's history. One of the best places to gain an understanding of the life of a coal miner is on the Lackawanna Coal Mine Tour at McDade Park in Scranton. Here visitors ride 250 feet down into a real underground coal mine. Former miners and sons of miners tell the story of what a typical workday was like for the men and boys (as young as seven years old!) of the mines. According to Barbara Colangelo, director of the mine, most children's favorite part of the tour is when the guide turns out the lights and the group stands in total darkness for a long couple of seconds. "They think the total darkness is awesome," she says. "Children

who get scared of the dark should be prepared!"

The tour is partially handicapped accessible, as long as the person can move from a wheelchair to the car. It's chilly and damp down below (fifty-five degrees year-round), so be sure to bring along a sweatshirt.

McDade Park

The Lackawanna Coal Mine may be the main attraction, but there's lots more to do in McDade Park. Next door to the mine is the Anthracite Heritage Museum, which traces the history of coal and its influence on the people of this area, including immigrant workers in the coal mines. Call (570) 963–4804 for more information.

McDade Park is also home to a summer theater festival, a fall balloon festival, and other special events. In addition, it's a great place for a family picnic and outdoor play. For more information and a schedule of upcoming events, call (570) 963–6764.

MONTAGE MOUNTAIN (ages 2 and up)

1000 Montage Mountain Road; (800) GOT–SNOW or (570) 969–7669; www.skimontage.com. The summer park is open from mid-June to Labor Day, weekdays noon to 5:00 P.M. and weekends 11:00 A.M. to 5:00 P.M.

Another center of family-oriented activity is Montage Mountain, located right off exit 182 of I-81. Summer activities include water slides, batting cages, chairlift rides, children's activity park, playground, and more. During the colder months, Montage is home to a top ski resort offering skiing, snowboarding, and snowtubing. Saturday night is Family Night.

ALSO IN THE AREA

Lackawanna County Stadium (ages 5 and up), *Montage Mountain Road; (570) 969–BALL.* Home to the Red Barons, an AAA farm club for the Philadelphia Phillies. Call for game information and schedules for the upcoming season.

Everhart Museum (all ages), *Nay Aug Park, 1901 Mulberry Street, Scranton; (570) 346–7186; www.everhart-museum.org. Open year-round. Admission is $$ for adults, $ for seniors and children; children under 5 are* Free. Permanent exhibits include a dinosaur hall, rocks and mineral display, a bird gallery, and children's gallery, as well as examples of American and European painting, prints, and more. The Everhart often attracts high-quality traveling exhibits, so be sure to call ahead and see what will be there during your stay.

Annual Armed Forces Air Show, *Wilkes-Barre/Scranton International Airport, Avoca; call (877) 2–FLYAVP for information, dates, and admission prices.* If your family enjoys air shows, schedule a visit to the Scranton area for mid-August to coincide with the Annual Armed Forces Air Show, billed as the premier air show in the Northeast. Precision formation flying, parachuters, aerial ballet, tactical demonstrations, and other in-the-air performances complement a full array of land-based exhibits of aircraft.

Eckley Miners' Village, *RR 2, Box 236, Weatherly; (570) 636–2070; www. phmc.state.us. Open daily year-round. Admission: $ per person, $$ for families.* Just 9 miles east of Route 81, Eckley Miners' Village offers the chance to visit an authentic nineteenth-century "patch" town. The town was originally built in 1854 by the mining firm of Sharpe, Leisenring and Co. for its workers, mostly new immigrants to the States. The town, which was restored in the late 1960s for the filming of the movie *The Molly Maguires,* is now a historic site, administered by the Pennsylvania Historical and Museum Commission. Throughout the summer season the village holds various special events, including Patch Town Days, a Living History Weekend, and Family Sunday, which features a community picnic typical of the 1800s.

The Lehigh Gorge and Surrounding Area (White Haven, Jim Thorpe, Lehighton)

The Lehigh River cuts through the section of the Pocono Plateau south of Wilkes-Barre and creates a gorge that has become a mecca for recreation enthusiasts. A bike path along the river is a dramatic but easy ride (especially going north to south), and the river itself offers challenging white water for boating. There's also great skiing in the area, as well as some terrific resorts for families.

For a family that wants to combine outdoor activities like biking, hiking, and swimming with more urbane pursuits such as museums, shops, and restaurants, the town of Jim Thorpe has a winning combination.

MAUCH CHUNK LAKE PARK (all ages)

625 Lentz Trail, Jim Thorpe; (570) 325–3669. Open year-round.

In the late 1800s and early 1900s, tourists flocked to Mauch Chunk (now Jim Thorpe) to ride the famous Switchback Railroad. This 18-mile figure-eight of track was more like a roller coaster than a train ride—at some points on the trip, cars reached speeds of 60 miles per hour. Now, a century later, the Switchback is again attracting tourists. Although the railroad has not operated in many years, its railbed has been transformed into one of the best-known mountain-bike trails on the East Coast.

Much of the Switchback trail is located within or near Mauch Chunk Lake Park, a county park that offers more than a vacation's worth of activities. The park features nice campsites, a sandy beach on a beautiful lake, excellent programs at the environmental center, picnic pavilions, food and refreshment stand, and 18 miles of biking, hiking, or cross-country skiing trails. Trails include scenic overlooks, one of which offers a spectacular view of the Lehigh Gorge and Glenonoko Falls. On weekends during the month of October—peak foliage time—the park offers hayrides along the Switchback Trail.

Other special attractions of the park include handicapped access to the lake, a handicapped-accessible fishing pier, bathrooms with changing tables, and a nice playground for kids. Fees are charged for many of the park's activities, including swimming, hayrides, equipment rentals, and camping. Eight camping cottages are available for rent.

MAUCH CHUNK MUSEUM AND CULTURAL CENTER (ages 4 and up)

41 West Broadway, Jim Thorpe; (570) 325–9190. Open Tuesday through Sunday year-round. Call ahead for current hours. Admission is $.

Stop here to learn about the history of the Switchback Railroad and the town that grew up around it. Exhibits portray the history of the coal mining industry in Mauch Chunk (the town's former name), the Leni Lenape Indians, and more. There's also a display about the life of Jim Thorpe, the Native American Olympic athlete for whom the town was renamed in the 1950s. Although Thorpe was never a resident of the town, his widow heard of the area's efforts to revitalize its economy and offered her husband's memorabilia in exchange for naming the town in his honor.

The museum is housed in a beautiful redbrick Victorian church built in 1843.

THE OLD JAIL MUSEUM (ages 6 and up)

128 West Broadway, Jim Thorpe; (570) 325–5259. Open daily except Wednesday, Memorial Day through Labor Day. Open weekends only in September and October. Admission is $.

Asked what kids like best about his museum, Thomas McBride answers, "It's a real jail and it's spooky. Real 'bad guys' were here!" Indeed, this building served as the Carbon County jail from 1871 to January 1995. It was also the site of the hanging of the Molly Maguires. Purchased by Thomas and Betty Lou McBride in 1995, it has now been preserved as a museum. Tour guides take visitors through the kitchen, cell blocks, and even down to the dungeon, where prisoners were kept in solitary confinement. Yes, it's a bit spooky, but there are lessons to be learned here. Older kids especially seem fascinated. Look for the "mysterious handprint" left by a prisoner in 1871. No matter how many times the room is repainted, the ghostly handprint always bleeds through!

BLUE MOUNTAIN SPORTS AND WEAR (ages 8 and up)

Route 209, Jim Thorpe; (800) 599–4421); www.bikejimthorpe.com. Open daily.

If mountain biking or other outdoor sports are your pleasure, stop in at the Blue Mountain Sports and Wear shop for information about the excellent trails in the area. The store offers top-quality bike rentals and shuttle service to various trailheads. Tell the experienced staff your skill level and how much time you want to spend, and they'll guide you to the right trail. In addition to bike rentals, the store has camping equipment, kayaks, rowboats, canoes, cross-country skis, and snowshoes for rent.

POCONO WHITEWATER ADVENTURES (ages 5 and up)

Route 903, Jim Thorpe; (800) WHITEWATER or (570) 325–8430; www. whitewaterrafting.com.

Another option for outdoor enthusiasts is a rafting trip down the Lehigh River. Pocono Whitewater Adventures offers "Family-Style Floatrips" for kids from "five to eighty-five," including riverside barbecue. One child per two paying adults rides **Free**.

RAIL TOURS, INC. (ages 4 and up)

P.O. Box 285, Jim Thorpe; (888) 546–8467 or (570) 325–4606. Admission: $$–$$$ for adults, $–$$ for children 2 through 11.

The visitors center in the old Jersey Central Railroad Station is the starting point for a number of special train-ride excursions. The schedule changes throughout the season, but rides take place on most weekends from April to October and the first two weekends of December.

ASA PACKER MANSION (ages 8 and up)

Packer Hill, Jim Thorpe; (570) 325–3229. Open daily Memorial Day through October 31. Call ahead for hours. Admission is $$ for adults and $ for children under 12.

Although not a place to take your wound-up preschooler, older kids will enjoy ogling over the opulence of the furnishings in this Victorian mansion.

OLD MAUCH CHUNK H.O. SCALE MODEL TRAIN DISPLAY (all ages)

41 Susquehanna Street, Jim Thorpe; (570) 386–2297 or (570) 325–4371. Open year-round. Hours vary. Admission is $; children under 4 enter **Free***.*

Across the street from the visitors center, in the Hooven Mercantile Co. building, head up to the second floor to see the Scale Model Railroad Display. With 1,000 feet of track, 60 cars, 200 miniature buildings, and 100 bridges, it sure is an impressive display.

THE INN AT JIM THORPE (all ages)

24 Broadway, Jim Thorpe; (570) 325–2599; www.innjt.com.

With a restaurant on-site and kid-friendly policies, this is a great place to stay right in Jim Thorpe. You can walk to all the sights. Suites have dining areas, whirlpools, VCRs, refrigerators, microwaves, and coffeemakers—things that make a family vacation much easier.

ALSO IN THE AREA

Big Boulder and Jack Frost Ski Resorts, *Lake Harmony; (570) 722–0100 or (800) 468–2442; www.big2resorts.com.* Big Boulder and its neighbor, Jack Frost, offer a great vacation deal for families. Families can try skiing (downhill and cross-country), snowtubing, snowboarding, and paintball and stay in a vacation home on the property. Even better, kids under five stay **Free**. Both resorts also offer baby-sitting, ski lessons, and nightlife. Jack Frost has TRAXX, a 15-mile course through the woods with divisions for motocross, ATV, and BMX bikes. This course is available for people ten and up. Bring your own equipment, but you can rent bicycles only. Also at Jack Frost is night-time snowtubing on Saturday nights.

Ashland

PIONEER TUNNEL COAL MINE & STEAM TRAIN (all ages)

Nineteenth and Oak Streets; (570) 875–3850; www.pioneertunnel.com. Open April through November. Call ahead for specific times. Mine tour: $$ for adults, $ for children under 12. Steam train: $$ for adults, $ for children under 12.

If you didn't visit the Lackawanna Coal Mine in Scranton—or if you and your kids enjoyed it so much you're ready for another mine tour— then head to Ashland and the Pioneer Tunnel Coal Mine. Like the Scranton mine, this is an actual coal mine. When the coal company shut it down, some local volunteers and former miners transformed it into a fascinating study of a coal miner's life. Visitors enter the mine in open mine cars, just as the miners did when they started their workdays.

After the thirty-five-minute mine tour, take a ride on a narrow-gauge steam locomotive, the Henry Clay. Along the 1½-mile round-trip, you'll see two other examples of coal mining: a strip mine and a bootleg coal mine, where men snuck past guards to get coal to sell or to heat their own homes. You can see the smoke rising from the ground as a result of the famous Centalia mine fire.

Red Rock

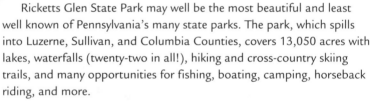

RICKETTS GLEN STATE PARK (ages 2 and up)
Route 487; (570) 477–5675 or (888) PA–PARKS; www.dcnr.state.pa.us. Open year-round. **Free**.

Ricketts Glen State Park may well be the most beautiful and least well known of Pennsylvania's many state parks. The park, which spills into Luzerne, Sullivan, and Columbia Counties, covers 13,050 acres with lakes, waterfalls (twenty-two in all!), hiking and cross-country skiing trails, and many opportunities for fishing, boating, camping, horseback riding, and more.

The Glens Natural Area, a registered National Natural Landmark, is the centerpiece of the park. Here, where two branches of Kitchen Creek create deep gorges, there are rare stands of virgin hemlock and other trees, some more than 500 years old. Much of the hiking in the park covers pretty steep territory, but with the help of a park ranger, you can choose trails that may be easier for children. For example, the Evergreen Trail, just ½-mile long, takes hikers through giant hemlocks and pine trees and to a view of several waterfalls. There are 120 tent and trailer campsites available year-round at the park. In summer there are flush toilets and hot showers. In winter, only pit toilets are available.

If camping sounds a bit too rustic, consider staying at one of the ten comfortable family cabins in the park. Each has a living area, kitchen, bath, and two or three bedrooms. Advance reservations are required for the cabins.

Hunting is permitted in parts of the park. If you visit during the hunting season (primarily in late fall), check in with park rangers to find out what safety precautions are appropriate.

Pennsylvania State Parks With 116 parks adding up to more than 277,000 acres, Pennsylvania has the largest state park system east of the Mississippi—and one of the best travel bargains anywhere. From the majesty of old growth forests to the drama of waterfalls, from the solitude of fishing to the camaraderie of a multi-generational family vacation, these parks offer something for just about everyone. And, admission is Free.

But while many families are aware of the recreational offerings of the state parks, many don't know about the cozy cabins and excellent campgrounds that offer an escape from ordinary life. Fifty-five of Pennsylvania's state parks offer camping. Located in the woods, on the edge of a lake, by a babbling brook, or at the edge of an inspiring vista, these accommodations are the stuff vacation dreams are made on—at prices that make wishes come true.

Cabin rentals include tiny rustic cabins for two and modern cabins with living room, bathroom, kitchen, and bunk beds for six. You'll have to reserve a weekday for the best rates, but even on weekends, the cabins are still a bargain. In summer, the cabins are available by the week. Bring your own food, linens, and cooking utensils, and you've got a terrific vacation.

Campsites start at about $$$ per night, even less for a primitive site. Some sites are equipped with electric and water hook-ups and are ideal for family travelers with a camper.

By calling (888) PA–PARKS, you'll be able to make reservations up to eleven months in advance at any of the state parks in Pennsylvania. If one park has no available cabins for the dates you select, the operator will locate another that does. You can also check the Web site at www.dcnr.state.pa.us.

Your best bet is to call the individual parks if you have specific questions. For general park information call (800) 63PARKS. But for cabin, campsite, or pavilion reservations, the number to call is (888) PA–PARKS.

A Paulsen Family Adventure The cabins in Pennsylvania's state parks are a great, inexpensive family vacation option. The cabins have beds, a family room with sofas, a bathroom, and a kitchen. But be sure to bring along bed linens, towels, and anything you might need to cook a meal. And I do mean anything.

When a friend of mine and I took Eli (eight months old) for a weekend at Ricketts Glen State Park, I thought I had remembered everything: sleeping bags, blankets, ingredients for dinner, pots and pans for cooking, even pancake mix for the morning. But at dinner, I discovered I forgot a can opener. So much for the soup I brought. When I went to take a shower, I discovered I forgot to bring a towel. Luckily, my friend had brought two. At breakfast, I discovered I forgot maple syrup. So much for the pancakes.

We had a great time anyway. We put Eli in the backpack and hiked through the woods in the snow. That night, we saw the comet Hale-Bopp in the dark night sky. Who needs soup anyway?

Forksville

WORLD'S END STATE PARK (ages 6 and up)

Route 154; (570) 924–3287 or (888) PA–PARKS; www.dcnr.state.pa.us. Open year-round. **Free**.

Despite its small size (less than 1,000 acres), it's easy to feel as if you're at the edge of the world in this remote valley. If you're looking for a good place to introduce your children to wilderness camping, this is the spot. There are seventy tent and trailer sites and nineteen cabins, equipped with refrigerator, range, fireplace, table, chairs, and beds. (There's a central shower facility.)

The park includes numerous hiking trails, including the Loyalsock Trail, a $59\frac{3}{10}$-mile hike, part of which runs through the park. Most of the trails are pretty steep, so this park is a better choice for older kids and more experienced hikers.

Festivals of Forksville *Sullivan County Chamber of Commerce (570–946–4160) or Endless Mountains Visitors Bureau (570–836–5431). Check the Web site www.endlessmountains.org. The calendar portion of this Web site can be searched like a database for events of special interest to you.*

Forksville might as well be called Festiville, with all the annual events planned for the fairgrounds and other locations around town. The fun starts in the winter with the annual Endless Mountains 50 Sled Dog Race. The 50-mile race, which is run in the state game lands near Forksville, attracts six-dog racing teams from as far away as Canada. When and if the weather gets cold enough, folks in the area start calling (570) 525-3255 to find out if the Ice Toboggan Slide has been set up in Eagles Mere.

In February the Forksville fairgrounds is the site of the Sullivan County Sleigh Ride and Rally. Here, horses pull the sleighs. In addition to divisions for men, women, and children, there's a timed obstacle-course race and a "Currier & Ives" class, where contestants are judged on the "postcard" quality of their sleighs. Visitors can get a ride in a bobsled. Labor Day weekend brings the Sullivan County Fair, held at the Forksville Fairgrounds. In October it's time for the Fall Festival, with demonstrations by quilters, wood-carvers, and apple-butter and apple-cider makers. There are wagon rides, draft horses, and lots of activities for children.

Where to Eat

IN THE DELAWARE WATER GAP AND STROUDSBURG AREA

Brandli's Pizzeria & Italian Restaurant, *6A Foxmoor Village, East Stroudsburg; (570) 223–1600; www.brandlis.com.* Family-oriented, casual Italian fare.

Brownie's, *Main and Oak Streets, Delaware Water Gap; (570) 424–1154.*

Brownie's in the Burg, *700 Main Street, Stroudsburg; (570) 421–2200.*

The Sarah Street Grill, *550 Quaker Alley, Stroudsburg; (570) 424–9120.* Casual dining including steaks, seafood, and pasta. Children's menu offers chicken fingers, grilled cheese sandwiches, and pizza.

IN THE MOUNT POCONO AND EASTERN POCONOS AREA

Memorytown, *Grange Road, Mt. Pocono; (570) 839–1680.* Shops, snack bar, restaurant, and amusement area all in one.

Smuggler's Cove, *Route 611, Tannersville; (570) 629–2277.*

IN THE HAWLEY-LAKE WALLENPAUPACK AREA

Ehrhardt's Lakeside Restaurant, *Route 507, 1 mile south of Route 6, Hawley; (570) 226–2124.* Dining with a view of Lake Wallenpaupack.

Falls Port Inn & Restaurant, *Main Street, Hawley; (570) 226–2600.* Children's menu, Sunday brunch, historic building.

IN THE HONESDALE AREA

Beach Lake Cafe, *Route 652, Beach Lake. Open year-round.* The most popular place around for weekend breakfasts, this little coffee shop serves up omelettes and pancakes. Get there early on Saturday to avoid a wait.

IN SCRANTON AREA

Cooper's Seafood House, *701 North Washington Avenue, Scranton; (570) 346–6883.*

The Mall at Steamtown, *Lackawanna Avenue, Scranton; (570) 343–3400.* Food court upstairs and two sit-down restaurants downstairs.

Pat McMullen's Restaurant, *217 East Market Street, Scranton; (570) 342–3486.*

Where to Stay

IN THE DELAWARE WATER GAP AND STROUDSBURG AREA

Ramada Inn, *Delaware Water Gap; (570) 476–0000.*

Shawnee Inn & Golf Resort, *River Road, Shawnee-on-Delaware; (570) 424–4000 or (800) SHAWNEE; www.shawneeinn.com.*

Sheraton Four Points, *1220 West Main Street, Stroudsburg; (570) 424–1930 or (800) 777–5453; www.quikpage.com/P/pocono.*

Timothy Lake, *RD 6, Box 6627, East Stroudsburg; (570) 588–6631 or for reservations (800) 588–2221.* Part of the "Outdoor World" group of camping resorts.

IN MOUNT POCONO AND EASTERN POCONOS

The Britannia Country Inn, *Upper Swiftwater Road, Swiftwater; (570) 839–7243. Open year-round. Rates are $$$$ per adult, $$$ for children 4 to 13. Children under 3 stay* **free.** If you can't bear to leave the pooch at home for your family vacation, consider a cottage at the Brittania Inn. Located on twelve acres with an outdoor pool, the inn serves up a taste of England in the Poconos. Modified American Plan (MAP) rates and ski packages available.

Hampton Court Inn, *Route 611, Mt. Pocono; (570) 839–2119.*

Mount Airy Lodge, *Route 611, Mt. Pocono; (570) 839–8811 or (800) 441–4410; www.mountairylodge.com.*

Pocono Super 8 Motel, *Route 611, Mt. Pocono; (570) 839–7728.*

IN THE SCRANTON AREA

Best Western University Inn, *320 Franklin Avenue, Scranton; (570) 246–7061.* Near Steamtown National Historic Site.

Holiday Inn Scranton-East, *200 Tigue Street, Dunmore; (570) 343–4771.* Indoor pool, newly renovated rooms.

Scotrun, *P.O. Box 428, Route 611, Scotrun; (570) 629–0620 or for reservations (800) 588–2221.* Part of the "Outdoor World" group of camping resorts.

IN THE HONESDALE AREA

Beach Lake is on Route 652, a great home base for exploring the Upper Delaware Valley and Honesdale.

Central House. *Off Route 652; (570) 729–4411 or (570) 729–8341. Open year-round.* An on-the-lake location, family-style meals, and on-site swimming pool and volleyball court—a nice spot for a value-priced vacation.

Pine Grove Cabins. *Off Route 652; (570) 729–8522. Open May through October.* For families who prefer to cook their own meals, these cabins can't be beat. Owners Jerry and Barbara Zimmerman keep this bungalow colony immaculate. Kitchens, small living rooms, bathroom with showers, and two bedrooms are crammed into each cabin. There's a beach for swimming and boats for guest use. Weeklong packages are available.

For More Information

Carbon County Visitor Center, *Broadway, Jim Thorpe; (888) JIM–THORPE; www.pavisnet.com/carbon. Open year-round.* Stop by to pick up brochures, ask questions, and check out the historic displays.

Endless Mountains Visitors Bureau, *RR 6, Box 132A, Tunkhannock PA 18657; (800) 769–8999 or (570) 836–5431; www.endlessmountains.org.*

Jim Thorpe Tourist Agency, *(570) 325–3673.*

Luzerne County Tourist Promotion Agency, *200 North River Street, Wilkes-Barre 18711; (570) 825–1635; www.bizwiz.com/ezcommerce/luzerne.*

Pennsylvania's Northeast Territory Visitors Bureau, *201 Hangar Road,* *Suite 203, Avoca 18641; (800) 22WELCOME or (570) 457–1320; www. visitnepa.org.*

Pocono Mountains Vacation Bureau, *1004 Main Street, Stroudsburg 18360; (800) 762–6667 or (570) 424–6050; www.poconos.org.*

Schuylkill County Visitors' Bureau, *91 South Progress Street, Pottsville 17901; (800) 765–7282 or (570) 622–7700.*

Upper Delaware Council, *Bridge Street, Narrowsburg, New York; (570) 252–3022.* An organization of businesses and individuals along the New York and Pennsylvania shores of the river. Contact them for more information about the area.

Central Pennsylvania

The center of Pennsylvania holds a wonderful array of cultural, historical, and recreational opportunities for families. Two cities, Williamsport and State College, have great museums, cultural events, and a wide variety of amenities, such as accommodations, shopping, and restaurants. Either one makes a good base for exploring the surrounding areas.

Dotted around the region are charming small towns, wonderful state parks, farms, and other rural attractions. Campgrounds are plentiful, and little bed-and-breakfasts often welcome families. The local county tourism organizations and chambers of commerce are great resources for planning your trip. Here are our recommendations.

Faith & Emily's Favorite Central Pennsylvania Attractions

1. Knoebels Amusement Park and Campground, Elysburg

2. Peter J. McGovern Little League Baseball Museum, Williamsport

3. Mountain Dale Farm, McClure

4. Shaver's Creek Environmental Center, State College

5. Bellefonte Museum for Centre County, Bellefonte

6. Children's Discovery Workshop, Williamsport

7. Clyde Peeling's Reptiland, Williamsport

8. T & D's Cats of the World, Mifflinburg

9. Historic Williamsport Trolleys, Wiliamsport

10. Walking tour of the Victorian downtown in Lewisburg

PENN'S CAVE

Williamsport

120   120
144
120
287
14
87
220
118
220
150
80
89
180
42
Lewisburg
Boalsburg   Bellefonte   Woodward   45   Mifflinburg   11   Elysburg
State College   45   61   42
35   522   225   125
322   522   35   104   147   225
655   17   147
22   35   17   22   11
Belleville
New Bloomfield
New Germantown
274   233

CENTRAL PENNSYLVANIA

Williamsport

If you have a child in Little League, then Williamsport—the home of the Peter J. McGovern Little League Baseball Museum—is a required stop on your vacation in central Pennsylvania. Once you get to the city, you'll find that the museum is a great destination, but there's more to Williamsport than baseball. To find out more, visit www.cityofwilliamsport.org.

PETER J. MCGOVERN LITTLE LEAGUE BASEBALL MUSEUM (ages 5 and up)

Route 15 South; (570) 326–3607; www.littleleague.org. Memorial Day through September 30: Open Monday through Saturday 9:00 A.M. to 7:00 P.M.; Sunday noon to 7:00 P.M. October 1 through Memorial Day: Open Monday, Thursday, and Friday 10:00 A.M. to 5:00 P.M., Saturday noon to 5:00 P.M., and Sunday noon to 4:00 P.M. Closed Tuesday and Wednesday and major holidays. Adults, $$; children 5 to 13, $.

The Peter J. McGovern Little League Baseball Museum traces the history of Little League from its founding in 1939 to the present, when more than two and a half million children in eighty countries participate in the program. There are interactive displays and batting and pitching cages with instant replay monitors so that kids can see themselves in action. You can watch highlights of the Little League World Series—a truly international sporting event that takes place here each August. The Hall of Excellence includes tributes to such famous former Little Leaguers as Tom Seaver, Kareem Abdul-Jabbar, columnist George Will, and former New Jersey Senator Bill Bradley.

Faith & Emily's
Favorite Events in Central Pennsylvania

- **Belleville Farmers Market** in Belleville (Wednesdays); (570) 248–6713.
- **Big Spring Festival** inn Bellefonte (mid-May); (800) 355–1705.
- **Mifflinburg Buggy Days** in Mifflinburg (end of May); (570) 966–1355.
- **Central Pennsylvania Festival of the Arts** in State College (July); (814) 237–3682.
- **Ag Progress Days** in State College (mid-August); (814) 865–2081.

CHILDREN'S DISCOVERY WORKSHOP (ages 3 to 11)

343 West Fourth Street at Elmira Street; (570) 322–5437; williamsportymca. com. Open September through May, Tuesday through Friday and Sunday 10:00 A.M. to 5:00 P.M., Saturday 11:00 A.M. to 5:00 P.M.; June through August, Tuesday through Friday and Sunday 9:00 A.M. to 4:00 P.M., Saturday 10:00 A.M. to 4:00 P.M. Admission: $ per person; children under 2 are Free.

Located inside the Williamsport YMCA, the Children's Discovery Workshop is a hands-on museum for children ages three to eleven. The interactive exhibits are designed to inspire children's imaginations, explorations, and discoveries. Features include a toddler area, bricks to build a castle, a pretend ice-cream parlor, and changing exhibits. One of the most popular features is the 129-foot-long "FUNnel," which children can crawl through.

If playing works up a family-size appetite, head across the street to the Hepburn Diner, known locally for its homestyle cooking.

 ### THOMAS T. TABER MUSEUM OF LYCOMING COUNTY (ages 5 and up)

858 West Fourth Street; (570) 326–3326; www.lycoming.org/lchsmuseum. Open Tuesday through Saturday year-round, Sunday from May to October. Adults $$, children 12 and under $.

Model-train enthusiasts will want to stop here to see the Larue Shempp Model Train exhibition, with more than 300 toy trains and two working layouts—reputed to be one of the finest displays of its kind in the country. There's a frontier room, which re-creates the furnishings from the county's first European settlement in 1769; a general store from the turn of the twentieth century; a one-room schoolhouse; a working gristmill; and a collection of farming, blacksmithing, and milling tools from the 1700s to 1900s.

HISTORIC WILLIAMSPORT TROLLEYS (all ages)

Downtown Williamsport; (800) CITYBUS or (570) 326–2500; www.citybus. org. Open Tuesday, Thursday, and Saturday during June, July, and August. Tours are $ per person.

The Historic Williamsport Trolleys are run by the City Bus company of the Williamsport Bureau of Transportation. The three trolleys, the *Herdic,* the *Weightman,* and the *Stotz,* are actually replicas of historic streetcars. Each makes a ninety-minute narrated trip around the historic areas of Williamsport. The route takes you past Millionaire's Row (6 blocks of magnificent mansions), the field where the first Little League game was played, and other sights of the city. Riders can get on and off at one of the downtown stops and each of the two outlying stops. On Tuesday and Thursday you can get off the trolley and onto the *Hiawatha* for a cruise—another great way to tour the sights of this city.

HIAWATHA CRUISES (all ages)

Susquehanna State Park; (570) 326–2500 or (800) 248–9287. In season only (570) 326–1221; www.williamsport.org. Cruises operate Tuesday through Sunday, May through mid-October. Public cruises: Adults $$, children 3 to 12 $. Family Night cruises: Adults $$, children 3 to 12 $. First come, first served after tickets go on sale day of sale 10:30 A.M.

The other way to tour the town is aboard the *Hiawatha*, a paddlewheeler that plies the Susquehanna River. The hour-long public cruise includes a narration that relates the history of the area, from the time when the Susquehannock Indians lived along these shores through the European settlements and boom years of the lumber industry. On Tuesday nights in June, July, and August, come aboard for a special cruise just for families, ninety minutes long, with a different featured activity every night. Sunday brunch cruises, for $$$ per person, will sail you to the Antlers Country Club for brunch, then take you back by Historic Williamsport Trolley.

CLYDE PEELING'S REPTILAND (ages 4 and up)

Route 15, south of Williamsport; (570) 538–1869; www.reptiland.com. Open daily 9:00 A.M. to 7:00 P.M. May through September. October to April, open daily 10:00 A.M. to 5:00 P.M. Admission is $$; children under 4 are **Free***.*

Don't miss Clyde Peeling's Reptiland, an accredited zoo with a collection of sixty different species of reptiles and amphibians. Poison dart frogs, a giant toad, a gaboon viper, a green tree python, a king cobra, alligators (including the 800-pound "Ivan"), giant tortoises, turtles, iguanas—they're all here. There are educational programs five times during the day that give visitors a chance to see and touch the animals up close.

Although it doesn't offer wheelchair rentals, Reptiland is wheelchair accessible.

Elysburg

KNOEBELS AMUSEMENT PARK AND CAMPGROUND (ages 2 and up)

Route 487, about 12 miles south of Bloomsburg; (800) ITS–4FUN or (570) 672–2572; www.knoebels.com. Open weekends in April, May, and September; daily in June, July, and August. Admission **Free** *to park; camping and cabins are $$$$. Individual ride prices are $.*

If you've ever wondered what happened to the traditional amusement parks you remember from your own childhood, head to Knoebels (pronounced with a hard "k"). This park got its start at the turn of the twentieth century, when Henry Hartman Knoebel charged 25 cents to water, feed, and brush the horses that brought groups to swim on his property. After a few years he added picnic tables and sold ice cream and other snacks to the visitors. A pool, overnight cottages, and a carousel were added in 1926. By the 1940s Knoebels had graduated to an amusement resort.

At present Knoebels offers fifty rides (including two world-class wooden roller coasters, the Phoenix and the Twister), a huge swimming pool, and many rides, especially for the younger set. There are several restaurants, snack bars, and picnic areas as well as a collection of shops and regularly scheduled entertainment. All of this is nestled among natural streams and shady hemlock trees that keep the temperatures here a good ten degrees lower than elsewhere in the area.

If this sounds like too much for a day trip, stay the night—or longer—at one of 500 campsites and log cabins. Cabins sleep six and have electricity. Call (570) 672-9555 for campground information.

Lewisburg

A pretty Victorian town that is home to Bucknell University, Lewisburg is a good place to stop and stretch the legs or grab some lunch. Pick up a walking-tour brochure from the Union County Tourist Agency at 418 Market Street (570-524-2815). There are some great historic homes in town that are open for tours. Although not geared for small children, older ones enjoy the tours.

Because it is home to Bucknell University, this is a good place to find a place to stay or have a bite to eat. The Union County Tourist Agency can point you in the right direction.

SLIFER HOUSE MUSEUM (ages 6 and up)

1 River Road; (570) 524–2245; http://slifer.albrightcare.org. Open April 15 through December 31, Tuesday through Sunday 1:00 to 4:00 P.M.; January 1 through April 14, Tuesday through Friday 1:00 to 4:00 P.M. or by appointment. Admission is $; children under 10 are Free.

House tours aren't on most kids' top ten list, but the Slifer House has several exhibits that children six and older enjoy. An artifact quiz is designed to stimulate minds, both young and old. Among the favorites are the children's bedroom and old toys, a Regina music box, and the doctor's office, with antique medical tools. In summer there's an outdoor concert series, followed by Free ice cream. A sure hit with kids. Slifer House also hosts family activities such as Civil War encampments, storytelling, and workshops. The house is wrapped in Victorian excess for the Christmas holidays, including a floor-to-ceiling tree with nineteenth-century ornaments and garlands of roses over the dining-room table. Recent workshop topics have included gingerbread house making and origami.

PACKWOOD HOUSE MUSEUM (ages 6 and up)

15 North Water Street; (570) 524–0323. Open Tuesday through Saturday 10:00 A.M. to 5:00 P.M. Admission is $; children under 6 are Free.

Christmas is a special time for children at the Packwood. Even younger children love seeing the decorations and lights. The rest of the year, the museum is more geared for school-age children. There is an impressive collection of antique furniture, glass, ceramics, textiles, and more at the Packwood.

Mifflinburg

In addition to the following sights, Mifflinburg serves as the headquarters for no fewer than four Pennsylvania state parks: McCalls Dam State Park (known for its fishing); R. B. Winter State Park (with lake swimming, environmental education, and camping); Ravensburg State Park (fishing, hiking, and camping); and Sand Bridge State Park (known for snowmobiling trails). For information on any one of these parks, call (570) 966–1455 or (800) 63–PARKS.

MIFFLINBURG BUGGY MUSEUM (ages 3 and up)

598 Green Street; (570) 966–1355; www.lycoming.org/buggy. Open May through October, Thursday through Saturday 10:00 A.M. to 5:00 P.M., Sunday

1:00 to 5:00 P.M. Visitors center open November through April, Thursday through Saturday 10:00 A.M. to 5:00 P.M. Admission is $$ for adults and $ for children 6 to 17. Children under 6 enter Free. Free *parking.*

The Mifflinburg Buggy Museum gives you a chance to see horse-drawn buggies up close. Through the late nineteenth century, Mifflinburg earned the nickname "Buggy Town" by producing roughly 5,000 horse-drawn vehicles a year, more per capita than any other town in Pennsylvania. Over an eighty-year period, the town was home to seventy-five separate buggy makers. Only one of these factories remains, the W. A. Heiss Coachworks, now part of the museum. The Mifflinburg Buggy Museum is believed to be the only museum in the United States housed in an original carriage factory with original contents.

First, stop at the new visitors center to view the seven-minute introductory video and self-guided exhibit. The hands-on workbench includes a wheel that can be disassembled, tools to handle, a buggy engraving, coloring and word-find sheets kids can complete at the museum or take home, and more.

Then, take a guided tour of the original factory, complete with tools and supplies; the Repository (showroom) with vehicles on display; and the family home. Recent renovations include not only the new visitors center but also improved wheelchair accessibility and the opening of a second floor in the repository. Accessibility for the visually and hearing-impaired has also been upgraded, as has the gift shop. Each May the museum hosts the annual Mifflinburg Buggy Day Festival, featuring craft vendors, antiques dealers, live entertainment, food, activities for children, demonstrations, and buggy rides.

CHRISTKINDL MARKET (ages 2 and up)

Downtown Mifflinburg; (570) 966–1666.

Another Mifflinburg traditional celebration is Christkindl Market, held the Thursday through Sunday after Thanksgiving each year. The festival re-creates a traditional German Christmas, with authentic food, seasonal music, and handmade gifts for sale. There's also a Santa's Workshop with crafts and games just for kids.

 ### T&D'S CATS OF THE WORLD

Penn's Creek; (570) 837–3377; www.tdscats.com. Open weekends May through September noon to 6:00 P.M. Admission is $$; children under 2 enter Free. *Group tours can be arranged throughout the year.*

The purpose of T&D's Cats of the World is to rescue wildlife, especially exotic felines, from situations of abuse, mistreatment, and abandonment, or when they are no longer wanted as "pets." This effort began as a labor of love when the Mattive family (Terry, Donna, Jennifer, and T. J.) discovered how many exotic animals are abandoned when they outgrow the baby stage. Today, the entire Mattive family is involved in the care of eleven Bengal tigers, one Siberian tiger, eight African lions, thirteen cougars, four bobcats, and a leopard, plus smaller mammals such as skunks, coyotes, raccoons, river otters, and more.

McClure

MOUNTAIN DALE FARM (all ages)

Rural Route 2; (570) 658–3536; www.pafarmstay.com. Open year-round.

If your family wants to experience farm life firsthand, then a vacation at Ken and Sally Hassinger's Mountain Dale Farm is just the ticket. This 175-acre farm is surrounded by state forest and game land, making it a complete getaway from civilization. But you don't have to rough it completely. The farm offers accommodations in a variety of cabins and efficiencies. There is a 200-year-old restored log house that has four bedrooms and sleeps up to fourteen people. Children under twelve are half price, and those under two years old stay **free**. Meals are provided at an extra cost upon request, but most visitors enjoy cooking in their own kitchens or in the common kitchen.

Kids love helping out with the barn chores and getting to know the farm animals. Other activities include boating, fishing, swimming, or ice skating on three ponds; cross-country skiing or hiking in the woods; or just relaxing on the front porch of your cabin. Come before Christmas and choose your own tree from the Christmas tree farm.

New Bloomfield

LITTLE BUFFALO STATE PARK (all ages)

Off Route 34; (570) 567–9255; www.dcnr.state.pa.us/stateparks/parks/ buffalo.htm. Open year-round. **Free** *for most activities.*

In Perry County 830-acre Little Buffalo State Park has both historic and natural attractions. There's an eighty-eight-acre lake, a swimming pool (fee charged), hiking trails, fishing, and picnic areas. But there are also a covered bridge, a working gristmill from the 1800s, and an old tavern, all of which have been restored (or are in the process). In winter there are 7 miles of cross-country trails, a sledding and tobogganing area, and a skating area on the lake (the rest of the lake is open for ice fishing in winter). There is no camping in the park, but the park ranger can furnish names of other campgrounds in the area.

BOX HUCKLEBERRY NATURAL AREA (all ages)

Route 34; (570) 536–3191; www.parec.com. Open year-round. **Free**.

Just a few miles south of Little Buffalo State Park on Route 34 is the Box Huckleberry Natural Area, a special reserve for a box huckleberry plant estimated to be 1,300 years old. A short interpretive nature trail around the area is a favorite of small children. This is a good place to teach your kids about the importance of preserving our natural resources. Trail maps and a written history of the plant are available on-site.

New Germantown

TUSCARORA STATE FOREST (all ages)

Route 274, southwest of New Germantown; (570) 536–3191; www.dcnr. state.pa.us/forestry/forests.tuscar. Open year-round. **Free**.

Traveling southwest on Route 274 from New Germantown, you'll come upon the entrance to the Tuscarora State Forest—90,512 acres of amazing vistas, undisturbed areas, trout streams, state parks, hiking, snowmobiling, and more. The forest roads are well maintained, making a great route for a mild "off-road" driving experience. The Bureau of Forestry has developed a brochure that will guide you on a 26-mile auto tour of the forest. The dirt roads are in good shape, so you shouldn't need four-wheel drive to navigate the route in good weather.

Highlights in and around the state forest include: Hemlocks Natural Area, a 131-acre area of virgin hemlock forest with 3 miles of hiking trails; the Iron Horse Trail, a rails-to-trails project that provides 10 miles of hiking with only moderate climbing necessary; the Tuscarora Trail, a 22-mile side trail of the Appalachian Trail; Fowler Hollow State Park, with eighteen campsites and fishing in the creek; and Colonel Denning State Park, with fifty-two trailer and tent sites, excellent hiking, and an extensive environmental education program during summer months. For more infor-

mation about the state forest and natural areas, contact the Bureau of
Forestry, RD 1, Box 42-A, Blain 17006. For more information about the
state parks within the forest, call (570) 776-5272 or (800) PA-PARKS.

Belleville

Everyone loves a farmers' market: rows of fresh vegetables, home-baked
goods, handmade crafts, and the chance to meet the people who produce
them. The town of Belleville may have the ultimate farmers' market.

BELLEVILLE FARMERS MARKET (all ages)

*Route 655; (717) 935–2146. Open year-round Wednesday during daylight
hours.* **Free** *admission.*

   The Belleville Farmers Market takes place every Wednesday from six
in the morning to six at night. The ten-acre Amish market has livestock
yards, auction barns, and 400 flea-market stalls. It's a popular event, so
be prepared to walk a ways from your car to the auction areas. For
more information about the area, call the Juniata Valley Area Chamber
of Commerce at (570) 248-6713. For information on this and other
farmers' markets, check www.ams.usda.gov/farmersmarkets/states/
penna.htm.

ALSO IN THE AREA

Mifflin County Trout Hatchery (ages 4 and up), *Route 655, between Belleville and
Reedsville; open Wednesday and Saturday.* While you're in the area, check out the
Mifflin County Trout Hatchery, where children can fish for trout and pay only
for what they catch. Fishing poles and bait are provided.

State College

A visit to a college campus is a great way to inspire a child's educational
dreams. The home of Penn State University, one of the country's best public
universities, State College has much to offer families.

   Bolstered by the university population, State College is a thriving town
with many hotels, shops, and restaurants. Many of the area's attractions are
within an easy drive, making the town an ideal base for your explorations.

A Paulsen Family Adventure The first rule of traveling with children should be: if possible, get a hotel with a pool.

Most kids love the water. At the Holiday Inn in State College, Eli (eighteen months) learned how to jump from the edge of the pool into our arms. He thought this was great fun and jumped and jumped until his lips turned blue.

Eli was totally wound up from a day of sight-seeing and visiting with his grandparents. He wanted to run around, but the confines of a small hotel room, the car, or a restaurant didn't allow this. The pool let him get his ya-yas out.

Which leads to the third benefit of a pool: It wears kids out. After playing in the pool, we put him in his pajamas and put him in his portacrib. He was out like a light in a matter of minutes. No mean feat for a kid who was bouncing off the walls earlier in the day.

 CENTRAL PENNSYLVANIA FESTIVAL OF THE ARTS (all ages)
Downtown State College; (814) 237–3682; www.arts-festival.com. Five days in July. **Free** *admission.*

State College is the site of the Central Pennsylvania Festival of the Arts, a five-day celebration that takes place in July each year. The first day of the festival is traditionally Children and Youth Day, featuring the creations of local children ages eight through eighteen and a wonderful procession through town in which children wear masks and carry their works of art. Life-size puppets also take part in the procession. Storytelling, marionette performances, concerts, and more round out this not-to-be-missed event. Organizers have made special attempts to include people with special needs, including visual impairments.

 FROST ENTOMOLOGICAL MUSEUM (ages 5 and up)
Headhouse 3, halfway between Shortlidge and Bigelar Roads; (814) 863–2865; www.ento.psu.edu/home/frost/index.html. Open Monday through Friday 9:30 A.M. to 4:30 P.M. **Free**.

The Insect Zoo features a functional beehive plus a variety of insects and other arthopods such as scorpions, tarantulas, and cockroaches. Kids will get a kick out of it; parents may or may not.

EARTH AND MINERAL SCIENCES MUSEUM (ages 5 and up)

122 Spiedle Building, Pollock Road; (814) 865–6427; www.ems.psu.edu/ museum. Open year-round Monday through Friday 9:30 A.M. to 5:00 P.M. Closed holidays. **Free.**

The halls of the Spiedle Building are lined with crystals, gems, carvings, and fossils. Kids especially like the ultraviolet light room that highlights minerals invisible under normal incandescent lights. The shrunken heads also get an enthusiastic reception from most kids.

GREENBERG INDOOR SPORTS COMPLEX (ages 2 and up)

Pollock and McKean Streets; (814) 865–4102.; www.psu.edu/deptice_pavilion. Open to the public for part of most days. Call ahead for current hours. Admission is $. Skate rental is $.

After checking out the museums, you might want to take a spin around the indoor ice-skating rinks at the Greenberg Indoor Sports Complex. The complex offers two rinks with superior surfaces.

BEAVER STADIUM (ages 5 and up)

University Drive and Curtin Road; (814) 863–1000 or (800) 833–5533. Various prices.

Of course, for many people the most famous aspect of Penn State is its football team. The Nittany Lions play in the Big Ten College Football League, and sports fans come from around the country to see a game at Beaver Stadium. For current schedules and tickets, call the aforementioned phone numbers or log onto www.psu.edu.

BRYCE JORDAN CENTER (ages 5 and up)

University Drive and Curtin Road; (814) 865–5555 or (800) 863–3336.

Men's and women's basketball as well as a variety of special events take place across the street from Beaver Stadium at the Bryce Jordan Center. Call for schedules and tickets.

COLLEGE OF AGRICULTURAL SCIENCES (all ages)

Agriculture Administration Building, University Park; (814) 865–4433. Open 9:00 A.M. to 4:00 P.M. **Free.**

Check out the animals at the agricultural facilities of the College of Agricultural Sciences, near Beaver Stadium. See white-tailed deer, sheep, cattle, horses, and pigs. There's also an exhibit of flowering plants and vegetables.

Throughout the year special events are scheduled for the nearby Ag Arena. Check the marquee outside to see what's scheduled or call ahead. Children especially enjoy the shows of horses or dairy cattle. Around Christmas, the Festival of Trees features more than one hundred different trees, decorated by area businesses and organizations.

AG PROGRESS DAYS and the JEROME K. PASTO AGRICULTURAL MUSEUM (all ages)

Russell E. Larson Agricultural Research Center, Route 45; (814) 865–2081; www.cas.psu.edu/docs/AGIS/APD.html. **Free**.

Penn State's Ag Progress Days is one of the largest agricultural shows in the country. It takes place in mid-August each year and features live animal exhibitions, a petting zoo, computer-based games, demonstrations of the latest farming technologies, and displays of antique farm equipment. The Family and Youth Building has special programs just for kids.

On the same site as the Larson Agricultural Research Center, the Jerome K. Pasto Agricultural Museum traces the history of farming in America with displays of old tools and appliances from the days before electricity. It's open April 15 to October 15. Call ahead for scheduling information (814–865–8301). Admission is **Free**, but donations are encouraged.

MILLBROOK MARSH NATURE CENTER (all ages)

Puddintown Road, State College; (814) 863–2000. Open year-round. Call ahead for current hours. **Free** *admission.*

A cooperative venture of many local educational organizations, this is the site for several nature programs conducted by the Shaver's Creek Environmental Center. The mission of the center is to educate and inspire people about the natural world and to instill a passion for the environment through science, history, culture, and art. Call for updated information and a schedule of events.

STONE VALLEY RECREATION AREA (all ages)

State Route 1029, off Route 26 South; (814) 863–1164; www.psu.edu/dept/ stone_valley. Open year-round sunrise to sunset. **Free**.

After the hubbub of the active campus, this is a great place to come and wind down. Administered by Penn State, the Stone Valley Recreation Area has a wide variety of activities for all ages. Depending on the season you can enjoy boating (canoes, rowboats, or sailboats—all of which are available for rent), fishing (trout and bass), hayrides, hiking, ice skating (rentals available), sledding, ice fishing, or cross-country skiing (lessons available). There are eleven handicapped-accessible cabins for overnight accommodations. The one-room cabins are equipped with bunk beds, refrigerator, electric range top, electricity, and gas heat. There are central bathroom and shower facilities nearby. Bring your own linens and cooking and eating utensils. Call for rates and reservations.

SHAVER'S CREEK ENVIRONMENTAL CENTER (all ages)

State Route 1029 (Charter Oak Road) off Route 26 South; (814) 863–2000; www.shaverscreek.org. Open mid-January to mid-December. Call ahead for current hours. Visitor and Raptor Center admission is $ per person; children under 3 are Free.

At the Environmental Center, learn about the local wildlife and how injured eagles, hawks, owls, reptiles, and amphibians are cared for at this lovely environmental center. There's a bookstore with a good selection of books for children; you'll also find other wildlife accessories there. Special gardens attract butterflies, bees, and hummingbirds.

Shaver's Creek is the site of a wonderful day camp program for children six and up. For children six to eleven, the Discovery and Explorer Camps run from Tuesday through Friday and end up with a family overnight at the camp.

Children twelve and up can choose from several different camp experiences, including Raptor and More Camp (in which campers work with rehabilitated birds of prey), which is for campers ages fourteen to seventeen.

Boalsburg

Looking for a special way to spend an upcoming three-day weekend? The town of Boalsburg has several claims to fame that make it a good destination any time of year. For Memorial Day weekend, how about visiting the place where the holiday got its start? Boalsburg has been commemorating this day since 1864, and today there are community picnics and parades to enjoy.

In July Boalsburg is the site of the **Peoples' Choice Festival of Pennsylvania Arts and Crafts.** The weekend of activities includes free museum tours for children, a petting zoo, and a stuffed-animal vet.

Columbus Day weekend coming up? What better place to get in touch with the discoverer of the New World than at the **Christopher Columbus**

Family Chapel, part of the Boal Mansion and Museum. And, for Veterans Day, learn the history of our nation's veterans at the Pennsylvania Military Museum across Route 322.

BOAL MANSION AND MUSEUM (ages 6 and up)

300 Old Boalsburg Road; (814) 466–6210; www.boalmuseum.com. Open Tuesday through Sunday noon to 5:00 P.M. summer to Labor Day; 1:30 to 5:00 P.M. in spring and fall; closed Monday. Admission is $$$ for adults and $$ for children 7 to 11; children under 7 enter Free.

This historic house has an added attraction: original objects belonging to Christopher Columbus. Originally part of the Columbus family castle in Spain, the chapel contains heirlooms that date back to the 1400s. The *Wall Street Journal* called the collection "a strong tangible link to Columbus in the New World." Kids especially enjoy looking at the antique weapons and dresses and hearing stories about nine generations of the Boal family, across 210 years in the same house, continuing today.

PENNSYLVANIA MILITARY MUSEUM (ages 5 and up)

Route 45 and Business Route 322; (814) 466–6263; www.psu.edu/dept/ aerospace/museum/armor.html. From April through October open Tuesday through Saturday, 9:00 A.M. to 5:00 P.M.; Sunday noon to 5:00 P.M. Closed Monday except for Memorial Day, July 4th, and Labor Day. From November through March call ahead for hours. Admission is $; children under 6 are Free.

Starting with Ben Franklin's first military unit, the museum traces the history of the military—and Pennsylvanians' involvement—all the way through the Vietnam conflict. A tour of this museum is highlighted by a 100-foot-long re-creation of a front-line trench from World War I. The museum building is surrounded by a sixty-five-acre park that includes equipment, monuments, and memorials. There are daily living-history demonstrations and many special celebrations during the year. On Memorial Day each year, the museum is the site of a Civil War encampment.

TUSSEY MOUNTAIN SKI RESORT (ages 3 and up)

301 Bear Meadows Road; (800) 733–2754 or (814) 466–6810. Open year-round.

Heading east from State College on Route 322 is Tussey Mountain Ski Resort, a great place for family skiing and snowboarding. At the Kid's Mountain Learning Center, children ages three to six can ski in a specially designed learning area. They can even join a Paw Prints group and enjoy instructed play and an introduction to skiing. The Mountain

Lion group, for children six to ten years old, is aimed at building children's skiing skills. Both classes run two hours and are scheduled twice a day on weekdays and three times a day on weekends. Tussey Mountain has recently added Avalanche Canyon, a snowtubing area.

Eastern Centre County

Just east of State College are several small towns with worthwhile attractions for families. Here are a few of the best.

PENN'S CAVE (ages 4 and up)

Route 192, 5 miles east of Centre Hall; (814) 364–1664; www.pennscave.com. Open 9:00 A.M. to 5:00 P.M. February 15 to December 31 (weekends only in December). Admission is $$$ for adults and $ for children 2 to 12.

Kids love caves. Penn's Cave has been attracting visitors for centuries, since the Seneca Indians discovered it. It has been a tourist attraction since the late 1800s, when a hotel was built on the site.

Penn's Cave is the country's only water-filled cave, and tours are given by motorboat. Along the hour-long ride you'll see amazing stalactites and stalagmites in a series of "rooms." Colored lights illuminate formations with names like the Statue of Liberty, Chinese Dragon, and Niagara Falls.

If you're lucky, you'll spot some of the bats that live in the cave.

No matter what the temperature outside, it's always fifty-two degrees inside the cave, so bring a jacket in summertime. Some children are initially scared by the dark and the idea of being underground; however, most become more comfortable as they get involved in spotting the formations

Cave Exploration Woodward

Cave and Penn's Cave may get most of the attention, but Central Pennsylvania actually has hundreds of fascinating caves and caverns. If you're interested in doing some cave exploring that's a bit off the beaten path, contact the Nittany Grotto, headquartered in State College. This group of enthusiastic cave explorers encourages safe and responsible cave exploring. Its members are pleased to arrange Beginner Trips. In order to take advantage of this service, families may be asked to join the group at a cost of $10.00 a year. For more information contact the group at (814) 238-2057 or check out the organization's Web site at www.clubs.psu.edu/nittanygrotto.

and enjoying the colored lights. According to tour guides, the temperament of the child is more of a factor than age.

But there's more to Penn's Cave than the cave. There's also 1,000 acres with an operating farm and a wildlife sanctuary with elk, mountain lions, deer, wolves, and mustangs. Professional guides take you through the park in four-wheel-drive vehicles, pointing out animals and telling about their habits. Tours last about one and a half hours. The sanctuary is open daily March through November. Call ahead for rates and reservations.

In September Penn's Cave is also the site of the Nittany Antique Machinery annual show. Model trains, tractor parades, demonstrations of antique machinery, toy tractors, and a children's pedal pull are among the attractions.

A Paulsen Family Adventure

We weren't sure how eighteen-month-old Eli would react to being in a small boat, let alone how he would like being in a cave. But at Penn's Cave, the country's only water-filled cave, we got to try both.

There was just one other family and a couple on the tour with us. The other children were about eight and ten—the perfect age for looking for bats and spooking each other. Eli, on the other hand, wasn't so sure about this darkness stuff. He whimpered a bit as the driver pushed off from the dock.

He squirmed out of my lap and into my husband's, then back to mine, as if searching for a place where he might feel safe. I wondered to myself if they've ever had to turn a boat back when a child got scared of the dark.

Once the light show started, Eli started to calm down. He wasn't exactly enjoying himself, but he wasn't complaining either.

At the end of the cave, the driver gave us the option to pull out onto the lake that borders the Penn's Cave Wildlife Sanctuary. Even though it was drizzling, the group gave unanimous approval. As we pulled into the daylight, Eli perked up. At the sight of a group of very ordinary ducks, his eyes lit up, and he pointed and started making quacking sounds. He smiled and laughed.

Even though we were outside maybe five minutes, that glimpse of the the ducks and the daylight was all he needed to reassure him as we headed back into the cave. On the way back, he stayed interested, turning around to see what the guide was talking about. I guess the dark isn't so intimidating once you know it's not forever.

WOODWARD CAVE AND CAMPGROUND (ages 4 and up)

Route 45, Woodward; (814) 349–9800; www.woodwardcave.com. Open daily 9:00 A.M. to 7:00 P.M. in summer, 10:00 A.M. to 5:00 P.M. in spring and fall. Admission is $$$ for adults, $$ for seniors and children 2 to 12, and Free *for children under 2.*

If Penn's Cave has whet your appetite for spelunking, head back to Route 45 and continue east to Woodward Cave and Campground, one of the largest caverns in Pennsylvania. A sixty-minute tour takes you through the five rooms of the cavern, each filled with rock formations. The Hanging Forest features a large collection of stalactites. In the Hall of Statues, see one of the largest stalagmites in the United States: the Tower of Babel. If you're planning to camp in the area, inquire about the nineteen-acre campground with sites for tents as well as RVs. Cabin rentals are also available.

Bellefonte

About 12 miles north of State College on Route 26, Bellefonte is the county seat for Centre County. This lovely Victorian town celebrated its bicentennial in 1996, and things are hopping still. A new museum, a restored theater, and several festivals have been added to the list of attractions for families.

With a historic district of more than 300 buildings, taking a walking tour through this town is like taking a walk back in time. Pick up a copy of *Historical Walking Tour of Bellefonte,* a brochure you'll find at the train station on High Street. The town is especially beautiful when decked out for a Victorian Christmas each December (call 814-353-8074 or check www.bellefonte.com for more information).

BELLEFONTE MUSEUM FOR CENTRE COUNTY (ages 5 and up)

Allegheny Street; (814) 353–1473; www.bellefonte.org/museum. Open year-round. Admission charged. Call for schedule and rates.

An innovative new museum, the Bellefonte launched well before it recently found a home in one of the town's historic buildings. The goal of the museum is to promote appreciation of the area's heritage, especially among children. The hard-working volunteer staff visits schools and has set up exhibits around town.

The museum is now housed in the historic Linn House, donated to the town by the Omega Bank next door. The exhibits change at least three times per year and are designed for both children and adults.

This museum is not only great fun for kids, it's a fount of information and inspiring ideas for parents and others who might want to start something similar in their own communities.

BELLEFONTE HISTORICAL RAILROAD (all ages)

Train Station, High Street; (814) 355–0311. Various excursions throughout the year, mostly on weekends. Call for schedules and prices.

When you're tired of walking, climb aboard one of the rail excursions offered by the Bellefonte Historical Railroad. The train station is located across the High Street Bridge. On weekends from Memorial Day to Labor Day, the railroad offers trips to Curtin Village, Sayers Dam (a nice place for a picnic), the town of Lemont, or the gliderport at Julian. In fall the route takes you to Bald Eagle Ridge, aflame with autumn leaves. The Santa Claus Express in December features a visit from you-know-who. Other excursions are offered throughout the year.

EAGLE IRON WORKS AND CURTIN VILLAGE (ages 4 and up)

Route 150, 2 miles north of Route 80; (814) 355–1982. Open weekends in May, September, and October; daily during summer. It is also open in mid-December for Christmas at Curtin. Call for current hours and rates.

Heading north on Route 150 from Bellefonte, stop off at Eagle Iron Works and Curtin Village, a historic site that gives a glimpse of life in the 1800s. There's a restored iron furnace, the iron master's mansion, and a worker's log cabin. Throughout the year the museum holds special events, including craft shows, Civil War encampments, and antique tool demonstrations.

***B*ellefonte Festivals** The Victorian Christmas is the biggest festival in Bellefonte's schedule, but there are several more that are worth checking out. In mid-May come for the Big Spring Festival, which celebrates the spring that supplies the town with water. For more information and this year's schedule, call (800) 355–1705.

In June the streets of Bellefonte fill with antique and vintage automobiles as the town re-creates a Historic Cruise, that lapping-the-block ritual favored by teens in the 1950s. For more information contact Historic Bellefonte at (814) 355–3692. August brings the annual Bellefonte Arts and Crafts fair, with area craftspeople exhibiting and selling their creations and with special events for children. Once again, Historic Bellefonte organizes this annual event.

GARMAN OPERA HOUSE (ages 4 and up)

Across the street from the County Court House; (814) 355–7884. Call for schedule and ticket prices.

Recently restored, this former vaudeville house now offers live theater, concerts, and other events, including performances for families and children.

Where to Eat

IN THE WILLIAMSPORT AREA

Bonanza Steak House, *1503 East Third Street; (570) 326–7114.*

Chi-Chi's Mexican Restaurant, *2502 East Third Street; (570) 321–9208.*

Heavenly Pasteria, *135 West Third Street; (570) 327–9035.* Casual Italian food. Children's portions of pasta and pizza.

Hoss's Steak and Sea House, *1954 East Third Street; (570) 326–0838.*

Manhattan Bagel, *1790 East Third Street; (570) 322–4500; e-mail: yrgyo3@prodigy.com.*

Olive Garden, *1825 East Third Street; (570) 321–9250.*

Peter Herdic House, *407 West Fourth Street; (570) 322–0165.* A little more formal but family-oriented, offering a variety of traditional meats, seafood, pasta, and salad.

Red Lobster, *1951 East Third Street; (570) 323–0423.*

Vinnie's Italian Eatery, *44 West Fourth Street; (570) 326–1998.*

IN STATE COLLEGE

Backstage at Michael's, *240 South Pugh Street; (570) 238–8454.* Breakfast and family dinner daily.

Chili's Grill & Bar, *139 South Allen Street; (570) 234–5922.* Mexican fare.

The Tavern Restaurant, *220 East College Street; (570) 238–6116.* Offers a variety of steaks, seafood, chicken, and salads. Children's menu has chicken nuggets, burgers, etc. and side dishes. Relaxed atmosphere.

Whistle Stop Restaurant, *Pennsylvania Avenue; (570) 364–2544.* "Meat and potatoes and nothin' fancy." Children's menu.

Where to Stay

IN THE WILLIAMSPORT AREA

Genetti Hotel, *200 West Fourth Street, Williamsport; (717) 326–6600 or (800) 321–1388.* Located in downtown Williamsport, this full-service historic hotel offers suites as well as standard guest rooms. An on-site pool and restaurant make it a good choice for families.

Holiday Inn & T.G.I.Friday's Complex, *1840 East Third Street, Williamsport; (717) 326–1981 or (800) 36–WILPA; www. holiday-wilpa.com.* This hotel complex offers some great features for families—an outdoor pool, Free Disney channel, on-site restaurants—plus kids stay and eat Free. In summer a "Poolside King Room" may be the best choice for families. Features include a king-size bed plus pull-out sofa just steps from the pool.

Sheraton Inn, *100 Pine Street, Williamsport; (800) 325–3535 or (717) 327–8231.* The Sheraton has two clinchers that make this hotel a hit with kids: an indoor pool and Nintendo-equipped televisions. And the hotel's kids-eat-Free policy at the on-site restaurant makes it a hit with parents, too.

IN THE LEWISBURG AREA

B/W Country Cupboard Inn, *Route 15 North, Lewisburg; (717) 524–5500.* Hotel, restaurant, and gift shop all in one complex.

Days Inn–Lewisburg, *Route 15, Lewisburg; (717) 523–1171.* Perkins Family Restaurant on premises.

IN THE STATE COLLEGE AREA

Many of the major hotel/motel and restaurant chains have facilities in and near State College. Here are a few to check out:

Bellefonte/State College KOA Campground, *2481 Jacksonville Road, Bellefonte ; (814) 355–7912 or (800) KOA–8127.* Full-service campground with cabin rentals available.

Best Western State College Inn, *1663 South Atherton Street, Business Route 322, State College; (814) 237–8005 or (800) 635–1177.* Breakfast is included, and there is a twenty-four-hour restaurant on premises.

Courtyard by Marriott, *1730 University Drive, State College; (814) 238–1881.* An indoor pool, suites, and an on-site restaurant make this a good choice for families.

Days Inn Penn State, *240 South Pugh Street, State College; (814) 238–8454 or (800) 258–DAYS.* Just blocks from campus, the Days Inn has on-site parking, a restaurant/sports bar, and an indoor pool. Continental breakfast is included.

Holiday Inn State College, *1450 South Atherton, State College; (814) 238–3001 or (800) HOLIDAY.* Two outdoor swimming pools make this an especially good choice in the summer.

The Nittany Lion Inn, *200 West Park Avenue, State College; (814) 231–7500 or (800) 233–7505.* Colonial-style inn on the Penn State campus.

For More Information

Bellefonte Tourism Commission, c/o *Chamber of Commerce, Train Station, Bellefonte 16823; (814) 355–2917; www.bellefonte.com.* Call ahead for recommendations on accommodations, train schedules, and other events in the area.

Centre County Lion Country Visitors and Convention Bureau, *1402 South Atherton Street, State College 16801; (814) 231–1400 or (800) 358–5466.* Pick up a **Free** visitors guide and campus map at one of the many information booths on campus or at the Lion Country Convention and Visitors Bureau. Call ahead for lists of restaurants, hotels, bed-and-breakfasts, events, and attractions.

Columbia-Montour Tourist Promotion Agency, *121 Papermill Road, Bloomsburg 17815; (800) 847–4810 or (570) 784–8279.* Call for more information about accommodations, restaurants, and the twenty-four covered bridges in the area.

Lycoming County Tourist Promotion Agency, *454 Pine Street, Williamsport 17701; (800) 358–9900 or (570) 326–1971; www.williamsport.org.* Call or write for more information about things to do and see in Williamsport, as well as a list of restaurants, motels, and other accommodations.

Perry County Tourist and Recreation Bureau, *Courthouse Center Square, P.O. Box 447, New Bloomfield 19068; (717) 582–2131.* Call ahead for lists of campgrounds, restaurants, and other accommodations in the area.

Susquehanna Valley Visitors Bureau, *219D Hafer Road, Lewisburg 17837; (800) 525–7320 or (570) 524–7234.* Call for more information about attractions, accommodations, and upcoming events in Northumberland, Snyder, and Union Counties.

Pennsylvania's Northern Tier

Pennsylvania has the largest rural population in the country. That means there are more people living in towns of fewer than 2,500 people here than in any other state in the country. Although all of the regions covered in this book have many towns that meet that description, along Pennsylvania's Northern Tier, it's hard to find towns that don't. There are large stretches of this region that remain wilderness—and provide wonderful opportunities for camping, boating, hiking, skiing, and more.

Scenic Route 6 traverses the Northern Tier of Pennsylvania, passing some of the region's best-loved sights and towns. For information about scenic Route 6, call 1-87-PAROUTE6 or check the Web site www.pa route6.com. Pine Creek Gorge, billed as Pennsylvania's Grand Canyon, is a spectacular achievement of nature. Allegheny National Forest is one of only fifteen

Faith & Emily's
Favorite Attractions in Pennsylvania's Northern Tier

1. Pine Creek Gorge, Ansonia

2. Ole Bull State Park, Cross Fork

3. Crook Farm and Country Fair, Bradford

4. Knox Cane Railroad, Marienville

5. exPERIEence Children's Museum, Erie

6. *Appledore* Cruises, Erie

7. Heart's Content National Natural Landmark, Warren

8. Cook Forest Sawmill Center for the Arts, Cooksburg

9. Presque Isle State Park, Erie

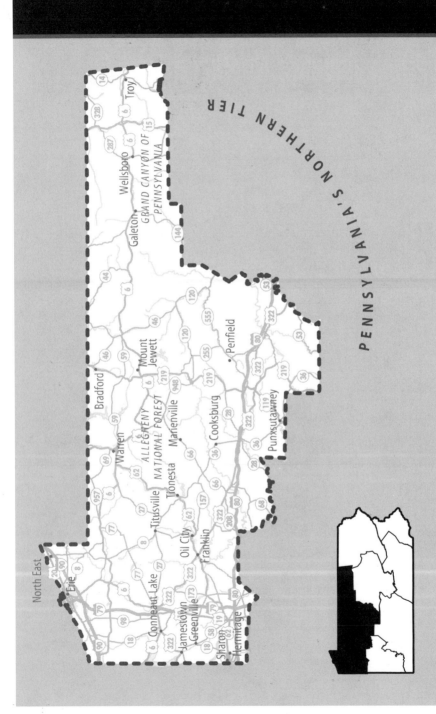

PENNSYLVANIA'S NORTHERN TIER

national forests in the eastern United States and harbors some of the last remaining virgin stands of northern hardwoods left in the East.

This is a big area. Our advice would be to keep your ambitions within limits. Pick a state park, a town, or a sight that interests you most, and build your vacation around it. Try to see more than a portion of this region, and you'll spend more time in the car than enjoying its many offerings. You can always come back to see more at another time.

Faith & Emily's
Favorite Events in Pennsylvania's Northern Tier

- **Bobsled Festival** in Wellsboro (February); (570) 724-1926.
- **Teddy Bear Weekend** in Cooksburg (end of July); (570) 744-9670.
- **We Love Erie Days** in Erie (August); (570) 454-7191.
- **Fabulous 1890s weekend** in Mansfield (end of September); (570) 662-3442.

Troy

We start our tour of Pennsylvania's Northern Tier in the town of Troy, located on Route 6 just west of the Susquehanna River.

BRADFORD COUNTY HERITAGE MUSEUM (all ages)

Route 14 North, ½-mile from Troy; (570) 297–3410 or (570) 297–3405 during the off-season; www.pavisnet.com/troy/farmmuseum. Open late April through October, Friday to Monday and holidays 10:00 A.M. to 4:00 P.M. Admission is $; children under 6 are **Free**.

Young and old alike will enjoy "The Farm Museum," established by the Bradford County Heritage Association on the Troy Fairgrounds. Local resident and dairy farmer Wilmer Wilcox's impressive collection of farm antiques is on display. The displays work together to tell the story of rural farm life in Bradford County. There's a kitchen and antique clothing and an old country store. The association has recently begun work to restore the oldest house in Troy Township, built in 1822, adjacent to the current museum. Formerly an inn on the stagecoach route, it houses period furniture, glassware, and antique toys and clothing. Portions of this house are open for tours.

During the Fall Carriage, Wagon, and Sleigh Festival in mid-September, children six and older enjoy the flax demonstration, blacksmithing, carpentry, tinsmithing, and stories of how chores were done in the past—from butter making with a dog-treadle butter churn to laundry with washboards and wringers. Throughout the season the heritage gardens display heirloom varieties of vegetables, plants used to make dyes, herbs, and perennials.

The museum is open daily during the Troy Fair, a typical country fair with farm animals, agricultural displays, and amusements, which has usually been held each year, for more than one hundred years, toward the end of July. For more information about the Troy Fair, call (570) 297-3648.

Wellsboro Area

Located on scenic Route 6 in Tioga County, Wellsboro is an ideal base for adventures in Pine Creek Gorge, Pennsylvania's Grand Canyon. Forty-seven miles long with a maximum cliff height of 1,450 feet, this majestic canyon is surrounded by four state parks and hundreds of thousands of wilderness acres to explore by boat, foot, horseback, snowmobile, cross-country skis, mountain bike, and more. For information check www.visittiogapa.com.

COLTON POINT STATE PARK (ages 8 and up)

Five miles south of Route 6 at Ansonia; (570) 724–3061; www.dcnr.state.pa. us/stateparks/parks/leon.htm. Open year-round.

Perhaps the easiest way to get a glimpse of the **Pine Creek Gorge** is to head south from Route 6 at Ansonia. There's a sign there that directs you to the park. The drive follows the rim, with short trails that lead to views over the canyon. Although there are guard rails at official overlooks, make sure children don't run ahead or rough-house near the edge.

In addition to great views, Colton Point offers family camping, hiking trails, snowmobiling, and picnic areas. Most of the trails involve steep terrain and are recommended for experienced hikers aged eight and up.

LEONARD HARRISON STATE PARK (ages 8 and up)

Route 660, 10 miles west of Wellsboro; (570) 724–3061; www.dcnr.state.pa.us/ stateparks/parks/leon.htm. Open year-round.

Leonard Harrison State Park is on the east rim of the canyon. It offers one of the best views of the canyon anywhere. Stop at the visitors center to learn about the history of the canyon. Camping is available, and there are hiking trails of varying length and difficulty. Experienced family hikers (ages eight and up) won't want to miss the Turkey Path, a steep, 1-mile journey that takes you from the rim of the canyon down to Pine Creek.

Festivals Sponsored by Greater Mansfield Chamber of Commerce

Home to Mansfield University, part of the Pennsylvania state university system, the town of Mansfield hosts a series of events and festivals throughout the year. Call (570) 662–3442 or check www. mansfield.org for more information. The town and university team up to host two great festivals in September: the Northern Appalachian Storytelling Festival and the Fabulous 1890s weekend. The first attracts storytellers and enthusiasts from across the country. The second commemorates the first night football game, in which Mansfield University played Wyoming Seminary on September 28, 1892. The entire Mansfield community comes out to celebrate with a motorless parade, a balloon rally, a football reenactment, and fireworks.

PINE CREEK TRAIL (all ages)

Trailheads at Route 6 in Ansonia and at Route 414 in Blackwell. Open year-round. Bathrooms at trailheads. Call (570) 724–3061.

In an ongoing rails-to-trails project, 22 miles of the abandoned Conrail Railway along Pine Creek have been converted into a trail for hiking, biking, horseback riding, and other nonmotorized transportation. The relatively flat, groomed trail is wonderful for family hiking. The trail is handicapped accessible and perfect for all-terrain strollers. The less strenuous Ansonia access is recommended for families.

If you'd like to tour Pine Creek Trail on a covered wagon, call Mountain Trail Canyon Wagon Rides (570) 376–5561 or (877) 376–5561.

PINE CREEK OUTFITTERS (ages 6 and up)

RR4, Box 130B, Wellsboro 16901; (570) 724–3003; www.pinecrk.com.

Whether you're looking for trail maps, equipment rentals, shuttles to trailheads, camping permits, guide service, or you-name-it, the folks at Pine Creek Outfitters are the ones to talk to. From kayaking to canoeing, biking to hiking, if they can't provide it themselves, they'll point you in the right direction. For families with young children, they particularly recommend their Upper Pine half-day trip, which navigates a calm section of the creek. There is no minimum age on this trip; others have a minimum age of seven. Pine Creek also rents bikes. When you're planning your trip, send for the current edition of the *Outdoor Adventure Guide for Pennsylvania's Grand Canyon,* published by Pine Creek Outfitters.

A Paulsen Family Adventure Pine Creek Canyon is often called Pennsylvania's Grand Canyon. It is a sight to behold almost any time of the year. But if you're not a hunter, it's probably not a good idea to visit the Monday after Thanksgiving, the first day of deer season in Pennsylvania.

We made that mistake when Eli was just six months old. We were returning home from the holiday with my husband's family in Ohio. It seemed a shame to let a little thing like the first day of hunting season get in the way of doing some research for this book.

Although there were few hunters in Colton Point State Park, we could hear the rifles in the distance. We wanted to check out each of the overlooks, but we didn't want to spend much time out in the open. "Wow, that's beautiful," I said. "Now let's get back in the car!"

TIOGA TRAIL RIDES (ages 8 and up)

RD 106, Route 105; (570) 724–6592; www.pavisnet.com/ttr/.

Tioga Trail Rides offers western riding on day rides or overnight trips. Children without experience must be at least twelve years old; younger children are allowed on shorter rides if they can control their horses and have an inseam of at least 21 inches (gotta be able to reach the stirrups!). Sunset and supper rides are also available. During winter Tioga Trail Rides offers bobsled rides.

MOUNTAIN TRAIL HORSE CENTER (ages 8 and up)

Wellsboro; (570) 376–5561; www.mountaintrailhorse.com; e-mail: maier@epix.net. Open spring, summer, and fall.

Mountain Trail Horse Center offers a wide variety of horseback rides designed as wilderness adventure. Covered-wagon rides are good for families of varying ages and abilities. There's no age minimum on the rides through the gorge. During the twice-yearly Family Vacation Horseback Adventures, the minimum age for overnight trips is dropped to eight (from the usual twelve). Longer trips are available. Rates go down per person with groups of more than four people.

STORMS HORSE DRAWN RIDES (all ages)

RD 4, Box 1031, Little Marsh; (570) 376–3481; www.stormshorsedrawnrides. com. Open spring through fall. Groups of ten to twelve people or more.

Scenic views, a comfortable horse-drawn wagon, home cooking over a campfire—this is a backcountry adventure with style!

TIOGA CENTRAL RAILROAD (all ages)

P.O. Box 269, Wellsboro 16901; (570) 724–0990. Various rates.

Take the 24-mile round-trip excursion from the station near Wellsboro to the north end of Hammond Lake, near the New York State border. The trip takes about an hour and twenty minutes and runs three times a day on weekends.

Wellsboro Festivals Wellsboro has several top-notch festivals and fairs throughout the year. Check out the Bobsled Festival and Winter Weekend in February, the Pennsylvania State Laurel Festival in June, and the Canyon Country Blue Grass Festival in July.

ALSO IN THE AREA

Hills Creek State Park, *East of Wellsboro; (570) 724–4246; www.dcnr.state.pa.us/ stateparks/parks/hillscreek.htm.* One hundred ten campsites, cabins available, 137-acre lake.

Little Pine State Park, *Waterville; (570) 753–8209.* One hundred four campsites; ninety-four-acre lake; hiking, biking, and cross-country ski trails; nature programs and swimming in summer.

Galeton Area

Home of the Pennsylvania Lumber Museum and headquarters for four state parks, Galeton has a full roster of events and activities for families.

PENNSYLVANIA LUMBER MUSEUM (ages 6 and up)

5660 US 6 West, P.O. Box 239, Galeton 16922; 12 miles west of Galeton; (814) 435–2652; www.lumbermuseum.org. Open daily April through November

9:00 A.M. to 5:00 P.M. Closed major holidays. Admission is $; children under 6 are **Free**.

From Wellsboro head west on Route 6 to the Galeton area to enjoy a visit to the Pennsylvania Lumber Museum. Antique tools and other logging artifacts tell the story of this area's logging history. Tour a real logging camp and sawmill. A restored Barnhart Log Loader has been added to the display. The museum is the site for several unusual special events throughout the year, including the Bark Peeler's Convention the weekend closest to July 4th.

LYMAN RUN STATE PARK (all ages)

RR 1, Box 136, Galeton; (814) 435–5010. Open year-round.

Lyman Run acts as the headquarters for three other state parks in the area: Cherry Springs, Patterson, and Prouty Place. Lyman Run offers trout fishing, ice fishing, swimming, and camping. Cherry Springs has picnic areas, hiking trails, hunting, snowmobile trails, and a campground. It's also the site of the Woodsmen's Carnival in early August. Patterson State Park offers picnicking, hiking, and camping. Prouty Place State Park is known for its picnic areas, cold-water fishing, hiking, and camping.

OLE BULL STATE PARK (all ages)

Off Route 144, Cross Fork; (814) 435–5000 or (888) PA–PARKS for reservations. Open year-round.

About 20 miles south of Galeton is the Lodge at Ole Bull State Park, voted by *Condé Nast Traveler* magazine as Pennsylvania's top getaway. The lodge is actually a three-bedroom log cabin built by the Civilian Conservation Corps in the 1930s. It sleeps ten comfortably and is well equipped with everything you need for a woodsy adventure. It even has a playground out back for the kids. The first floor is handicapped accessible. Book your reservations early (up to eleven months in advance). This is the kind of place where people come back each year. (Best bets: February and March, says Mary Herrold, park manager. You can book the lodge for as few as two nights and as many as fourteen, and the cross-country skiing is great.)

Even if you're not lucky enough to book a week at the lodge, Ole Bull is still a great place for a family adventure. There are eighty-one tent and trailer sites along Kettle Creek, some with electrical hookups. Swimming, hiking, fishing, and biking also are all available in the secluded

125-acre park. During summer weekends there's a full schedule of environmental education programs.

Penfield

PARKER DAM STATE PARK and S. B. ELLIOT STATE PARK (all ages)

Off Route 153, Penfield; (814) 765–0630 or (888) PA–PARKS for reservations; www.dcnr.state.pa.us/stateparks/. Open year-round.

There are some great family programs available at Parker Dam State Park and S. B. Elliot State Park. Parker Dam offers a variety of naturalist programs for families, starting with maple sugar weekends in March all the way through apple cider Sundays in October. During summer there are bat programs, evening campfire talks on the weekends, and even a guided trip to see the elk herd. In summer you can swim in the twenty-acre lake.

The camping here is class A, which means hot showers are available. There are also rustic log-frame and stone cabins available for rent year-round. There's no running water in the cabins, but there's a separate building with showers. A big fireplace supplies the heat, and you can cook with an electric stove and refrigerator.

S. B. Elliot State Park offers a quieter setting on top of a hill. There are six cabins here and some class B campsites, but no flush toilets or showers.

Bradford

PENN-BRAD OIL MUSEUM (ages 6 and up)

Route 219; (814) 362–5984; http://bradford-online.com/pennbrad. Open daily Memorial Day through Labor Day. Monday through Saturday 10:00 A.M. to 4:00 P.M. and Sunday noon to 5:00 P.M. Admission is $$ for adults and $ for seniors; children under 12 are Free.

Just as eastern Pennsylvania has coal, the northwestern part of the state is oil country. This museum traces the state's involvement in oil drilling and includes a working example of the 1890s-style wooden oil rig that once dotted the countryside.

Sights of St. Marys

Sights of St. Marys From Bradford head south on 219 into Elk County, home of one of the two free-roaming elk herds east of the Mississippi—and the only one in Pennsylvania, now numbering more than 700. One of the best places to spot the herd is near the airport in St. Marys. The Dent's Run viewing area is located near the town of Benezette, near Elk State Forest on Route 555. Early morning or late afternoon are the best times to see them. For information check the Web site www.pagreat outdoors.com. Remember, feeding the elk is against the law.

For up-to-date information on elk sightings, stop by the Benezette Store & Restaurant on Route 555 (814-787-7456).

CROOK FARM AND COUNTRY FAIR (all ages)

Route 219, third exit north of Bradford; (814) 368–9370. Open Tuesday through Friday afternoons during May through September and various times throughout the year. Call ahead for hours and admission prices.

The Crook Farm is a collection of restored buildings from the 1800s, including a farmhouse, a one-room schoolhouse, barn, herb garden, tool house, train depot, and outbuildings. At the end of August, join the celebration at the Crook Farm Country Fair with crafts, food, entertainment, and special events for children.

ZIPPO/CASE VISITOR CENTER (ages 6 and up)

1932 Zippo Drive, off Route 219; (888) 442–1932; www.zippo.com and www.wrcase.com. Open Monday through Saturday 9:00 A.M. to 5:00 P.M. and Sunday noon to 4:00 P.M. Admission is Free.

Here's something you don't see every day: a collection of antique and rare Zippo lighters and cases. For the uninitiated, Zippo Manufacturing has been making "windproof" lighters with a lifetime guarantee since 1932. The company also makes steel tape measures, knives, money clips, pens, and key holders. Zippo products are popular among collectors, with swap meets and collector's clubs around the world. The Zippo/Case Visitor Center is the most-visited museum in Pennsylvania's Northern Tier.

In 1996 the museum was expanded into a 15,000-square-foot facility with more than 2,000 Zippo products on display. New exhibits include "ZAC" (the Zippo/Case audio kinetic sculpture) and a 14-foot flag made entirely of Zippo lighters. Definitely not just another roadside attraction.

ALSO IN THE AREA

Holgate Toy Store and Museum (all ages), *Wetmore Avenue, Kane; (814) 837–7600.* Open daily year-round. Windows and a video allow you to see toys being made at the toy factory. Kids love the trolley cars based on Mr. Rogers's Village of Make-Believe.

Allegheny Arms and Armor Museum (ages 5 and up), *Route 46, Smethport; (814) 362–2642.* Call for hours and admission prices. Handicapped accessible. Kids love this military museum with its changing displays of helicopters, tanks, vehicles, armor, and more. "Living History Days," during the third week in June, offers the chance to see actual encampments and reenacted battles.

Warren

ALLEGHENY NATIONAL FOREST (all ages)

P.O. Box 847, 222 Liberty Street; (814) 726–5150; www.pavisnet.com/ alleghenynationalforest/ or www.fs.fed.us/r9/allegheny/. Open year-round.

With more than a half million acres, there's room for many a family adventure within the boundaries of Allegheny National Forest, the only national forest in Pennsylvania.

You will find a working forest when you visit the Allegheny. Congress mandates that national forests be managed for a variety of uses, using techniques that ensure future generations will be able to enjoy the benefits of these lands. Recreation, wood production, and wildlife habitat improvements are just some of the many activities going on in Allegheny National Forest.

Several towns act as good bases for explorations of the forest, including Warren, Marienville, Bradford, Ridgway, Tionesta, and Kane. Warren serves as the headquarters for the park, but there are information centers in Marienville, Ridgway, and Marshburg. Before planning your trip, be sure to get a copy of the 𝐅𝐫𝐞𝐞 Outdoor Recreation Map of the Allegheny National Forest Region, available at tourist information centers or by calling ahead. It displays the small roads of the forest much more clearly than most road maps.

The forest has just about everything a family adventurer looks for: camping (developed and backwoods), fishing, hiking, ATV trails, horseback riding, snowmobiling, cross-country skiing, and hunting. There are nearly 200 miles of trails, 700 miles of streams, two Wild and Scenic Rivers, and several lakes and reservoirs within the forest.

A Paulsen Family Adventure

A Paulsen Family Adventure What do you do with a baby on a trip to a place like Allegheny National Forest? Well, lots of things. My husband and I have realized that, although having a child changes many aspects of our lives and our travel habits, there are still a lot of outdoor activities and adventures we can include Eli in.

Hiking: We started hiking with Eli soon after he was born. We put him in a front pack facing out. He insisted on this fairly early on, even if it meant we had to hold his head up for him. Most of the time, he would fall asleep fairly quickly. But at the Heart's Content section of the Allegheny National Forest, he stayed awake for a 2-mile hike through the old growth forest. He seemed aware that it was a rare treat to see trees hundreds of years old.

Cross-country skiing: By the time Eli was nine months old, he graduated from the front pack to the back pack. We bought a top-of-the-line model with all sorts of straps and supports. Snapped into the pack, Eli accompanied us not only on hikes, but also cross-country ski trips. We made sure he was dressed very warmly, and we didn't stay out as long as we did without him, but he loved getting outside, even on a winter's day. As Martin headed down a gentle slope, Eli said "WEEEE" and clapped his hands in the air.

Driving long distances: Lots of people dread taking their kids on long car trips, but (knock on wood) so far so good. Our secret: get on the road early; I mean really early. We usually take off on a long trip by 4:30 in the morning. We just move Eli from his bed to the car seat. Although he wakes up for a bit, he's usually back to sleep within a half hour and stays asleep until 6:30 or 7:00. Entertain him for an hour, and we've done half of a six-hour drive before stopping for breakfast.

But if you only have a few hours to explore the park, head to **Heart's Content,** a National Natural Landmark that harbors one of the last stands of old-growth forest in the eastern United States. The turnoff from Route 62 is easy to miss (it's just before the bridge to Tidioute). Stop at the Tidioute Overlook, where an easy path leads to two vistas over the river gorge. Look carefully; it's not unusual to see a bald eagle circling over the river. At Heart's Content, there's a 1-mile interpretive trail. White pines and hemlocks that are hundreds of years old reach high into the sky.

Although no motorized vehicles are allowed in the old-growth forest, there are several excellent scenic drives through other parts of the forest.

Route 62 follows the Allegheny River from Tionesta to Warren; the Allegheny Reservoir Scenic Drive circles the large lake formed by the Kinzua Dam, and the Longhouse Scenic Drive starts at the Kinzua Dam and includes other area highlights.

Marienville

KNOX KANE RAILROAD (all ages)

P.O. Box 422, Route 66; (814) 927–6621. Various schedules June through October. Rides cost $$$$ for adults; $$$ for children 3 through 12.

One way to enjoy the beauty of the forest without expending too much energy is a ride on the Knox Kane Railroad. But just because you aren't hiking or biking doesn't mean you're not going to have an adventure on this 96-mile ride from Marienville to Kinzua Bridge and back. The train is pulled either by a diesel engine or a steam locomotive. If you're lucky enough to ride when the steam engine is used, don't sit in the open-air car unless you don't mind water and soot from the stack ending up on you. Riders have a thirty- to forty-minute break to picnic or walk around while the engine is switched to the opposite end for the return trip.

Mount Jewett

KINZUA BRIDGE STATE PARK (all ages)

Off Route 6, Ormsby Road, Mount Jewett; (814) 965–2646. Open year-round.

Even if you can't take the Knox Kane Railroad, stop at the state park and take a look at the bridge. It's an engineering feat that will take your breath away. The brave can walk across the bridge. Others can just gawk from the overlook.

Tionesta

FLYING W RANCH (all ages)

Tionesta; (814) 463–7663. Children must be 4 feet, 6 inches tall.

Another highlight of the Allegheny National Forest is the Flying W Ranch, west of Marienville in Tionesta. This 500-acre working ranch sits within the boundaries of the national forest and offers countless opportunities for adventure. Spend an hour or a week here taking western riding lessons, canoeing on the Allegheny River, hiking, fishing, and more. In July come for the professional Allegheny Mountain Championship Rodeo. For a real adventure go on one of the overnight horseback trips into the national forest.

Accommodations range from bunkhouses to cabins, or you can bring your RV and hook up at the campground. In summer the ranch offers a western riding camp for children ages nine through sixteen.

Cooksburg

Not only does this area harbor one of the largest stands of virgin hemlock and pine forests in the East, it is also home to a thriving arts center. The combination is unbeatable for a family vacation.

COOK FOREST SAWMILL CENTER FOR THE ARTS (ages 6 and up)

Breezemont Drive; (814) 744–9670 (year-round) or (814) 927–6655 (May through October); www.sawmill.org. Open summer and fall. Admission Free. *Ticket prices for live theater and special events and fees for classes vary.*

Cook Forest Sawmill Center for the Arts has two buildings full of crafts, art and craft classes, various special events, and more. (Site I, which offers crafts, is open only in the summer.) Festivals include a Herb Festival in June, Wood Competition and Show in July, Forest Fest and Quilt Show in August, and Dulcimer and Folk Music Gathering in September. In the summer, children ages six to twelve can participate in a morning arts program. There's also Creative HeARTS, for the mentally and physically challenged, and a young people's drama workshop and dance camp.

COOK FOREST STATE PARK (all ages)

Exit 8, 9, or 13 off I–80 (P.O. Box 120); (814) 744–8407; www.dcnr.state. pa.us

Named one of the nation's top fifty parks, Cook Forest contains one of the last remaining old-growth forests of 200- to 350-year-old white pine and hemlock that reach 200 feet into the sky. At the Log Cabin Inn Visitor's Center, check out the Historical Room, which displays logging and rafting tools as well as models and other artifacts of the logging industry.

There are 27 miles of trails that are wonderful for hiking, cross-country skiing, and more. Many of the trails are less than a mile in length—a distance that's just right for little hikers. During the summer season nature programs are offered on Friday and Saturday nights, and guided walks are conducted regularly. The easy-flowing Clarion River is a great way to introduce yourself and your family to tubing or canoeing.

The twenty-four rustic cabins in the forest are a popular vacation option. The cabins are grouped in two areas. There are eleven small, one-room cabins in the Indian area, located by the park office and near the accessible fishing pier. Flush toilet and shower facilities are nearby. The thirteen River cabins are located on a hillside overlooking the Clarion River. Twelve of these are some of the largest models built by the CCC, with a living room, kitchen, and two bedrooms. Recently the park has completed work on two cabins to make the doors and kitchen appliances accessible to people in wheelchairs. Another bonus of these larger cabins: cold running water. But you'll still have to use the composting toilets.

PINE CREST CABINS (all ages)

Cook Forest; (814) 752–2200.

For families who want to combine horseback riding with their vacation, one of the best choices is Pine Crest Cabins. Don't let the name fool you: There is a campground on the property as well as stables. There are also canoes, go-carts, bumper boats, and long-putt golf—all on a seventy-five-acre family-oriented resort. More than half of the land has been preserved in its natural state and provides great hiking territory for families. Log cabins sleep eight to ten people and have indoor and outdoor fireplaces and two or three bedrooms.

DOUBLE DIAMOND DEER RANCH (all ages)

Route 36, south of Cook Forest; (814) 752–6334; www.usachoice.net/dddr. Open year-round. Call for current hours and admission prices.

If you want to see your wildlife up a little closer, check out the Double Diamond Deer Ranch, near the entrance to the state park on Route 36 South. Here a herd of twenty-five deer have been raised since birth. The deer are tame, so they'll come right up and greet you, eat from your hand, and enjoy a good scratch behind the ears. Fawns are born each spring, and during June through August they are bottle-fed. Children are welcome to hold the bottles. A new Whitetail and Wildlife Education

Center offers a chance to learn about the animals you've seen in the woods.

Punxsutawney

On Groundhog Day each year, the world focuses its attention on the little town of Punxsutawney and on a groundhog named Phil. If he climbs out of his burrow on Gobbler's Knob and sees his shadow, the story goes, winter will be sticking around for a while longer. Phil's an old hand at this prediction stuff: He (or his ancestors) has been doing it every year since February 2, 1887.

PUNXSUTAWNEY GROUNDHOG ZOO (all ages)

124 West Mahoning Street; (800) 752–PHIL; www.groundhog.org or www.penn. com/punxsycc. Open year-round. Admission Free.

You don't have to wait until February to get a glimpse of Phil. He can be found living with his family at the Punxsutawney Groundhog Zoo at the Civic Complex in town. Each summer the town celebrates its favorite son with a weeklong Groundhog Festival in July. Parades, dances, contests, flea markets, and lots of food are all part of the festivities.

This is also the site of the Punxsutawney Chamber of Commerce, (124 West Mahoning Street; 800-752-PHIL or 814-938-4303; www.punxsutawney.com), your source of information on accommodations, restaurants, attractions, and, of course, all things groundhog.

PUNXSUTAWNEY HISTORICAL AND GENEALOGICAL MUSEUM (ages 6 and up)

401 West Mahoning Street; (814) 938–2555; www.users.penn.com/~mweimer. Call for hours and admission charges.

Lest you think that groundhogs are all there is to Punxsutawney, check out the Punxsutawney Historical and Genealogical Museum. Of course, a good bit of the museum is devoted to groundhog history and lore, but there are other treasures from the town's past as well.

Franklin

Franklin is a great area for biking, hiking, and camping. Here are a couple of outfitters to help you plan your trip:

- **Outer Limits (ages 8 and up),** *Route 322 East, Franklin; (814) 432–8432 or (800) 707–6520; www.bikeandfloat.com.* Outer Limits offers customized outdoor adventures for families and other groups. From hiking, biking, and backpacking to canoeing and fishing, the guides provide everything you need, including equipment, meals, and transportation. All tour guides are certified in first aid and CPR.

- **Country Peddlers Recreational Rentals and Sales (ages 8 and up),** *Route 322 East, Franklin; (814) 432–8055; www.bikeandfloat.com.* Located on the Allegheny River at the trailheads for two excellent family adventure trails: the Samuel Justus Recreational Trail (5 $^8/_{10}$-miles) and the Allegheny River Trail (14 miles). Country Peddlers rents the bikes, skates, or canoes you need to enjoy this beautiful area.

ALSO IN THE AREA

Dandy's Frontier Family Fun Park (ages 2 and up), *Route 322, Cranberry; (814) 677–5278. Open Friday 4:00 to 11:00 P.M., Saturday 11:00 A.M. to 11:00 P.M., and Sunday 11:00 A.M. to 7:00 P.M. during the school year; open daily 11:00 A.M. to 11:00 P.M. during summer. Admission is* **Free**. From the easygoing tyke train to the exhilarating Rodeo Raceway, this family fun park has something for everyone in the family. There's an indoor play area and video arcade for rainy-day amusement.

Oil City and Titusville

To get a better picture of the history of oil in this area, head to Oil City and Titusville.

OIL CREEK & TITUSVILLE RAILROAD (all ages)

7 Elm Street, Oil City; (814) 676–1733; www.octrr.clarion.edu. Open mid-June through October. Call for current fares.

You can board the Oil Creek & Titusville Railroad through "the valley that changed the world." The two-and-a-half-hour narrated trip describes the world's first oil boom. Stations are at Rynd Farm, 5 miles north of Oil City, as well as the Drake Well Museum, Petroleum Centre, and Perry Street Station in Titusville.

OIL CREEK STATE PARK (all ages)

Off Route 8, between Oil City and Titusville; (814) 676–5915; www.dcnr. pa.state.us. Open year-round.

The 9½-mile paved bicycle trail through Oil Creek Gorge is the main attraction here. Bike rentals are available from the concession at the Old Egbert Oil Office. Hikers and, in winter, cross-country skiers are also welcome to use the trail.

DRAKE WELL MUSEUM (ages 6 and up)

Off Route 8, south of Titusville; (814) 827–2797; www.usachoice.net/drakewell. Open year-round. Adults $$, children 6 to 12 $.

Heading up Route 8 toward Titusville, stop at the Drake Well Museum, where Edwin Drake drilled the first oil well and launched the petroleum industry in 1859. Here you'll find exhibits, videos, historic buildings, and operating oil machinery. Kids can make plastic, enjoy the fire-engine display, and blow the steam whistle in the full-size replica of Drake's engine house. Have fun "feeding" the horses in the oil transportation exhibit, but watch out for the nitro explosion! Trails in adjacent Oil Creek State Park provide great hiking, and there's a picnic pavilion.

CASEY'S CABOOSE STOP (all ages)

221 South Monroe Street, Titusville; (814) 827–6597 or toll-free (866) 275– 9821.

Got a train lover in your family? Stay at this twenty-one-caboose motel, where cabooses have been converted into accommodations complete with cable TV, heat, air-conditioning, telephones, and computer data ports. Pretty cool. It is adjacent to Molly's Mill, a renovated mill, which has family dining.

Greenville

There are a couple of museums worth a look-see in Greenville. For information try Mercer County Tourism at www.merlink.org.

THE CANAL MUSEUM (ages 6 and up)

60 Alan Avenue; (724) 588–7540. Call for hours and admission.

This museum traces the history of the Erie Extension Canal. You can see a full-size replica of a packet boat and a working model of a canal lock.

GREENVILLE RAILROAD PARK AND MUSEUM (all ages)
314 Main Street; (724) 588–4009. Open weekends only in May, September, and October 1:00 to 5:00 P.M. Open Tuesday through Sunday during summer months, 1:00 to 5:00 P.M. Admission is **Free***, but donations are gladly accepted.*

Here your kids can climb aboard the largest steam switch engine ever built in the United States. There are also railroad cars, a 1914 Empire automobile, and the world's first parachute on display.

 GREENVILLE FARMERS' CURB MARKET (all ages)
Corner of Penn Avenue and Main Street. Open Wednesday and Saturday 7:00 A.M. to 2:00 P.M.

If you're in town on a Wednesday or Saturday, check out this outdoor market that features the produce of farmers within a 20-mile radius of town.

 BRUCKER GREAT BLUE HERON SANCTUARY (all ages)
Route 18, south of Greenville. Open year-round. Admission is **Free***.*

More than 400 of these majestic birds nest at this wildlife reserve—the largest colony of herons in the state.

Sharon and Hermitage

Chocolate lovers will want to stop by two unusual factories in the towns of Sharon and Hermitage, both south of Greenville on Route 62. These towns are also known for their shopping malls, and they make great home bases for explorations of this area.

DAFFIN'S CANDIES (all ages)
496 East State Street, Sharon; (877) 323–3465 or (724) 342–2892; www.daffins.com. Store is open daily year-round. Factory tours are available Monday through Friday 9:00 A.M. to 3:00 P.M.

Daffin's Candies Chocolate Kingdom is a sight to behold. The display area is filled with giant rabbits, turtles, elephants, and more—all made of chocolate. The rabbit alone required 700 pounds of chocolate to create. If you make arrangements in advance, you can tour the chocolate factory, located on Route 60, south of Sharon.

PHILADELPHIA CANDIES (all ages)

1546 State Street, Hermitage; (724) 981–6341. Open daily year-round. Admission is ℱᵣₑₑ.

In Hermitage tour the 30,000-square-foot facility at Philadelphia Candies, a company that's been making fine chocolates and other confections since 1919. The retail store is located right at the factory, so you can bring home a sample for all your friends back home (if the candies make it that far!).

AVENUE OF FLAGS (all ages)

2619 State Street, Hermitage; (724) 345–3818. Open daily year-round. Admission is ℱᵣₑₑ.

Before you leave Hermitage, take a walk down the Avenue of Flags. The street is lined with 444 flags, making it the world's largest display of American flags.

Conneaut Lake Area

You'll find lots of family fun around Pennsylvania's largest lake.

CONNEAUT LAKE PARK (all ages)

12382 Center Street, Conneaut Lake; (814) 382–5115. Open daily early summer to late fall. Admission is ℱᵣₑₑ.

For more than one hundred years, families have come to Conneaut Lake Park to enjoy the lake, ride the rides, and just plain have fun. There is a 167-room historic hotel, a 105-site modern campground with camping cabins, and a full range of rides and amusements. The classic Blue Streak wooden roller coaster is sure to thrill, and the Waterpark is a hit with most kids. When you've had enough of the rides, relax on the lake beach or take a ride on the stern-wheeler *Barbara J.*

Admission to the park is ℱᵣₑₑ—you pay only for the rides you want.

PYMATUNING STATE PARK (ages 5 and up)

Route 58, Jamestown; (724) 932–3141. Open year-round.

With the 27-square-mile Conneaut Lake as its centerpiece, the park offers boating, hiking, fishing, camping, and winter sports.

PYMATUNING DEER PARK (all ages)

Route 58, Jamestown; (724) 932–3200. Open weekends in May and daily Memorial Day through Labor Day. Call for current admission prices.

This small zoo offers train and pony rides as well as an opportunity to pet and feed the animals. Small children especially seem to enjoy this stop. The park has added more animals, including lions, tigers, bears (oh my!), wallabies, kangaroos, and camels in addition to the favorite farm animals.

Erie

Erie is the area's largest population center, the state's only Great Lake port, and the home of former governor Tom Ridge. The city celebrated its bicentennial in 1995, and things have been booming ever since. With a newly opened Bayfront Highway, several new or refurbished museums and historical sights, and a vibrant arts program, Erie has never been better.

 PRESQUE ISLE STATE PARK (all ages)

 Peninsula Drive (P.O. Box 8510); (814) 833–7424. Open year-round. **Free** *admission.*

Presque Isle State Park is one of the most remarkable aspects of Erie. This narrow spit of sand *(presque isle* literally means "almost an island") juts out into Lake Erie, providing an unusual environment for wildlife and a beautiful retreat for humans. To plan your day at the park, stop at the interpretive center, where there is a wonderful nature gift shop and bookstore as well as exhibits about local wildlife.

Choose the calm waters of Presque Isle Bay for boating or the almost oceanlike waves of Lake Erie for swimming. Water enthusiasts can rent canoes, rowboats, or motorboats to explore the waters on their own, whereas landlubbers can enjoy 13 miles of hiking trails. Bring your binoculars; Presque Isle is touted as one of the best bird-watching sites in the country. More than 300 species live in or pass by the park.

B.O.A.T. (Best of All Tours, Inc.) runs the forty-nine-passenger *Lady Kate* from the Perry Monuments at Presque Isle. There's also a thirty-six-passenger water taxi, Presque Isle Express, that runs between Presque Isle and Dobbins Landing in downtown Erie. It's a great way to pack in a full day of Erie sights and fun.

Although busiest in summer, there's something to do year-round at the park. In winter hiking trails turn to cross-country ski trails, and Presque Isle Bay provides great ice fishing.

WALDAMEER PARK AND WATER WORLD (ages 3 and up)

220 Peninsula Drive; (814) 838–3591. Open Tuesday through Sunday, mid-May through Labor Day. Individual-ride and combo tickets available. **Free** parking and admission.

Right outside the entrance of Presque Isle State Park is Waldameer Park and Water World. If you don't spot it, your kids definitely will. There are five body slides, three double-tube slides, the Wild River tube slide, free-fall slide, speed slide, Endless River ride, three "tad pool" areas, and a heated pool. The amusement park has sixteen major rides and ten rides for children, including the fantastic log flume ride, Thunder River. Use of tubes and life jackets is **Free**, and there is a variety of gift shops, snack bars, and midway games at the park. Or you can bring your own picnic. Puppet shows and musical shows are offered throughout the day.

ERIE MARITIME MUSEUM (ages 6 and up)

150 East Front Street; (814) 871–4596. Open seven days a week year-round. Open Monday through Saturday 9:00 A.M. to 5:00 P.M., Sunday noon to 5:00 P.M. Last tickets sold at 4:00 P.M. Admission: adults $$, family ticket $$$, youth 6 to 12 $; children under 6 are **Free**.

The maritime attractions of downtown Erie have been united in the Erie Maritime Museum. This state-of-the-art facility features exhibits about the ecology of the Great Lakes; Lake Erie; Pennsylvania's North Coast maritime history's *Wolverine* and interactive Fighting Sailing Deck; several video displays about the *Niagara*, the Battle of Lake Erie, reconstruction of the *Niagara;* and a live fire exhibit. In addition, when it is in port, tour O. H. Perry's flagship.

You can take a look at the *Wolverine*—at least what's left of it. The ship, originally christened the USS *Michigan,* was the first iron-hulled ship ever built. Now the bow is all that remains of this impressive part of maritime history.

When it's in port, you can tour the flagship *Niagara,* a brig built to fight the naval battles of the War of 1812. To avoid disappointing children with their hearts set on seeing this boat, call ahead.

BICENTENNIAL OBSERVATION TOWER (ages 3 and up)

Dobbins Landing; (814) 455–6055 or (814) 455–7557; www.eriepa.com/ tower. Open year-round. Call for current hours and days. Admission is $; children under 6 are **Free**. *Admission is* **Free** *for all ages on Tuesday.*

This 185-foot-tall tower gives an amazing view over Presque Isle, downtown Erie, and Lake Erie. Take the 210 stairs to the top observation deck or take the elevator. If you take the stairs, follow the sixteen stations that point out historic, geographic, and other landmarks.

APPLEDORE CRUISES (ages 3 and up)

17 State Street at Dobbins Landing; (814) 459–8339; www.bbyc.com; e-mail: baybreeze@bbyc.com. Summer only. Two-hour cruise: adults $$$$, children 12 and under $$$.

Enjoy a hands-on sailing adventure on the beautiful 85-foot schooner *Appledore*—truly an unforgettable experience for all members of the family.

ERIE ART MUSEUM (ages 8 and up)

411 State Street, Discovery Square; (814) 459–5477; www.erieartmuseum.org. Open Tuesday through Saturday year-round. Admission is $. **Free** *admission on Wednesday.*

The Erie Art Museum offers changing exhibitions, concerts, classes, and children's activities. During the first weekend of August the museum hosts the Erie Art Museum Blues & Jazz Festival, which draws 10,000 people to Frontier Park for the **Free** event.

expERIEnce CHILDREN'S MUSEUM (all ages)

420 French Street, Discovery Square; (814) 453–3743; www.ohwy.com. Open year-round Tuesday through Saturday 10:00 A.M. to 4:00 P.M., Sunday 1:00 to 4:00 P.M. Closed Monday year-round and Tuesday during school year. Admission is $.

For small children the highlight of Erie is the expERIEnce Children's Museum, housed in an old livery stable. The museum is aimed at kids ages two to twelve, but those under age eight seem to enjoy it the most. According to one of the museum's curators, "This is a hands-on museum, which means that kids can come in and break things, and after they leave, we fix them."

There's a Gallery of Science on one floor and a Gallery of the Human Experience on the other. You can also see a simulation of a cave, in which children learn about cave painting, cave exploration, and fossils. At the Wegman's Corner Store, children can shop in a re-creation of a supermarket, complete with scanners, shopping carts, and very real-looking groceries. Youngsters may want to pick out a funny outfit from the costume closet and put on a show on a real stage.

WATSON-CURTZE MANSION AND ERIE PLANETARIUM (all ages)

356 West Sixth Street; (814) 871–5790. Open Tuesday through Sunday afternoons year-round. Call for current hours. Museum admission is $.Planetarium admission is $. Children under 2 are admitted **Free** *to both exhibits.*

Kids of all ages love planetarium shows. Even toddlers will point out the moon and the stars. Call ahead for schedule of shows.

ERIE ZOO (all ages)

423 West Thirty-eighth Street; (814) 864–4091; www.eriezoo.org. Open year-round. Call for admission prices and hours.

More than 300 animals representing nearly one hundred different species live in this fifteen-acre park. There's a children's zoo and a train ride around the zoo.

ALSO IN THE AREA

Wooden Nickel Buffalo Farm and Shop (all ages), *5970 Koman Road, Edinboro; (814) 734–BUFF; www.woodennickelbuffalo.com. Open year-round.* **Free** *admission.* A herd of more than fifty buffalo roam on this fifty-acre ranch outside Erie. It's quite a sight to see. Who knows, you might get inspired to get into buffalo farming yourself. The Wooden Nickel says it is "thinning the herd": You can buy a two and one-half-year-old breeding bull for $3,000. You can also purchase bison meat, "the healthy red meat for the millennium."

North East

About 20 miles east of Erie on Route 20 is the historic village of North East. Take a walking tour of the historic district (brochures are available at local stores and museums).

HORNBY SCHOOL MUSEUM (ages 4 and up)

11573 Station Road; (814) 725–5680. Open Sunday 1:00 to 5:00 P.M. or by appointment. Admission is 𝕱𝖗𝖊𝖊, *but donations are accepted.*

If you call ahead and make arrangements, your children can experience what it was like to learn in a one-room schoolhouse built in the 1870s. Even the books and slates are original equipment.

 LAKE SHORE RAILWAY HISTORICAL SOCIETY MUSEUM (ages 2 and up)

Corner of Wall and Robinson Streets; (814) 825–2724 or (814) 725–1191. Open Wednesday through Sunday afternoons from Memorial Day to Labor Day. Call for exact hours and admission.

Another historical sight of interest to children is the Lake Shore Railway Historical Society Museum. Here, you can see a variety of train equipment, including a Pullman car, a caboose, and a dining car. Located on a busy stretch of railroad track, the site practically guarantees that your children will get to see several modern trains pass by during your visit.

Where to Eat

IN THE COOKSBURG AREA

Americo's Italian Restaurant, *Cooksburg-Vowinckel Road, 1¼ mile north of Sawmill Theatre, Cook Forest; (814) 927–8516.* Open April through October for lunch and dinner. Children's menu. Near attractions.

Cook Forest Country Inn, *Cooksburg-Vowinckel Road; (814) 927–8925 or (800) 830–6133.* Home-style cooking, homemade rolls and pies.

The Farmer's Inn, *Two miles north of Sigel on Route 949, near Clear Creek State Park; (814) 752–2942.* Restaurant, ice cream, bakery, gift shop, Amish furniture, horse-drawn wagon and pony rides, miniature golf, animal exhibits, petting zoo.

Gateway Lodge Country Inn and Restaurant, *Route 36 in the heart of Cook Forest; (814) 744–8017 or (800) 843–6862.* Dine by kerosene light. Staff dressed Colonial-style. Breakfast and lunch daily. Dinner daily except for Monday.

Mama Doe's Restaurant, *Shiloh Ranch Resort, Route 36, Cook Forest; (814) 752–2361.* Fine dining and Italian cuisine. Breakfast, lunch, and dinner; daily specials, Sunday buffet. Also campground, cabins, and lodge.

Sawmill Restaurant, *Intersection of Routes 36 and 66 at the blinker light, Leeper; (814) 744–8578.* Soft ice cream, fresh baked goods, home of the Sawdustburger. Open daily, year-round, 7:00 A.M. to midnight.

The Trails End, *Cooksburg-Vowinckel Road, near Cook Forest State Park; (814) 927–8400.* Steaks, seafood, sandwiches. Near theater and park attractions.

Vowinckel Hotel, *corner of Route 66 and Cooksburg-Vowinckel Road, 5 miles from Cook Forest; (814) 927–6610.* Homemade bread and pizza dough. Voted "Best Wings in Clarion County." Fireplace.

IN ERIE

Applebee's Restaurant, *7790 Peach Street; (814) 866–8210.*

Backstage Grill, *2025 Peach Street; (814) 452–1356.*

Bagel Basket, *3 East Eighteenth Street; (814) 452–2435.*

Bob Evans Restaurant, *8041 Peach Street; (814) 864–5444.*

Caffe Royale, *25E Tenth Street; (814) 455–2243.*

Calamari's Restaurant, *1317 State Street; (814) 459–4267.*

The Carriage House, *1535 West Twenty-sixth Street; (814) 623–1174.*

China Garden Restaurant, *6801 Peach Street; (814) 868–2695.*

Chuck E Cheese, *7200 Peach Street, Summit Towne Center; (814) 864–3100.*

Connie's Ice Cream, *6032 Peach Street; (814) 866–1700.* Take-out homemade ice cream made with the freshest ingredients.

Hoss's Steak & Sea House, *3302 West Twenty-sixth Street; (814) 835–6836.*

Italian Oven, *2709 West Twelfth Street; (814) 835–6836.*

Julio's Family Restaurant & Pizzeria, *29 South Jared; (814) 455–6301.* Family-friendly bar and restaurant serving sandwiches, burgers, wings, and more. Children's menu; high chairs available.

Old Country Buffet, *7200 Peach Street; (814) 866–5671.*

The Olive Garden, *5945 Peach Street; (814) 866–1105.*

Pio's Italian Restaurant & Pizzeria, *815 East Avenue; (814) 456–8866.* Pastas, pizza, and other casual Italian-style choices. Children's menu.

Porter's Taproom, *123 West Fourteenth Street; (814) 452–2787.*

Smuggler's Wharf, *3 State Street; (814) 459–4273.*

Where to Stay

IN THE WELLSBORO AREA

Comfort Inn Canyon Country, *300 Gateway Drive, Mansfield; (717) 662–3000 or (800) 822–5470.* Conveniently located for events in Mansfield as well as touring nearby Pine Creek Gorge.

IN THE BRADFORD AREA

Howard Johnson Lodge and Restaurant, *100 Davis Street South;* *(800) 344–4656.* Open year-round. A good base for Bradford and Allegheny Forest area explorations. Outdoor pool, special combination packages for the Knox Kane Railway excursions, skiing, and golf.

IN THE ALLEGHENY NATIONAL FOREST AREA

Kane View Motel, *Route 6 East, Kane;* *(814) 837–8600.* The Allegheny National Forest is in the backyard of this convenient motel.

IN WARREN

Super 8, *Warren, US Routes 6 and 62N;* *(814) 723–8881.* Near major attractions and downtown. Continental breakfast.

Holiday Inn–Warren, *210 Ludlow Street, Warren; (814) 726–3000.* On-site restaurant, indoor pool, and a three-diamond rating from AAA make this a good choice for families exploring the national forest and other area attractions.

IN THE COOKSBURG AREA

Clarion River Lodge, *River Road in Cook Forest; (814) 744–8171 or (800) 648–6743.* Magnificent view of Clarion River. Guest rooms available. Open year-round.

IN PUNXSUTAWNEY

Pantall Hotel, *downtown; (814) 938–6600.* Beautifully restored Victorian hotel; restaurants on-site.

IN FRANKLIN

Inn at Franklin, *downtown; (814) 437–3031 or (800) 535–4052.* **Free** continental breakfast; restaurant, tavern, family plans.

IN OIL CITY AND TITUSVILLE

Holiday Inn–Oil City, *1 Seneca Street, Oil City; (814) 677–1221 or (800) HOLI-DAY.* Kids stay **Free**. Full-service restaurant, lounge, entertainment.

IN THE CONNEAUT LAKE AREA

Days Inn–Meadville, *just off exit 36A off I–79, Meadville; (814) 337–4264.* Minutes from Conneaut Lake. Family restaurant on-site.

IN THE HERMITAGE AND SHARON AREAS

Holiday Inn of Sharon/Hermitage, *3200 South Hermitage Road, Route 18 North; (412) 981–1530 or (800) HOLI-DAY.* Full-service hotel.

Radisson Hotel Sharon, *Route 18 and I–80, West Middlesex; (412) 528–2501 or (800) 333–3333.* On-site restaurant, indoor pool, hot tubs.

IN CLARION

Comfort Inn, *I–80 exit 9, north on Route 66; (814) 226–5230.* **Free** continental breakfast, outdoor pool.

Holiday Inn of Clarion, *Route 68 and I–80, exit 9; (814) 226–8850 or (800) 596–1313.* **Free** breakfast buffet. Tropical courtyard with indoor pool and saunas, restaurant, and lounge. Kids stay and eat **Free**.

Super 8 Motel—Clarion, *I–80, exit 9;* (814) 226–4550. AAA-rated, first-floor, and nonsmoking rooms. **Free** continental breakfast and local calls, cable television, outdoor pool.

IN THE ERIE AREA

Erie has an impressive array of hotels and motels—with just about all the major chains represented. Most of the big-name places are equipped with indoor pools, definitely good news for families traveling in winter or when bad weather interrupts sight-seeing plans. Here are a few highlights:

The Glass House Inn, *3202 West Twenty-sixth Street (Route 20); (814) 833–7751 or (800) 956–7222; www. velocity.net/~ghilel.* A family-friendly, family-run, colonial-style inn with outdoor pool and lots of room to play.

Marriott Residence, *8061 Peach Street; (814) 864–2500; www.ncinter.net/ ~erieinns/.* This all-suite hotel has kitchens in the rooms, an indoor pool, and a breakfast buffet. (Web site serves three other big hotels, so do some online comparison shopping.)

Presque Isle Cottage Court, *320 Peninsula Drive; (814) 833–4956.* Located close to Waldermeer Water World and Presque Isle State Park.

For More Information

Allegheny National Forest Vacation Region, *P.O. Drawer G, Junction 219 and 770, Custer City 16725; (814) 368–9370; www.allegheny-vacation.com.* Call ahead or drop by for information about things to do and see and places to stay and eat in McKean County.

Cameron County Tourist Promotion Agency, *P.O. Box 118, Driftwood 15832; (888) 25–CCTPA or (814) 546–2665; www.pavisnet.com/camtpa.*

Crawford County Tourist Promotion Agency, *Box 786, Meadville 16335; (800) 332–2338 or (814) 333–1258; www.visitcrawford.org.* Call ahead for information about Crawford County.

Elk County Visitors Bureau, *P.O. Box 838, St. Marys 15857; (814) 834–3723.* Call ahead for an information packet with things to do and see and places to stay in Elk County.

Erie Area of Chamber of Commerce, *downtown office: Scenic Route 5, the Pennsylvania Seaway Trail. Mailing address: 1006 State Street, Erie 16501; (800) 542– ERIE or (814) 454–7191; www.eriepa.com; e-mail: Erie-chamber@erie.net.* Visit the extensive Web site, call ahead for information, or stop by one of several information centers along major routes for up-to-the-minute details on attractions, accommodations, and events in the Erie area. Some major festivals in the area include the Erie Summer Festival of the Arts (end of June) and We Love Erie Days (August). Both feature special events for children.

Galeton Chamber of Commerce, *P.O. Box 176, Galeton 16922; (814) 435–2321.* For information on accommodations and the lowdown on what's happening in town, contact the chamber before your visit.

The Magic Forests Visitors Bureau, c/o Brookville Office, RR 5, Brookville 15825; (800) 348–9393 or (814) 849–5197; www.magicforests.org. Covering Clarion, Clearfield, and Jefferson Counties, this tourist organization can supply you with information about attractions, accommodations, and more.

Mercer County Convention and Visitors Bureau, 835 Perry Highway, Mercer 16137; (800) 637–2370 or (412) 748–5315; www.mercercountypa.org. Your source for information on accommodations and attractions in Greenville, Sharon, Hermitage, Grove City, and all of Mercer County.

Northern Allegheny Vacation Region, 315 Second Avenue, Warren 16365; (800) 624–7802 or (814) 726–1222; www.northernalleghenies.com. Tourist information for Forest and Warren Counties.

Oil Heritage Region Tourist Promotion Agency, Inc., National City Bank Building, Third Floor, 248 Seneca Street, Oil City 16301; (800) 483–6264 or (814) 677–3152; www.usachoice.net/oilregion tourist. Call ahead for an information packet with brochures about attractions and accommodations in Venango County.

Potter County Recreation, Inc., P.O. Box 245, Coudersport 16915; (888) POT-TER–2 or (814) 435–2290. For more information on recreational opportunities in Potter County, give this tourist organization a call.

Tioga County Tourist Promotion Agency, 114 Main Street, Wellsboro 16901; (800) 332–6718 or (717) 724–0634. Call ahead or stop by for area information.

Wellsboro Chamber of Commerce, 114 Main Street, Wellsboro 16901; (717) 724–1926. For more information about festivals, accommodations, and other attractions in Wellsboro, this is your source.

General Index

Activities Index